Critical Views:
Essays on the Humanities and the Arts

THE TOWNSEND PAPERS IN THE HUMANITIES *No. 4*

Critical Views: Essays on the Humanities and the Arts

Published by
The Townsend Center for the Humanities
University of California | Berkeley

Distributed by
University of California Press
Berkeley, Los Angeles, London | 2011

ISBN 978-0-9823294-3-6

Library of Congress Cataloging-in-Publication Data

Critical views : essays on the humanities and the arts / editor, Teresa Stojkov. — 1st ed.
p. cm. — (Townsend papers in the humanities ; v. IV)
ISBN 978-0-9823294-3-6
1. Arts. 2. Humanities. I. Stojkov, Teresa R. II. Title: Essays on the humanities and the arts.
NX60.C75 2012
001.3—dc23
2011042478

Inquiries concerning proposals for the Townsend Papers in the Humanities from Berkeley faculty and Townsend Center affiliates should be addressed to The Townsend Papers, 220 Stephens Hall, UC Berkeley, Berkeley, CA 94720-2340, or by email to townsend_papers@lists.berkeley.edu.

Design and typesetting: www.mattinglydesign.com

Manufactured in the United States of America

Photo credits appear on page 344.

Table of Contents

Preface

THIS VOLUME of the Townsend Papers in the Humanities commemorates the twenty-fifth year of the Doreen B. Townsend Center for the Humanities at the University of California, Berkeley. As such, the volume is an attempt to capture the breadth and depth of lectures and events presented by the center, many of which were documented in the center's *Occasional Papers* series between 1994 and 2002. In all, twenty-seven *Occasional Papers* were published under the editorship of Christina Gillis (Associate Director, 1988–2004). While this represents just a fraction of the activity in the humanities at Berkeley in the past quarter-century, the challenge of making a limited selection from the previously published material was no less daunting.

We present here fourteen offerings. Many are revised versions of lectures and presentations organized in connection with the annual appointment of the Avenali Professor in the Humanities at Berkeley (generously funded by Joan and Peter Avenali), or Berkeley's Una's Lecturer (endowed in the memory of Una Smith Ross, Class of 1911); several are based on other events presented by the center over the years, such as the "Humanities Perspectives on Aging" program or the "Futures" lecture series organized to commemorate the center's tenth anniversary. All are the reflection of a public event before a live audience. We have chosen to retain references to the live event where they occur, though space limitations would not permit the inclusion of audience questions.

Part 1 reproduces ten cohesive lectures in chronological order of original publication, beginning with "Identity Against Culture," Kwame Anthony Appiah's 1994 examination of multiculturalism. Appiah questions the possibilities of maintaining a pluralistic culture of many identities and subcultures while retaining the civil and political practices that sustain national life. Opera and theater director Peter Sellars follows with his thoughts on art and inspiration in a world without government funding; his 1997 vision of an artistic engagement that can proceed with or without the National Endowment for the Arts (NEA) is once again to the point in 2012, as the NEA is threatened with its biggest cut in sixteen years.

Following on the heels of Sellars's post-NEA America, Mike Davis analyzes apocalyptic Los Angeles as rendered in film and literature. In "Golden Ruins/Dark Raptures: The Literary Destruction of Los Angeles" he explores the underlying politics and recurring tropes of Los Angeles disaster fiction and ultimately identifies race—and racial fear—as that which best explains the genre.

Arthur Danto continues with "The Work of Art and the Historical Future," also presented in 1997. According to Danto, the contemporary art world, as a model of a pluralistic society, has dissolved all barriers and boundaries and given rise to "unlimited lateral diversity." One can no longer give art's progression a narrative direction or form, leading to what Danto describes as the liberation of art beyond history.

Czech writer Ivan Klíma, who has lived through many of the events that shaped midcentury Europe, states: "In modern Czech history there has been no shortage of great dramatic events. In such a situation it is difficult to write a novel and pass over these moments." While in residence in Berkeley in 1998, Klíma delivered the lecture included here, "Living in Fiction and History," an inquiry into the relationship between these two different areas, especially in times of political turmoil.

Taking the life and work of philosopher Isaiah Berlin as his subject, Michael Ignatieff muses on the relationship between philosophy and aging in "Berlin in Autumn: The Philosopher in Old Age," and in doing so examines how that relationship may have contributed to Berlin's equanimity at the end of his life.

In "The Novel in Africa" J. M. Coetzee cleverly imbeds a lecture in a fiction—the tale of two emblematic characters, an Australian novelist and a Nigerian author, who are engaged by a cruise ship to present contrasting lectures on the novel, "The Future of the Novel" and "The Novel in Africa," respectively.

Kenzaburō Ōe asks a related question: "Will literature, specifically the novel, hold its ground for the next hundred years until writers of the future...have their centennial celebrated?" Ōe's "From the Beginning to the Present, and Facing the End: The Case of One Japanese Writer" chronicles the diverse influences in his own work and his development as a writer.

Anthony Grafton returns to Western philosophy in his 1999 investigation of Descartes's philosophical conversion from what was portrayed as doubtful belief to certain knowledge. Historian Randolph Starn, then Townsend Center director, noted at the time that Grafton's investigation of Descartes "encourages us to look with eyebrows raised at the tales we tell about how Western philosophy and science came to be modern."

Michael Pollan first posed the question, "Just what is the knowledge held out by a plant such as cannabis?" in his best-selling book, *The Botany of Desire: A Plant's-Eye View of the World*. His 2002 lecture "Cannabis, Forgetting, and the Botany of Desire" delves deeper into what has been learned about cannabis, the cannabinoid network, and memory since the book's publication and raises provocative questions about our understanding of consciousness and drugs.

Part 2 shifts registers to include several of the many dialogues and conversations organized by the Townsend Center. The first in this section, "Grounds for Remembering," is the transcribed proceedings of a symposium on monuments and the act of memorializing, organized in conjunction with the visit of architect Maya Lin in 1995. The symposium brought Lin into conversation with four Berkeley scholars, Thomas Laqueur (History), Andrew Barshay (History of Modern Japan), Stephen Greenblatt (English), and Stanley Saitowitz (Architecture). Collectively they discussed topics that include how a name relates to place and to memory, the artistic and technical issues of building, and the political nature of public spaces dedicated to mourning.

Maurice Sendak, the author and illustrator of many beloved children's books, was in residence at Berkeley in February 1996, an occasion that featured several panel discussions and conversations. In "They Know Everything: Children and Suffering," Sendak and Dr. Herbert Schreier of Oakland's Children's Hospital discuss the durability of early childhood trauma from two different points of view. Both raise questions about the transformation of childhood suffering in art.

"Sounding Lines: The Art of Translation" captures the lively exchange between Irish poet Seamus Heaney and Robert Hass, Poet Laureate of the United States (1995–97), both not only eminent poets but also assiduous translators. Heaney and Hass discuss approaches to translation as well the variations of meaning generated in the act of translating a poem.

The final piece in this volume reproduces Brazilian photographer Sebastião Salgado's commentary on his monumental touring exhibit *Migrations,* which was presented at the Berkeley Art Museum in 2002. Salgado discusses his attempt to document the nearly epic displacement of the world's people at the close of the twentieth century and engages in conversation with Orville Schell, former dean of the UC Berkeley Graduate School of Journalism, on the broader topics of cynicism, hope, and the language of photography.

Twenty-five years on, words of gratitude are in order. First, to the former directors of the Townsend Center for providing the exciting intellectual and academic agenda from which this volume derived: Paul Alpers, Randolph Starn, Thomas Laqueur, Candace Slater, and Anthony J. Cascardi. I also want to acknowledge Christina Gillis for her editorial work on the original *Occasional Papers*, and the Office of the Vice Chancellor for Research at Berkeley for contributions that make possible the Townsend Papers in the Humanities. Finally, I would like to express appreciation to Jean Day for her expertise and indispensable assistance in the preparation of this volume.

Teresa Stojkov
Associate Director
Doreen B. Townsend Center for the Humanities

Part I: Lectures

Kwame Anthony Appiah

Identity Against Culture

Introduction

IT IS A TRUISM that in the United States of America "we live in a multicultural society." But the obviousness and apparent clarity of this truism, like the apparent clarity and obviousness of most such truisms, dissolves upon inspection. To begin with what is perhaps the least patent difficulty, what people normally have in mind when they pronounce this slogan is that the United States is a multicultural state. This is by no means obviously the same thought, since that we in America constitute a state is, so to speak, a juridical and constitutional fact; and that juridical fact is neither necessary nor sufficient for our being a society.

The word "society," used in this context, means something like *a group of people with a shared social geography,*[1] *and certainly shared institutions and a common culture*; and, granted the geographical unity of the (continental) United States and the existence, under the constitution, of American institutions, the question whether we are a society in this sense is the same as the question whether there is such a thing, at some level, as a shared American culture.[2] To speak of American society as multicultural in this sense, as composed of groups of people with distinct cultures, might seem to be, at best, confusing, at worst, actually contradictory: the American state can be multicultural; but unless Americans also share a culture, there is no American society.

Such problems as flow from the coexistence of the many cultures within the boundaries of the American state are the consequence of the yoking together of societies, groups of people with a common culture and common institutions, within a single set of political institutions and in a shared social space.

The diversity of America's societies should not blind us to their interdependence. We think of ourselves as a nation of immigrants—thus erasing, of course, the Native American peoples and cultures who predated the immigrations we have in mind. This "nation of immigrants" talk has advantages as well as disadvantages however; one of which is that it records an understanding that the dominant cultural groups in this nation have no special claim upon the American soil, an understanding that is a powerful tool in resisting the regular upsurges of American nativism. The "nation of immigrants" story has another important consequence: it has accustomed us to the idea that the diversity of cultures within the United States is the natural consequence of the importation of different cultures from different societies elsewhere. But while *some* of the cultural variety of the current United States arises from the presence of people who grew up and were acculturated in other places,[3] most of America's cultures have been largely shaped by experience in the United States: if there is an overarching set of beliefs, ideas, and practices that make up an American culture, most of America's cultures were shaped by that common culture. And even if that common culture is pretty thin gruel, America's cultures have mostly been shaped by interaction with each other. America's many cultures, its various societies, have grown up together, belong in a single system of cultures: they are not the mere logical sum of a series of unrelated historically independent elements.

If, as I have suggested, a society is a group of people with a shared geography, and certainly shared institutions and a common culture, then understanding whether we are *a* society will depend on both

a. whether there are American institutions and
b. whether there is *an* American common culture.

I have already relied upon the obvious answer to first of these questions: the political institutions of the American state are shared by all who live in the United States.[4] If we had only these institutions in common, we would have common institutions.

The difficult question, then, would seem to be the second question: the question of an American culture. Suppose it is correct to speak, as many do, of American culture as centrally constituted in part by, for example, democratic and republican values. Then, so it seems, something central to American culture may not be held in common by all who live within the American state. Or suppose that the English language is the American language, defining the American system of communication: then there are juridical Americans who do not participate in American culture for that reason. And so, in the relevant sense, there may be no American society, nothing bound together both by the American institutions, whose existence I have granted, and by an American culture, about whose existence I am suggesting we may need to inquire further.

Approaching Culture

But we will not get much further with that inquiry until we explore the idea of culture, which immediately reveals itself to be extremely elastic. In my dictionary I find as a definition for "culture": "The totality of socially transmitted behavior patterns, arts, beliefs, institutions, and all other products of human work and thought."[5] This is not, I think, quite right. There is, to begin with, no obvious incoherence in the idea of a nonhuman culture: we can reasonably speak of the culture of some primates or imagine, in science fiction, the culture of nonterrestrial creatures.

But the definition surely picks out a familiar constellation of ideas. "Culture," in one sense, does indeed name all the "products of human work and thought." That is, in fact, the sense in which anthropologists largely use the term nowadays. The culture of the Ashanti or the Zuni, for the anthropologist, includes every object they make (clothing, pottery, houses—which, taken together, we call their "material culture") and everything they think and everything they do; or, more precisely, everything that they do that is the product of thought (which is to say, invoking a distinction familiar to philosophers, not every bodily movement, but every action).

You will notice, however, that the dictionary definition could have stopped there, leaving out the talk of "socially transmitted behavior patterns, arts, beliefs, institutions" because these are all products of human work and thought. They are mentioned, of course, because they are the residue of an older idea of culture than the anthropological one. Here what the dictionary draws attention to is something more like the idea of a civilization: the "socially transmitted behavior patterns" of ritual, etiquette, religion, games, arts; the values that they engender and reflect; and the institutions—family, school, church, state—that shape and are shaped by them.

There are two tensions between the anthropologists' idea of a culture and the idea of a civilization. First, there is nothing in the anthropologists' idea that requires that the culture of a group should be a totality in any stronger sense than being what I called the mere logical sum of all the things they make and the actions they undertake.

American civilization, on the other hand—if there were such a thing—would not be just a simple logical sum of the doings and thoughts of Americans. It would have to have a certain coherence. Some of what is done in America and by Americans would not belong to American civilization because it was too individual (the particular bedtime rituals of a particular American family); some would not belong because it was not properly American, because (like a Hindi sentence made in America) it does not properly cohere with the rest.

The second, connected, difference between what I am calling the anthropological idea of culture and the idea of a civilization is that the latter takes values to be more central to the enterprise in two ways. First, the civilization of a group is centrally defined by its moral and aesthetic values, and the coherence of a civilization is, primarily, the coherence of those values with each other and, then, of the group's behavior and institutions with its values. Second, civilizations are essentially to be evaluated: they can be better and worse, richer and poorer, more and less interesting. Anthropologists, on the whole, tend now to avoid the relative evaluation of cultures, adopting a sort of cultural relativism whose coherence philosophers have tended to doubt. And they do not take values as more central to culture than, for example, beliefs, ideas, and practices.

Because there are these differences I want to reserve the word "culture" for the anthropologists' notion; henceforward I shall use the word "civilization" for the older notion I have been sketching. The habit of shaking hands at meetings belongs to culture in the anthropologists' sense; the works of Sandro Botticelli and Martin Buber and Count Basie belong to culture also, but they belong to civilization as well.

The Move to Culture

I am using the words "civilization" and "culture" to distinguish two ways of thinking about the products of human work and thought; I don't claim that these words now mark that distinction in ordinary speech. And I want to point out now that the move from the cluster of ideas I have labeled the concept of "civilization" to the cluster I have called "culture" was the result of arguments, not a simple drift of usage. The move away from evaluation came first, once people recognized that much evaluation of other cultures by the Europeans and Americans who invented anthropology had been both ignorant and biased. Earlier criticisms of "lower" peoples turned out to involve crucial misunderstandings of their ideas (Levy-Bruhl's talk of a "pre-logical" mentality, for example); and it eventually seemed clear enough, too, that nothing more than differences of upbringing underlay the distaste of some Westerners for unfamiliar habits. It is a poor move from recognizing certain evaluations as mistaken to giving up evaluation altogether, and anthropologists who adopt cultural relativism often preach more than practice it. Still, this cultural relativism was a response to real errors. That it is the wrong response doesn't make the errors any less erroneous.

The arguments against the ethnocentrism implicit in the "civilization" concept were in place well before the midcentury. More recently, anthropologists began to see that the idea of the coherence of a civilization got in the way of understanding important facts about other societies (and, in the end, about our own). For even in some of the "simplest" societies, there are different values and practices and beliefs and interests associated with different social groups (women as opposed to men; elders as opposed to young men; chiefs as opposed to commoners; one clan as opposed to another). To think of a civilization as coherent was to miss the fact that these different values and beliefs were not merely different but actually opposed.[6] Worse, what had been presented as the coherent unified worldview of a tribal people often turned out, on later inspection, to be merely the ideology of a dominant group or interest.

I believe there is much of value in these anthropological criticisms of the idea of a civilization.[7] I shall refer back to the idea of civilization from time to time, however, where it helps to understand some of our contemporary debates.

Multiculturalism Defined

I am going to call the *shared* beliefs, values, and practices of a socially recognized subgroup a subculture.[8] And I shall say that a state that contains subcultures wider than the family is *multi-*

cultural. This is a *stipulation*: I am aware of other uses of the word "subculture" and other understandings of the multicultural. These understandings I propose, I propose for the purposes of making an argument today; and I don't want us to be distracted by questions about whether I am accurately reflecting someone's current usage of these terms, not least because I doubt that most current uses of the term are particularly stable.

Since this definition is going to do some work later, let me point out at once some things that it does not entail. On this way of thinking of subcultures, there doesn't have to be one common culture shared by the members of all the national subcultures taken together. A subculture is "sub" because it belongs to a recognized subgroup of the nation, not because its members share the national culture *plus* some other more specific culture. My definition doesn't assume there is some culture in common to all the national subcultures: but it isn't meant to rule that out either.[9]

It is also important that the overarching group is the nation, not the society. For in the way I have been using the word "society," it is an open question whether fellow citizens share a society because it is an open question whether there is a national common culture.

No one is likely to make much fuss about the fact that a nation is multicultural in this sense. For in this sense, many simple and all large-scale societies have been multicultural. Once you have division of labor and social stratification, there will be people who do and people who don't know about music and literature and pottery and painting; if we call all these specialized spheres together the arts, then everyone will participate in the arts to varying degrees, and there are likely to be subgroups (opera lovers, say, or dedicated moviegoers, or lovers of poetry) who share significant practices and ideas with each other that are not shared with everyone else.

I associate cultures with social groups, not with nations, because I want to insist again that a group of persons living together in a common state, under common authorities, need not have a common culture. There is no single shared body of ideas and practices in India, or, to take another example, in most contemporary African states.

Thus many, but by no means all, Ghanaians know (some) English. There is no language known to all (or even most) of us. There are Muslims and Christians and practitioners of the traditional religions of many ethnic groups. There are matrilineal and patrilineal conceptions of family; there are traditions of divine kingship and less hierarchical notions of politics. The modern constitutional order—the presidency, the parliament, the courts—are not well understood by many and unknown to quite a few.[10]

Now I think it is fair to say that there is not now and there has never been a common culture in the United States either. The reason is simple: the United States has always been multilingual and has always had minorities who did not speak or understand English. It has always had a plurality of religious traditions; beginning with Native American religions and Puritans and Catholics and Jews and including now many varieties of Christianity, Judaism, Islam, Buddhism, Jainism, Taoism, Bahá'í ... and so on. And many of these religious traditions have been quite unknown to each other. More than this, Americans have also always differed significantly even among those who do speak English, from north to south and east to west, and from country to city, in customs of greeting, notions of civility, and a whole host of other ways.

To say this is not to deny that for significant parts of American history there has been a good deal of mutual knowledge across regional, religious, ethnic, and even linguistic barriers. My point is that the notion that what has held the United States together historically over its great geographical range is a common culture, like the common culture of a traditional society, is not sociologically plausible.

The notion that there is no American national culture will come as a surprise to many: observations about American culture, taken as a whole, are common. It is, for example, held to be individualist, litigious, racially obsessed. I think each of these claims is actually true, because what I mean when I say there is no common culture of the United States is not what is denied by someone who says that there is an American culture.

Such a person is describing large-scale tendencies within American life that are not necessarily participated in by all Americans. I do not mean to deny that these exist. But for such tendencies to be part of what I am calling the *common culture,* they would have to derive from beliefs and values and practices (almost) universally shared and known to be so. And *that,* they are not.

At the same time, it has also always been true that there was a dominant culture in these United States. It was Christian, it spoke English, and it identified with the high cultural traditions of Europe and, more particularly, of England. And, until recently, when most people here spoke of American culture, this is what they meant: this was the age of Eurocentrism.

This dominant culture included the common culture of the dominant classes—the government and business and cultural elites: but it was familiar to many others who were subordinate to them. And it was not merely an effect but also an instrument of their domination. Because the dominant norms of language and behavior were those of a dominant class, their children, for example, were likely to have preferred access to the best educations; educations which themselves led to dominant positions in business, in government, and in the arts.

As public education has expanded in the United States, America's citizens, and especially those citizens educated in public elementary schools in this country, have come to share a body of historical knowledge, and an understanding—however tenuous—of the American political system. And it is increasingly true that whatever other languages children in this country speak, they speak and understand English, and they watch many of the same television programs and listen to much of the same music. Not only do they share these experiences, they know that they do, and so they can imagine themselves as a collectivity, the audience for mass culture.

In that sense, most young Americans have a common culture based in a whole variety of kinds of English, but it is no longer that older Christian, Anglo-Saxon tradition that used to be called American culture.

The outlines of this almost universal common culture, to which only very few Americans are external, are somewhat blurry. But it includes, for example, in its practices, baseball; in its ideas, democracy; in its religion, Christianity;[11] in its arts, rap music and music videos and many movies. This culture is to a large extent, as I have implied, the product of schools and of the media. But even those who share this common culture live in subcultures of language, religion, family organization, and political assumptions.

Now I take it that multiculturalism is meant to be the name of a response to these familiar facts, that it is meant to be an approach to education and to public culture that acknowledges the diversity of cultures and subcultures in the United States and that proposes to deal with that diversity in some other way than by imposing the values and ideas of the hitherto dominant Anglo-Saxon cultural tradition. That, I think, is the common core of all the things that have been called multiculturalism.

Multiculturalism, in This Sense, Defended

I think this common idea is a good one. It is a good idea for a number of reasons. It is a good idea, first, because the old practice of imposing Christian, Anglo-Saxon tradition was rooted in racism and anti-Semitism (and sexism and heterosexism...but that is another story). But it is a good idea, second, because making the culture of one subculture the official culture of a state privileges the members of that subculture—gives them advantages in public life—in ways that are profoundly anti-egalitarian and, thus, antidemocratic.

Yet agreeing to this idea does not tell you much about what you should do in schools and in public culture. It tells you that you mustn't impose certain practices and ideas, but it doesn't tell you what you should do affirmatively. I want to suggest that one affirmative strategy in this area is a *bad* idea for public education and that there are other strategies that are better. And then, in closing, I want to say something about why living together in a multicultural society is bound to turn out to be difficult.

Identity Versus Culture

There is one final piece of apparatus I need, however. I have been talking of "subcultures" and defining what I mean by this. And it would be natural to assume that the primary subgroups to which these subcultures are attached will be ethnic and racial groups (with religious denominations conceived of as a species of ethnic group). It would be natural, too, to think that the characteristic difficulties of a multicultural society arise largely from the cultural differences between ethnic groups. I think this easy assimilation of ethnic and racial subgroups to subcultures is to be resisted.

First of all, it needs to be argued, and not simply assumed, that black Americans taken as a group, have a common culture: values and beliefs and practices that they share and that they do not share with others. This is equally true for, say, Chinese or Mexican Americans, and it is *a fortiori* true of white Americans. What seems clear enough is that being an African American or an Asian American or white is an important social identity in the United States. Whether these are important social identities because these groups have shared common cultures is, on the other hand, quite doubtful, not least because it is doubtful whether they *have* common cultures at all.

These issues matter in part because thinking in terms of cultural difference suggests different problems for political life than does an analysis in terms of identities. With differing cultures, we might expect misunderstandings arising out of ignorance of each other's values, practices and beliefs; we might even expect conflicts because of differing values or beliefs. The paradigms of difficulty in a society of many cultures are misunderstandings of a word or a gesture; conflicts over who should take custody of the children after a divorce; whether to go to the doctor or the priest for healing.

Once we move from talking of cultures to identities whole new kinds of problem come into view. Racial and ethnic conflicts, for example, have to do with the ways in which some people think members of other races and ethnic groups should be treated, irrespective of their cultural accomplishments. It isn't because a black man won't understand his daughter; or because he will value her differently from a white man; or because he does not know some important facts; or that Archie Bunker wouldn't want his daughter to marry one. Mr. Bunker's bigotry does not require him to differ culturally in any significant respect from black people. He would be as opposed to the marriage if the potential son-in-law had exactly the same beliefs and values (on non-race-related matters) as he had himself. Similarly, in Bosnia it is not so much that what Croats *do* makes them hateful to Serb bigots, or vice versa. It is rather that those things are hateful because Croats (or Serbs) do them.

These cases bring out the ways in which ethnic and racial identities are contrastive: it is central to being African American that you are *not* Euro-American or Asian American; *mutatis mutandis*, the same goes for being Euro-American or Asian American. And these distinctions matter because (some) people think it appropriate to treat people differently depending on which of these categories they fall into, and these ways of treating people differently lead to patterns of domination and exploitation. Racial and ethnic identities are, in this way, like genders and sexualities. To be female is not to be male; to be gay is not be straight; and these oppositions lead some to treat people differently according to their gender or sexuality, in asymmetrical ways that usually privilege men or straight people.

Now it is crucial to understanding gender and sexuality that women and men and gay and straight people grow up together in families, communities, denominations. Insofar as a common culture means common beliefs, values, and practices, gay people and straight people in most places have a common culture, and while there are societies in which the socialization of children is so structured by gender that women and men have seriously distinct cultures, this is not a feature of most "modern" societies.[12]

I take the fact that questions about feminism (gender) and gay and lesbian identity (sexuality) come up often in thinking about multiculturalism (especially in the university) as a sign that what many people are thinking about is not the multiple subcultures of the nation but its multiple identities. All I want to insist on for now is that these are not the same thing.

What Does All This Mean for Education?

Implicit in much multicultural talk is the thought that the way to deal with our many cultures in public education is to teach each child the culture of "its" group, in order, say, to define and strengthen her or his self-esteem. This is the strategy of some (but by no means all) Afrocentrists and of some (but by no means all) of those who have favored bilingual education for Hispanics.

This is the strategy I oppose.

To explain my first basis for objection, I need to elicit a paradox in this approach, which we can do by considering the answer this approach—I shall call it, tendentiously, Separatism—proposes to the question: Why should we teach African American children something different from what we teach other children? The answer will come in two parts: the first part says that we should do so because they already come from a different culture; the second part says we should do so because we should teach *all* people about the traditions from which they come.

It's the first answer that is paradoxical, at least if you think that the plurality of cultures is a problem. It is paradoxical because it proposes to solve the problems created by the fact that children have different cultures by emphasizing and entrenching those differences, not by trying to reduce them.

I should make it plain that I have no problem with the argument that children's home cultures need to be taken into account in deciding how to teach them: there's no point in giving kids information in languages or dialects they don't understand, or simply punishing them—rather than dealing with their parents or guardians—for behavior that they are being taught at home. But to admit *that* is to admit only that culture may sometimes make a difference to *how* you should teach, not that it should make a difference to *what* you should teach. And defending teaching children different histories (Afrocentric history) or different forms of speech or writing (Black English) on the grounds that this is *already* their culture simply begs the question: if we teach African American children different histories from other children, then, indeed, it will become true that knowing that history and not knowing any other history will be part of the culture of African Americans.

But the fact is that if we don't enforce cultural differences of this kind in the schools, surely they will largely disappear.

And what that means is that the *only* serious argument for Separatism that survives is the second answer I considered earlier: the claim that we must teach each child the culture of "its" group, because that is the right thing to do, because we should.

That idea is much more powerful. It is presumably at the basis of the thought that many nonobservant Jews share with observant Jews (who have other reasons for believing this), namely, that it is good to teach their children Jewish history and customs because they are Jewish children. It is the argument—"we have Plato to our father"—that led to the sense of exclusion that many African Americans felt when the history and culture of the United States was taught to them as the continuation of a white Western tradition, the argument against which so much Afrocentrism is a reaction.[13]

I myself am skeptical of all arguments of this form: my instinct is to believe that traditions are worth teaching in our public schools and colleges because they are beautiful and good and true—or at least interesting and important and useful—never because they are ours or yours, mine or thine. I was brought up a Protestant, but after my first Seder it struck me that this was a tradition worth knowing about for *every*body, Jew or Gentile, and I have always valued the experience of family community among my Muslim cousins at Ramadan.[14]

But I repeat that I do not think that it will help us in public education to add to our baggage of reasons for offering an element of a school curriculum to a child the thought that: I teach you, this particular child, this thing because it is *your* tradition.

This is because I think this an inadmissible ground for the curriculum of a *public* school, not because I think that we should *never* hear such arguments. Indeed, they are among the most compelling arguments that a family or a church or temple or mosque can offer to a child. "In our family," I might tell my nephew, "we have done this for many generations. Your great-granduncle did it, in Asante, in the late nineteenth century; your grandfather did it when he was a boy in Kumasi." There are things and practices I value because we—my ancestors and I—have done them for generations, because I take pleasure in the sense of continuity with them as *my* ancestors.

If I had been to a Catholic or a Jewish or a Muslim school, I would have learned such traditions, too, not as *my* traditions but as somebody else's. I would have learned them not because the teachers and the school believed in them as traditions, but because they believed in them *tout court*. And because one can value them not just as traditions but as truths, I could decide to make them mine.

In the modern world many have sought to hold on to the profound pleasures of tradition even after they have left their faith behind. But, to repeat, in most Catholic or Jewish or Muslim schools, before the modern period, what was taught was taught as the truth about life, the universe, and conduct, and though people might have taken pleasure in thinking of it as a matter of the tradition of a family and a community, if they had not thought it *true*, they would have thought it worthless. For these schools one notion of the good and the true, a contested notion, attached to one identity was a presupposition of the curriculum.

The public schools of a multicultural, multi-ethnic, religiously diverse society should not operate like these older religious schools: the public schools should not propagate one faith, support the traditions of one group, celebrate the heritage of one ethnicity. They should not teach particular traditions and religions, though of course they should teach about them.

The view I am articulating here is a view about the division between public and private spheres in the education of children: on such a view, ethnicity and religion are not to be transmitted by the organs of the state. Both, rather, are created and preserved outside the state by families and by wider communities, including religious ones. Because there are many such cultures—and identities—created outside the state, in civil society, and because for many of us they are central to our conceptions of ourselves and of our lives, the school must acknowledge them. Because they have a great deal of impact on our relations, in communities and in the political life of the state, we are all better prepared for life in this nation if we know something of the cultures and identities of others and if we learn to engage in respectful discourse with them. Outside the school, children can be preached a specific religion; within it, they can hear about their own traditions, along with others, but they should not be proselytized, even on behalf of their families.

I realize that I have been articulating rather than defending this view: I have not been making arguments from premises widely conceded. And I shall try to remedy that defect in a moment. But let me begin by noticing that my view does not have some of the obvious problems of Separatism. For consider what might happen if we adopted a policy in which the public schools set out to teach children according to their identities and subcultures, that not only taught *about* collective identities but set out to reinforce and transmit them. If carried to its ultimate, this policy would require segregation into cultural and religious groups either within or between public schools, in ways that would be plainly unconstitutional in the United States since the *Brown* decision. For if we did have unsegregated classes teaching Jewish history and African American history and Anglo history and Hispanic history and Chinese history in our schools, by what right would we forbid children from going to the "wrong" classes? Finally, too many of us have multiple identities—we would have to be in too many classrooms at once.[15]

Of course there are things that we surely all believe that we should teach all American children: in particular, we should teach them something of the history of the American political system. And here is a reason why we cannot hope to teach each child only "its" cultural tradition: for understanding the American constitutional system and its history requires us to know about slavery and immigration, about the Civil War and Reconstruction, the Underground Railroad and Ellis Island, the Chinese Exclusion Act and the Battle of Wounded Knee: if there is a sense in which each of these belongs more to the history of some social groups than others, there is also a clear sense in which they belong to us all.

And it is *that* idea that motivates the approach to dealing with our multicultural society that I favor, that undergirds *my* multiculturalism. For it seems to me that what is ideal in a multicultural society, whose multicultural character is created outside the state in the sphere of civil society, is that the state should seek in its educational systems to make these multiple subcultures known to each other. A multicultural education, in my view, should be one that leaves you not only knowing and loving what is good in the traditions of your subculture but also understanding and appreciating the traditions of others (and, yes, critically rejecting the worst of *all* traditions).[16]

Taylor Attacked (Gently)

I suspect that many will feel that a more substantial argument against the maintenance of identities by the state is in order. To make my case, I must spend a little time now somewhat out of the way of my main argument. What I want to do is to take on the most direct philosophical defense of ethnicity as a focus of state maintenance of which I am aware, namely that of Charles Taylor in his *Multiculturalism and "The Politics of Recognition."*[17]

Charles Taylor argues there that much of modern social and political life turns on questions of "recognition." In the Western liberal tradition we see recognition largely as a matter of acknowledging individuals and what we call their "identities," and we have the notion, which comes (as Taylor also rightly says) from the ethics of authenticity, that, other things being equal, people have the right to be acknowledged publicly as what they already really are. It is because someone is already authentically Jewish or gay that we deny them something in requiring them to hide this fact, to "pass," as we say, for something that they are not.

As has often been pointed out, however, the way much discussion of recognition proceeds is strangely at odds with the individualist thrust of talk of authenticity and identity. If what matters about me is my individual and authentic self, why is so much contemporary talk of identity about large categories—gender, ethnicity, nationality, "race,"[18] sexuality—that seem so far from individual? What is the relation between this collective language and the individualist thrust of the modern notion of the self? How has social life come to be so bound up with an idea of identity that has deep roots in romanticism with its celebration of the individual over against society?[19]

One strand of Charles Taylor's rich essay is a cogent defense of a set of answers to these questions.

The identities whose recognition Taylor discusses are largely what we can call collective social identities: religion, gender, ethnicity, "race," sexuality. This list is somewhat heterogeneous: such collective identities matter to their bearers and to others in very different ways. Religion, for example, unlike all the others, entails attachments to creeds or commitment to practices. Gender and sexuality, unlike the rest, are both grounded in the sexual body; both are differently experienced at different places and times; still, everywhere that I know of, gender identity proposes norms of behavior, of dress, of character. And, of course, gender and sexuality are, despite these abstract similarities, in many ways profoundly different. In our society, for example, passing as a woman or a man is hard, passing as straight (or gay) is relatively easy. There are other collective identities—disabled people, for example— that have sought recognition, modeling themselves sometimes on racial minorities (with whom they share the experience of discrimination and insult), or (as with deaf people) on ethnic groups. And there are castes, in South Asia; and clans in every continent; and classes, with enormously varying degrees of class consciousness, all over the industrialized world.

But the major collective identities that demand recognition in North America currently are religion, gender, ethnicity,[20] "race," and sexuality; and that they matter to us for reasons so heterogeneous should, I think, make us want to be careful not to assume that what goes for one goes for the others.

The connection between individual identity, on the one hand, which is the focus of Taylor's framing of the issues, and these collective identities, on the other, seems to be something like this: Each person's individual identity is seen as having two major dimensions. There is a collective dimension, the intersection of their collective identities, and there is what I will call a personal dimension, consisting of other socially or morally important features of the person—intelligence, charm, wit, cupidity—that are not themselves the basis of forms of collective identity.

The distinction between these two dimensions of identity is, so to speak, a sociological rather than a logical distinction. In each dimension we are talking about properties that are important for social life. But only the collective identities count as social categories, kinds of person. There is a logical category but no social category of the witty, or the clever, or the charming, or the greedy: people who share these properties do not constitute a social group in the relevant sense.

I shall return later to the question why these particular properties constitute the bases for social categories of the sort that demand recognition; for the moment, I shall rely on an intuitive grasp of the distinction between the personal and the collective dimensions of individual identity.

Let me turn now to "authenticity" in order to bring out something important about the connection between these two dimensions.

Authenticity

Taylor is right to remind us of Lionel Trilling's brilliant discussion of the modern self, and, more particularly, of the ideal of authenticity, whose roots are in romanticism. Taylor captures that idea in a few elegant sentences: "There is a certain way of being human that is *my* way. I am called upon to live my life in this way.... If I am not [true to myself], I miss the point of my life" (p. 30).

Trilling's theme is the expression of this idea in literature and in our understanding of the role of the artist as the archetype of the authentic person, and if there is one part of Trilling's picture that Taylor leaves out, it is the fact that, for romanticism, the search for authenticity is demonstrated at least as much in opposition to the demands of social life as it is in the recognition of one's own real self. In the precisely titled collection *The Opposing Self*, Trilling writes of "The Scholar Gipsy" (as the model of the artist) that "[h]is existence is intended to disturb us and make us dissatisfied with our habitual life in culture."[21]

Taylor's topic is the politics of recognition: attending to the oppositional aspects of authenticity would complicate the picture, because it would bring sharply into focus the difference between two levels of authenticity that the contemporary politics of recognition seems to conflate.

To elicit the problem, let me start with a point Taylor makes in passing about Herder, who is rightly regarded as one of the founders of modern philosophical reflection on the nation:

> I should note here that Herder applied his concept of originality at two levels, not only to the individual person among other persons, but also to the culture-bearing people among other peoples. Just like individuals, a *Volk* should be true to itself, that is, its own culture. (p. 31)

It seems to me that in this way of framing the issue less attention than necessary is paid to the connection between the originality of persons and of nations. After all, in many places nowadays, as I suggested earlier, the individual identity, whose authenticity screams out for recognition, is likely to have what Herder would have seen as a national identity as a component of its collective dimension. It is, among other things, my being, say, an African American that shapes the authentic self that I seek to express.[22] And it is, in part, because I seek to express myself that I seek recognition of an African American identity. This is the fact that makes problems for Trilling's opposing self: for recognition as an African American means social acknowledgment of that collective identity, which requires not just recognizing its existence but actually demonstrating respect for it. If, in understanding myself as African American, I see myself as resisting white norms, mainstream American conventions, the racism (and, perhaps, the materialism or the individualism) of "white culture," why should I at the same time seek recognition from these white others?

There is, in other words, at least an irony in the way in which an ideal—you will recognize it if I call it the Bohemian ideal—in which authenticity requires us to reject much that is conventional in our society is turned around and made the basis of a "politics of recognition."

Irony is not the Bohemian's only problem. It seems to me that this notion of authenticity has built into it a series of errors of philosophical anthropology. It is, first of all, wrong in failing to see, what Taylor so clearly recognizes, namely, the way in which the self is, as he says, dialogically constituted. The rhetoric of authenticity proposes not only that I have a way of being that is all my own, but that in developing it I must fight against the family, organized religion, society, the school, the state—all the forces of convention. This is wrong, however, not only because it is in dialogue with other people's understandings of who I am that I develop a conception of my own identity (Taylor's point) but also because my identity is crucially constituted through concepts (and practices) made available to me by religion, society, school, and state and mediated to varying degrees by the family. Dialogue shapes the identity I develop as I grow up, but the very material out of which I form it is provided, in part, by my society, by what Taylor calls its language in "a broad sense."[23] I shall borrow and extend Taylor's term "monological" here to describe views of authenticity that make these connected errors.

I used the example of African Americans just now, and it might seem that this complaint cannot be lodged against an American black nationalism: African American identity, it might be said, is shaped by African American society, culture, and religion. Some might say: "It is dialogue with these black others that shapes the black self; it is from these black contexts that the concepts through which African Americans shape themselves are derived. The white society, the white culture, over against which an African American nationalism of the counterconventional kind poses itself, is therefore not part of what shapes the collective dimension of the individual identities of black people in the United States." This claim seems to me to be simply false. And what shows that it is false is the fact that it is in part a recognition of a black identity by "white society" that is demanded by nationalism of this form. And "recognition" here means what Taylor means by it, not mere acknowledgment of one's existence. African American identity is centrally shaped by American society and institutions: it cannot be seen as constructed solely within African American communities.

There is, I think, another error in the standard framing of authenticity as an ideal, and that is the philosophical realism (which is nowadays usually called "essentialism") that seems inherent in the way questions of authenticity are normally posed. Authenticity speaks of the real self buried in there, the self one has to dig out and express. It is only later, after romanticism, that the idea develops that one's self is something that one creates, makes up, so that every life should be an artwork whose creator is, in some sense, his or her own greatest creation. (This is, I suppose, an idea one of whose sources is Oscar Wilde.)

Of course, neither the picture in which there is just an authentic nugget of selfhood, the core that is distinctively me waiting to be dug out, nor the notion that I can simply make up any self I choose, should tempt us. We make up selves from a tool kit of options made available by our culture and society, in ways that I pointed out earlier. We do make choices, but we don't determine the options among which we choose.[24]

If you agree with this, you will wonder how much of authenticity we should acknowledge in our political morality, and that will depend, I suppose, on whether an account of it can be developed that is neither essentialist nor monological.

It would be too large a claim that the identities that claim recognition in the multicultural chorus *must* be essentialist and monological. But it seems to me that one reasonable ground for suspicion of much contemporary multicultural talk is that the conceptions of collective identity they presuppose are indeed remarkably unsubtle in their understandings of the processes by which identities, both individual and collective, develop. And I am not sure whether Taylor would agree with me that collective identities disciplined by historical knowledge and philosophical reflection would be radically unlike the identities that now parade before us for recognition, and would raise, as a result, questions different from the ones he addresses.

In a rather unphilosophical nutshell: my suspicion is that Taylor is happier with the collective identities that actually inhabit our globe than I am, and that may be one of the reasons why I am less disposed to make the concessions to them that he does.

These differences in sympathy show up in the area of what Taylor calls group survival, and this is where we return, finally, to the questions I was raising about the role of the state in maintaining ethnic identity.

Here is Taylor defining what he means by group survival (and it is clear that he has the political life of his own native Quebec very much in mind).

> Policies aimed at survival actively seek to create members of the community, for instance, in their assuring that future generations continue to identify as French-speakers. (pp. 58–59)

Taylor argues that the reality of plural societies may require us to modify procedural liberalism. I think he is right in thinking that there is not much to be said for the view that liberalism should be purely procedural: I agree that we should not accept both (a) the insistence on the uniform application of rules without exception and (b) the suspicion of collective goals (p. 60); I agree that the reason we cannot accept (a) is that we should reject (b) (p. 61). There can be legitimate collective goals whose pursuit will require giving up pure proceduralism.

But Taylor's argument for collective goals in the vast majority of modern states, which are multicultural, is that one very strong demand, to which the state may need to accede, may be for the survival of certain "societies," by which he means groups whose continuity through time consists in the transmission through the generations of a certain culture, of distinctive institutions and values and practices. And he claims (p. 41n) that the desire for survival is not simply the desire that the culture which gives meaning to the lives of currently existing individuals should continue for them, but requires the continued existence of the culture through "indefinite future generations."

I would like to suggest a focus different from Taylor's in his discussion of this issue. To explain why, let me stress first that the "indefinite future generations" in question should be the descendants of the current population. The desire for the survival of French Canadian identity is not the desire that there should for the long future be people somewhere or other who speak that Quebec language and practice those Quebec practices. It is the desire that this language and practice should be carried on from one generation to the next. A proposal to solve the problems of Canada by paying a group of unrelated people to carry on French Canadian culture on some island in the South Pacific simply would not meet the need.

Why does this matter? Because it seems to me not at all clear that this aim is one that we can acknowledge while respecting the autonomy of future individuals. In particular families, it is often the case that parents want the children to persist in some practice that those children resist. This is true for arranged marriage for some women of Indian origin in Britain, for example. In this case, the ethical principles of equal dignity that underlie liberal thinking seem to militate against allowing the parents their way because we care about the autonomy of these young women. If this is true in the individual case, it seems to me equally true where a whole generation of one group wishes to impose a form of life on the next generation—and *a fortiori* true if they seek to impose it somehow on still later generations.

Of course, speaking abstractly, survival in this sense is perfectly consistent with respect for autonomy; otherwise every genuinely liberal society would have to die in a generation. If we create a culture that our descendants will want to hold on to, our culture will survive in them. But here there is a deep problem that has to do with the question of how a respect for autonomy should constrain our ethics of education. After all, we have it to some extent in our power to make our children into the kind of people who will want to maintain our culture. Precisely because the monological view of identity is incorrect, there is no individual nugget waiting in each child to express itself, if only family and society permit its free development. We have to help children make themselves, and we have to do so according to our values because children do not begin with values of their own. To value autonomy is to respect the conceptions of others, to weight their plans for themselves very heavily in deciding what is good for them; but children do not start out with plans or conceptions. It follows, therefore, in education in the broad sense—the sense that is covered by the technical notion of social reproduction—we simply must both appeal to and transmit values more substantial than a respect for liberal procedures. Liberal proceduralism is meant to allow a state to be indifferent between a variety of conceptions of the good: but what conceptions of the good there will be will depend on what goes on in education. Teach all children only that they must accept a politics in which other people's conceptions of the good are not ridden over, and there will soon be no substantive conceptions of the good at all.

In most modern societies, the education of most people is conducted by institutions run by the government. Education is, therefore, in the domain of the political. This is not just an accident: social reproduction involves collective goals. Furthermore, as children develop and come to have identities whose autonomy we should respect, the liberal state has a role in protecting the autonomy of children against their parents, churches, and communities. I would be prepared to defend the view that the state in modern society must be involved in education on this sort of basis, but even if someone disagrees with this they must admit that it currently does play such a role and that, for the reasons I have been discussing, this means that the state is involved in propagating elements, at least, of a substantive conception of the good.

That is one of the major reasons why I agree so wholeheartedly with Taylor's objections to pure proceduralism. I do not think that it is Taylor's reason, however, even though he does raise his objections to pure proceduralism in the context of a discussion of survival, that is, of social reproduction.

Proper Behavior

The large collective identities that call for recognition come with notions of how a proper person of that kind behaves: it is not that there is one way that gay people or blacks should behave, but that there are gay and black modes of behavior. These notions provide loose norms or models, which play a role in shaping the life plans of those who make these collective identities central to their individual identities.[25] Collective identities, in short, provide what we might call scripts: narratives that people can use in shaping their life plans and in telling their life stories. In our society (though not, perhaps, in the England of Addison and Steele) being witty does not in this way suggest the life script of "the wit." And that is why what I called the personal dimensions of identity work differently from the collective ones.

This is not just a point about modern Westerners: cross-culturally it matters to people that their lives have a certain narrative unity; they want to be able to tell a story of their lives that makes sense. The story—my story—should cohere in the way appropriate by the standards made available in my culture to a person of my identity. In telling that story, how I fit into the wider story of various collectivities is, for most of us, important. It is not just gender identities that give shape (through, for example, rites of passage into woman- or manhood) to one's life: ethnic and national identities too fit each individual story into a larger narrative. And some of the most "individualist" of individuals value such things. Hobbes spoke of the desire for glory as one of the dominating impulses of human beings, one that was bound to make trouble for social life. But glory can consist in fitting and being seen to fit into a collective history, and so, in the name of glory, one can end up doing the most social things of all.

How does this general idea apply to our current situation in the multicultural West? We live in societies in which certain individuals have not been treated with equal dignity because they were, for example, women, homosexuals, blacks, Catholics. Because, as Taylor so persuasively argues, our identities are dialogically shaped, people who have these characteristics find them central—often, negatively central—to their identities. Nowadays there is a widespread agreement that the insults to their dignity and the limitations of their autonomy imposed in the name of these collective identities are seriously wrong. One form of healing of the self that those who have these identities participate in is learning to see these collective identities not as sources of limitation and insult but as a valuable part of what they centrally are. Because the ethic of authenticity requires us to express what we centrally are in our lives, they move next to the demand that they be recognized in social life as women, homosexuals, blacks, Catholics. Because there was no good reason to treat people of these sorts badly, and because the culture continues to provide degrading images of them nevertheless, they demand that we do cultural work to resist the stereotypes, to challenge the insults, to lift the restrictions.

These old restrictions suggested life scripts for the bearers of these identities, but they were negative ones. In order to construct a life with dignity, it seems natural to take the collective identity and construct positive life scripts instead.

An African American after the Black Power movement takes the old script of self-hatred, the script in which he or she is a nigger, and works, in community with others, to construct a series of positive black life scripts. In these life scripts, being a Negro is recoded as being black, and this requires, among other things, refusing to assimilate to white norms of speech and behavior. And if one is to be black in a society that is racist, then one has constantly to deal with assaults on one's dignity. In this context, insisting on the right to live a dignified life will not be enough. It will not even be enough to require that one be treated with equal dignity despite being black, for that will require a concession that being black counts naturally or to some degree against one's dignity. And so one will end up asking to be respected *as a black*.

Let me rewrite this paragraph as a paragraph about gay identity: An American homosexual after Stonewall and gay liberation takes the old script of self-hatred, the script of the closet, the script in which he is a faggot, and works, in community with others, to construct a series of positive gay life scripts. In these life scripts, being homosexual is recoded as being gay, and this requires, among other things, refusing to stay in the closet. And if one is to be out of the closet in a society that deprives homosexuals of equal dignity and respect, then one has constantly to deal with assaults on one's dignity. In this context, the right to live as an "open homosexual" will not be enough. It will not even be enough to be treated with equal dignity "despite being homosexual," for that will require a concession that being homosexual counts naturally or to some degree against one's dignity. And so one will end up asking to be respected *as a homosexual*.

This is the sort of story Taylor tells, with sympathy, about Quebec. I hope I seem sympathetic to the stories of gay and black identity I have just told. I *am* sympathetic. I see how the story goes. It may even be historically, strategically necessary for the story to go this way.[26] But I think we need to go on to the next necessary step, which is to ask whether the identities constructed in this way are ones we—I speak here, for what it is worth, as someone who counts in America as a gay black man—can be happy with in the longer run. What demanding respect for people *as blacks* and *as gays* requires is that there be some scripts that go with being an African American or having same-sex desires. There will be proper ways of being black and gay: there will be expectations to be met; demands will be made. It is at this point that someone who takes autonomy seriously will want to ask whether we have not replaced one kind of tyranny with another. If I had to choose between the world of the closet and the world of gay liberation, or between Uncle Tom and Black Power, I would, of course, choose in each case the latter. But I would like not to have to choose. I would like other options. The politics of recognition requires that one's skin color, one's sexual body, should be politically acknowledged in ways that make it hard for those who want to treat their skin and their sexual body as personal dimensions of the self. And personal means: not secret, but not too tightly scripted. I think (and Taylor, I gather, does not) that the desire of some Quebeckers to require people who are "ethnically" francophone to teach their children in French steps over a boundary: and let me add (to pronounce on a topic Taylor does *not* address) that I believe it is, in some sense, the *same* boundary that is crossed by someone who demands that I organize my life around my "race" or my sexuality.

The relationship between these arguments and the issue of the role of the state in the maintenance of ethnic identities is complex. I have been arguing, in the name of liberal individualism, against a certain kind of enforcement of identity. John Stuart Mill wrote: "Society can and does execute its own mandates; and if it issues wrong mandates instead of right, or any mandates at all in things with which it ought not to meddle, it practices a social tyranny more formidable than many kinds of political oppression, since, though not usually upheld by such extreme penalties, it leaves fewer means of escape, penetrating much more deeply into the details of life, and enslaving the soul itself."[27] This passage should remind us that nongovernmental social enforcement of identities can be objectionable, even if my focus has been on limiting governmental enforcement.

But, as I have conceded, these arguments are hard to apply to young children since they are addressed to people possessed of an autonomy children do not (yet) possess. This might mean—since the state may have to protect both the autonomy of adults and the rights of nonautonomous persons, including children—that there can be a role for the state in relation to ethnicity, even if the state (like society) should not enforce ethnicities as it conceives of them. Indeed, if having the option of an ethnic identity is a good for an autonomous adult, might not the state owe to nonautonomous children an upbringing that permits them just such choices?

This is a complex issue: but let me say at least this much in answer to this obvious question. The sort of multicultural education I have been proposing will produce children knowledgeable about the meanings of many of the identities socially available around them: in that sense, so far as I can see, a state that offers multicultural education of this kind is meeting such obligations as the state has to make a range of identities available to children whose schooling it has in its charge.

A Final Argument

I have a final argument against Separatism. It is that it is dangerous, for reasons that have to do with the final point I want to make, which is about the difficulty of managing multicultural—plural—societies.

I said earlier that no one is likely to be troubled by the variety of subcultures in high culture. Why is this? Because however important our participation in high culture is, it is unlikely to be at the heart of our ethnicity. High culture crosses ethnic boundaries to an extraordinary degree. (The boundaries that it crosses with less ease are those of class.) The result is that subdivisions of high culture are not so likely to become central to the organization of political life. The United States is not threatened by the cultural autonomy of the American Philosophical Association or (even) the American Medical Association. In this respect the associations of high culture are like many elements of popular culture: the next New York mayoral election is not going to be between followers of the Mets and of the Yankees.

But differences in what I have called subcultures are rather different. We pass on our language to the next generation because we care to communicate with them; we pass on religion because we share its vision and endorse its values; we pass on our folkways because we value people with those folkways.

I have insisted that we should distinguish between cultures and identities, but ethnic identities are distinctive in having cultural distinctions as one of their primary marks. Ethnic identities are created in family and community life. These—along with mass-mediated culture, the school, and the college—are, for most of us, the central sites of the social transmission of culture. Distinct practices, beliefs, norms go with each ethnicity in part because people *want* to be ethnically distinct, because many people want the sense of solidarity that comes from being unlike others. With ethnicity in modern society, it is often the distinct identity that comes first and the cultural distinction that is created and maintained because of it, not the other way around. The distinctive common cultures of ethnic and religious identities matter not simply because of their contents but also as markers of those identities.

Culture in this sense is the home of what we care about most. If other people organize their solidarity around cultures different from ours, this makes them, to that extent, different from us in ways that matter to us deeply. The result, of course, is not just that we have difficulty understanding across cultures—this is an inevitable result of cultural difference, for much of culture consists of language and other shared modes of understanding—but that we end up preferring our own kind, and if we prefer our own kind, it is easy enough to slip into preferring to vote for our own kind, to employ our own kind, and so on.

In sum: Cultural difference undergirds loyalties. As we have seen repeatedly in recent years, from South Africa to the Balkans, from Sri Lanka to Nigeria, from South Central Los Angeles to Crown Heights, once these loyalties matter they will be mobilized in politics and the public square, *except to the extent that a civic culture can be created that explicitly seeks to exclude them*. And that is why my multiculturalism is so necessary: it is the only way to reduce the misunderstandings across subcultures, the only way to build bridges of loyalty across the ethnicities that have so often divided us. Multiculturalism of this sort—pluralism, to use an older word—is a way of making sure we care enough about people across ethnic divides to keep those ethnic divides from destroying us. And it must, I believe, be a central part of the function of our educational system to equip all of us to share the public space with people of multiple identities and distinct subcultures.

I insisted early on the distinction between cultures and identities. It is especially important here. Teaching young people to respect those with other identities is not the same thing as teaching them some of the central practices and beliefs of a different subculture. When we teach Toni Morrison to children with serious attention we are demonstrating respect for the cultural work of a black person in a culture where there is still pressure not to respect black people. We are showing that respect to black children; we are modeling that respect for other children. Each of these is something that a decent education can seek to do; neither is simply a matter of introducing people to a culture.

It seems to me that it will be important, too, to teach children to reflect critically on their identities, including their ethnic identities, if they care about them; and I accept that once we do this, we will inevitably change their identities or, at least, shape them in various ways. Once ethnic identities cease to be unreflective, as such reflection is bound to make them, I will come to see my identity as something that can be molded, if not individually then at least as part of a common political project, or indeed as something that can be put away altogether.

If I accept that the school in our society cannot simply leave everything ethnically where it is—accept that my earlier separation of ethnicity out of the public sphere in education was too simple—the question of a single common culture is likely to resurface. Why not argue out democratically a common culture, making sure to learn the lesson of multiculturalism that this must not simply be the cover for a sectional interest?

My answer is: because we do not have to do so. The question presupposes that what we *really* need is shared values, a common culture. I think this is a mistake: not least because, as I argued against Taylor, I am skeptical of the role of the state in enforcing identities.

But let me grant that we *do* need something in common if we are to live together, and try to say quickly what that something is.

What I think we really need is provided in a conjunct of our original definition of a society that was so obvious that we soon left it behind. "Common institutions and a common culture," I said, dropping talk of the common institutions almost immediately.

But to live together in a nation what is required is that we all share a commitment to the organization of the state—the institutions that provide the overarching order of our common life. This does not require that we have the *same* commitment to those institutions, in the sense that the institutions must carry the same meaning for all of us.

The first amendment separates church and state. Some of us are committed to this because we are religious: we see it as the institutionalization of a Protestant insistence on freedom of conscience. Some of us are committed to it because we are Catholics or Jews or Muslims, who do not want to be pressed into conformity by a Protestant majority. Some of us are atheists who want to be left alone. We can live together with this arrangement provided we all are committed to it, for our different reasons.

A shared political life in a great modern nation is not like the life of a traditional society. It can encompass a great diversity of meanings. When we teach children democratic habits, through practice in public schools, what we are creating is a shared commitment to certain forms of social behavior. We can call this a political culture, if we like. But the meanings citizens give to their lives, and to the political within their lives, in particular, will be shaped not only by the school, but by the family and church, by reading and by television, in their professional and recreational associations.

Maybe, in the end, there will be a richer American common culture; maybe it will lead to a consensus on the value of American institutions. Certainly cultural homogenization is proceeding apace. But it has not happened yet. And, so far as I can see, it doesn't have to happen for us to live together. Competing identities may be having a hard time living together in new democracies. But in this, the oldest democracy, so long as our institutions treat every significant identity with enough respect to gain its allegiance, we can muddle along in the meanwhile without a common culture. Is that not, after all, what we have been doing lo these many years?

Endnotes

1 The shared space is probably what distinguishes this sense of the term from the sense of society in the expression "international high society." We wouldn't normally speak of this as "a society," despite the shared institutions (Ascot, the Kentucky Derby, the fall fashions in Paris, the London season) and common culture (conventions of address).

2 My dictionary gives as the relevant sense of the word "society": "A group of human beings broadly distinguished from other groups by mutual interests, participation in characteristic relationships, shared institutions, and a common culture." *American Heritage Dictionary III for DOS*, 3rd ed. (Novato, CA, 1993), s.v. "society."

3 It is increasingly true, of course, that the cultures of other places are shaped by American culture—notably through the movies—so that the distinction between a culture shaped *in* the United States and one shaped *by* the United States is less sharp than it used to be.

4 Some of us live here without being citizens, and thus without being entitled to participate in those institutions as voters, jurors, and so on; but we all have the right to participate in other politically created institutions—heterosexual marriage, for example, or property-ownership—and the obligation to live under American laws.

5 *American Heritage Dictionary III for DOS*, s.v. "culture."

6 There is nothing absurd in holding that the different practices and beliefs of, say, women and men in a society cohere—not in the sense of forming a single logically consistent system, but in the sense that the reason why women engage in one practice is connected with the reason why men engage in another different practice and that a society in which women and men engage in these different practices is, in part, held together by that fact. But even that notion came under attack when the functionalist notion that every element of practice in a society was adaptive was subjected to criticism.

7 Though, as I say, I do not think you need to react by becoming a cultural relativist.

8 This is not the only way the term could be used. Some want to reserve the term for the culture of subordinate groups. I want to avoid that implication in my usage.

9 What I have been calling a subculture, then, consists of people who share specific practices, beliefs, and values that constitute the common culture of a subgroup of the nation.

10 Given that the constitution is about a year old as I write (it was promulgated in 1992 and came into full effect in 1993), this is not too

surprising, I suppose. But much of the structure has been in place since independence with few changes.

11 This is not, remember, to claim that most Americans are Christians by belief. It is to say only that some of the central ideas and practices of Christianity are known to and understood by most Americans.

12 Men and women may have characteristically distinct experiences, but that doesn't, by itself, guarantee distinct cultures.

13 There is another problem with this way of thinking: it suggests that Western culture belongs to some American children more than others *in virtue of their descent*. This is doubly troubling: first, because the culture we teach in school belongs only to those who do the work to earn it; second, because it proposes to exclude certain children from certain educational experiences on what look like racial grounds.

14 Of course, I do not think—absurdly—that everyone should become both a Jew and a Muslim while holding on to Protestantism. The sort of participation in Jewish or Muslim celebrations that I am talking about is the participation of a guest, a visitor, a friend.

15 A point made to me by Professor Elgin of the philosophy department at Wellesley College.

16 Postmodernism urges people to respond: "worst by whose criteria?" My answer is: in the real world of intercultural moral conversation, nobody—except a postmodernist—defends their position by claiming that it follows simply from their criteria and leaves it at that. If we argue with those who practice clitoral excision and say it ought to be stopped, we need to tell those who practice it why. If we argue that it causes pain to girls and years of low-grade infections to women and raises the risks of pregnancy; if we say that women who have not been circumcised are *not, ipso facto,* sexually insatiable; if we say that the practice deprives women of a source of pleasure; if we observe that the practice is *not,* in fact, recommended by the Koran: nobody, except in a rhetorical moment of weakness, is going to defend the practice by saying that these facts—if such they are—are relevant only by our criteria. And when they suggest to us that "we" mutilate women—through cosmetic surgery; or that "we" practice male circumcision, which also reduces men's capacity for pleasure; or that an uncircumcised girl cannot get a husband: these facts—if such they are—do not strike us as relevant only by *our* criteria. (And, in any case, there are people here who are not so sure about the badness of the practice and people there not so convinced of its goodness.)

And this is in a hard case of intercultural disagreement. Most American subgroups share so many substantial ethical assumptions that the "Says who?" response is usually offered only by those who are losing an argument.

17 Charles Taylor, *Multiculturalism and "The Politics of Recognition": An Essay* (Princeton, NJ, 1992).

18 I've spent enough time arguing against the reality of "races" to feel unhappy about using the term without scare quotes. See my *In My Father's House: Africa in the Philosophy of Culture* (New York, 1992), passim.

19 Taylor reminds us rightly of Trilling's profound contributions to our understanding of this history. I discuss Trilling's work in chapter 4 of *In My Father's House.*

20 In the United States we deal with what Herder would have recognized as national differences (differences, in Taylor's formulation, between one society and another within the American nation) through concepts of ethnicity.

21 Lionel Trilling, *The Opposing Self: Nine Essays in Criticism* (New York, 1955), p. xiv.

22 And, for Herder, this would be a paradigmatic national identity.

23 The broad sense "cover[s] not only the words we speak, but also other modes of expression whereby we define ourselves, including the 'languages' of art, of gesture, of love, and the like," p. 32.

24 This is too simple, too, for reasons captured in Anthony Giddens's many discussions of "duality of structure."

25 I say "make," here, not because I think there is always conscious attention to the shaping of life plans or a substantial experience of choice, but because I want to stress the anti-essentialist point that there are choices that can be made.

26 Compare what Sartre wrote in his "Orphée Noir," in *Anthologie de la Nouvelle Poésie Nègre et Malgache de Langue Française,* ed. Léopold Sédar Senghor (Paris, 1969), p. xiv. Sartre argued, in effect, that this move is a necessary step in a dialectical progression. In this passage he explicitly argues that what he calls an "antiracist racism" is a path to the "final unity ... [,] the abolition of differences of race."

27 John Stuart Mill, *On Liberty and Other Writings* (Cambridge, 1989), p. 8.

Peter Sellars

Getting Real: The Arts in Post-NEA America

IN MY LINE OF WORK truth is not arrived at by individuals sitting around saying what they think. Quite the opposite is true. Engagement, the discussion through sharing something in my life, is about going into a room with a bunch of other really interesting people and coming out with something more complex than any one of us would have imagined before we walked in. I assume the same thing tonight. So please, let's engage. I will say a series of irritating, indefensible things, and at some point people will respond to that.

Basically, in a friendly way, I want to talk about the current crisis. I'm not one of these people who just have to position everything as a crisis in order to talk about it, but I think it's not too far-fetched to suggest that the arts in America are in a rather crisis-oriented position. If we could just talk about Washington, DC. Everyone's favorite NEA chairman Jane [Alexander] testified today before the House Subcommittee on Appropriations, trying to keep the NEA budget at, I think, $163 million, which is what Mr. Clinton asked for last year but did not get. He's therefore asking for it again this year. I think people noted what is referred to as a plug for the arts in his State of the Union speech. In Washington even the infinitely hostile Mr. Newt has responded in a friendly way to the arts this week.

On the other hand, the Republican majority in the House a few months ago did openly target the National Endowment as something to be removed in this current session. By the time I was supplying the title for this evening, I figured that "post-NEA America" was not unduly apocalyptic, but kind of just what it feels like. The NEA had its guts ripped out of it a couple of years ago, and it's still on certain artificial life support systems, but I don't think it's really going to come back. So the question is: is there a public place, a public voice, a public space, a public identity in America, or is everything about to be privatized on our way into the next century?

Artists, of course, are very satisfied with the artistic equivalent of the Reaganomics trickle-down theory. They protest against Reagan, but in terms of the idea that "we're making art for a small handful of elite people who will be very pleased as they appreciate our work." Then somehow that will trickle down to the rest of society, and everyone will be happier for it. That seems to be accepted unquestioningly by a lot of artists, but I would suggest that it's perhaps not enough. One of the reasons why someone like Jesse Helms can actually corner the debate on art, define its terms, and, as soon as he's defined those terms can, of course, win the debate, is because artists themselves have not formulated counterterms in any way that has made an impact on the American public. I would *like* to blame the Satan of all Satans, Jesse Helms, but actually he has a sense for entertainment that so many artists lack. He has an ability to get space in the press, and also a sense of delicious outrage that is what the arts were supposed to be about. So, to my mind, Mr. Helms has won absolutely fair and square. The question is: do the artists want to roll over and play dead, or is a response going to be made?

There are several possibilities for the coming years. You could have what I think of as the Brezhnevization of the arts in America, where *Swan Lake* with the ironclad Plisetskaya will continue to be sponsored in the all-platinum version. This will be used as official culture the way they put those cement barriers in front of important office buildings to prevent suicide bombers from driving their trucks through. The idea is that you actually fund certain forms of culture because it is an impediment to thought and it discourages people from being creative. The Soviets have pioneered this, and in China and Vietnam you can see the vestiges of it. Obviously, though, in America we have our own form of major money being applied to mentally deadening activities.

I want to move on for one second to one interesting scenario. When Congress targeted the NEA, the message that was sent to artists in America was really simple: get a day job; there will be no such thing as a profession; art is something you do in your spare time. Now, for me, I would say this is not entirely a bad idea. I'd like to talk a little bit about that tonight because there are large stretches of the history of art where it's not a professional activity. During most of the history of theater, for example, people do other things with their lives and then happen to put on shows. The rise of the profession has not always been co-equaled with the rise of the standard of the art form. Music, of course, is a more complicated question. In a certain way this is because of the lifetime of commitment to technique that's required. So you need something to support you while you're learning. At the same time, when you look at the arts in many societies around the world, there's a very, very different attitude.

I was so interested in talking about Plisetskaya and the Bolshoi that I neglected to mention the actual art that was happening on a *samizdat* level. I do foresee this in America ten years from now. The way it was in Moscow in 1962: in Apartment Building Number 4 in the basement at ten o'clock, and if the police have heard about it, then it won't happen, and you'll be contacted. We have the Internet; so if it's not going to happen we can get that out an hour before. But the question is whether real artists might just have to go completely underground in the same manner that we saw in the Brezhnev years.

In the 1990 L.A. Festival, which was based around the Pacific Rim cultures, we invited a lot of artists from around Asia: aboriginal dancers, the Korean shaman from Chindo Island, the King Island Inupiat, the Jemez Pueblo from New Mexico, a lot of extraordinary drummers, dancers, and puppeteers from Japan. We had to convince the State Department that all of these people were world-class artists because, as you know, the rather evil immigration laws that have been coming through the last group of years make it almost impossible to bring a distinguished person from abroad to this country. We had to convince the State Department to grant H1 visas, saying that these are some of the last artists in their field keeping alive a tradition; these are world-class performers. So, of course, when they made their visa applications, we got these furious calls from the State Department saying, "You told us these were important artists, and it turns out on their visas they're all farmers."

This connects to a story that I heard in Bali a few weeks ago from a great elderly dance teacher, one of the most respected teachers on the island, who has now trained three generations of dancers. He said, "A good artist is someone who understands the gestures in the dance, knows the music, and has mastered the technique. A very good artist is someone who understands the gestures in the dance, understands the music, has mastered the technique, has spiritual insight, and understands the meaning. A great artist is someone who understands the gestures, understands the music, has mastered the technique, has spiritual insight, understands the meaning, and is a farmer."

I think our task right now is to recover from some bad decades. For example, the normally progressive critic Sir Herbert Read announced a few decades back that art begins where function ends; that is to say, as soon as you're certifiably nonfunctional, then that's an art, and we will reward that. But all the people who are doing things that you can use, making pots and so on, we'll put that by the elevator in the museum near the drinking fountains, or in the stairwell, because women and other people made those things, and they are deprioritized.

Obviously, in many cultures, that's not the way it functions. The first step is the artist's being part of a larger ecology. In an African village, culture is an artistic ecosystem. Your comb was carved by somebody who cares a lot about you. And in order to show you how much they care about you, they carved a beautiful comb for you. On the handle of the comb there's a picture, a representation of your grandmother, so that every time you comb your hair, you remember that the person who made this comb loved you. You realize that your ancestor is present with you, watching you and supporting you in every moment of your life. Meanwhile, it's a comb. All those things are happening. It is a total ecology. It is an ecology of meaning, of layers, of social engagement, that moves backwards and forwards in history, and it's a comb.

I think one of our key tasks right now is to reimagine this art ecology separated from high capitalism, which is essentially commodifying everything, but also reifying everything so that, for example, an artistic gesture now doesn't mean anything anymore. In theater, my line of work, presumably one of the things we're trying to do is to get people to feel something and cry. But it's AT&T who have perfected the ability to bring forth tears. In less than one minute you're in tears. "Oh, mama, the train station," and they've done it! There is no emotion that has not been used to sell products. So, therefore, all of it becomes totally suspect, and you say, "Wait a minute. What is this guy trying to do to me?" Then you really have to process it in a completely different way. So, again, in the arts our task is to surprise people somehow into feeling something, to come around the back. But this idea of coming around the back or, shall we say, proceeding by indirection, is, of course, what the arts exist in this society to inculcate. The ideal preparation for democracy is not the awareness of how business works. Maybe there has to be something else in order to sustain a democracy: the idea of what it takes to cultivate a voice, the idea of what it takes not only to cultivate a voice, but multiple voices, the idea of what happens when you have multiple voices. Even Bach's solo music is about multiple voices. It's the presence of multiplicity within each one of us and how that's organized, and how, in the course of a fugue, you end up somewhere that you couldn't have imagined because of all this participation. It's the participatory, engaged model.

I stage a lot of eighteenth-century oratorios. In the eighteenth century, the idea of oratory was exactly the idea that democracy is only functional if people can share the things that they most deeply believe. But actually, most people, when they're sharing the things they most deeply believe, exaggerate horribly. So you have this embarrassing image of Clinton holding a paraplegic kid and saying, "Vote for me." The rings of insincerity are really offensive. What about dealing with a paraplegic kid? How do we connect to Raphael's painting *The Transfiguration* and the moment when Jesus goes up on the mountain and is present with Elijah? Raphael treats that, of course, through the moment before Jesus has had to encounter the kid foaming at the mouth and his parents don't know what to do about it. Raphael paints this healing of a socially disruptive situation and the transfigurations which are adjacent to each other in the Book of Luke in the same painting. You need one for the other. The concept is transfiguration. The idea is that the world isn't just what it looks like. It's there to be transformed, to be transfigured. We transfigure things, and things are always in this state of transfiguration.

If I could just take Raphael as a good starting point to discuss real estate. Let's talk Florence, Italy. Let's talk a bunch of artists living there, working there, and let's talk about real estate values. It's now valuable property. The presence of artists raised the real estate value. Let's talk about one of my other favorite real estate bonanzas, Florence, Arizona. Have people been there? It's really very special. It's the maximum security prison capital of America. Prisons are the industry: the town industry. It's a town entirely devoted to prisons. There are seven of them. It's there where the famous "three strikes and you're out" people go. The prisons present a new level of specific cruelty that has been achieved by our yuppified society.

People are put in a tiny cement box, entirely painted white, with nothing allowed on the walls, and no reading material for twenty-three and a half hours a day. There is no human contact permitted whatsoever; that is to say, the food is distributed by a computerized dumbwaiter. At the time when you have your half-hour exercise, the door opens automatically and you move down a bend in the corridor to the exercise room, which is all cement and completely empty. The ceiling is covered over, and it's twice the size of your cubicle. When you go back, the door shuts automatically. You literally do not see another human being. This is also happening at Pelican Bay here in California. The inmates of Pelican Bay sued the US government for cruel and unusual punishment because, of course, they, like the child that Christ tried to heal and did heal, are going crazy. The deprivation of human contact is not, I think it's fair to say, rehabilitation.

Frankly, our task at this point in the arts is rehabilitation. One of the great things about being alive in America right now is there's no dearth of subject matter. There's plenty to work on. But the question is: what do people need, and how do you heal situations like that? How do you move in zones of violence? In L.A. we had a very intense example of that when a large section of the city erupted in flames over the course of three days and three nights. Some called it a riot. Some called it a rebellion. Some called it an insurrection. Some called it an uprising. George Bush, one of our recent presidents (who came up with a phrase that I particularly admire, "the vision thing"), had a response, which was to announce that "we will find whoever is responsible, and they will be prosecuted to the utmost of the law."

In the arts, of course, we're trained with Antonin Artaud to be sensitive to social disruption and to the literal meaning of what we're talking about when we say, "gesture through the flame." What is it when people are gesturing through the flames? What is it when a level of pain is such that people set fire to their own neighborhood? Are you reading the message? Or are you not? Do you know how to read the message in those flames? And, meanwhile, do you know how to treat the subject? The media did not, and for three days we had a spectacle of live television wires open all over America. Instead of any kind of teach-in about the issues of economic development and underdevelopment in South Central Los Angeles, we had three days of helicopters circling overhead with people going, "I don't know, Pete, it looks like it's on fire to me. I don't know. I can't tell. Oh, yeah, I guess it's burning. It looks like it's burning. Oh, okay. Back to the studio." It was a country that did not know how to read the flames, did not know how to read the gesture through the flames.

So one of our first tasks in the 1993 L.A. Festival was to respond to that gesture. We programmed the festival with a committee of artists drawn from all over the city, trying to say, "OK, how do we respond?" Since there was no response politically, since the media continued its course of predictable self-congratulation, there had to be some response. So a committee of artists met for a year and decided the themes of the 1993 festival would be home, place, and memory. What is your home? What do you think of as your home? Is it a place where you live? Or, in fact, is the place you live offensive to you and actually a betrayal of your idea of home? And, meanwhile, if you came from somewhere else, as most people in Los Angeles did, what is the role of memory, what memory of home are you carrying with you? Are you in some way maybe continuing to live it? Or indeed can you not live it because you're a refugee? Of course, as soon as you begin to propose—and this is really shocking in the century of formalism—that art is actually about subject matter, the gates are open for people to collaborate. That is: an artist, a musician, a dancer, and a poet can all talk about those issues, which is different from announcing an evening of dance, an evening of music, an evening of visual arts. It actually creates. We're out of our disciplinary boxes where we've been sent for our infractions, and we're actually permitted to talk to each other once there is subject matter.

We've come through a long period where teaching art has had nothing to do with subject matter; it has entirely to do with a formal set of considerations. I think that's a crisis, and I think that's one reason why the artists are so inarticulate when they have to speak to the rest of the country about what they're doing and why they're doing it; because art schools didn't train them to do that.

In any case, we ended up setting this festival at the intersection of Crenshaw Boulevard, where the first fires were lit. Over a five-week period of the festival, a large number of the four hundred events were headquartered there. It was very interesting to try to convince people in Los Angeles who would never dream of even driving through that neighborhood not only to drive, but to park their cars and get out. Of course, what they found was a beautiful neighborhood, a neighborhood just like their neighborhood. The difference was, what was marked in that neighborhood was everything that was owned outside the neighborhood. It was marked because it was burnt down. But a year later, in a festival, we were able actually to create a situation where people living in Beverly Hills could drive to this part of the city and see something that was, in fact, educational: educational in the sense that they had a good time and that they said, "Oh, right, this is not the war zone that I've seen pictured on the evening news. This is actually a place where people are raising their children and trying to get on with life. In fact, you can do fabulous Christmas shopping there."

Now, that was a year-long process of getting permission to work in that neighborhood, because you don't just show up and say, "Hi, we're going to save you now," but the opposite. The fact is that working with neighborhood associations, with merchants associations, with police, was a yearlong process of lots of stormy meetings, one on one, large groups, small groups, after work, during work, until gradually everybody had a reason to be at the table and to say, "Okay, we're inviting the rest of the city to come see our neighborhood."

When we first toured that area to begin thinking of putting a festival there, we noticed that there were no streetlights. It was dark at night, and so probably a lot of people would be frightened to be there in the evening. So agenda item number one was to get streetlights. There was garbage, and that's a problem. We needed to get that cleaned up. And there was a park, but the fountain had never been turned on, and the plants were just dead.

In fact, it turned out there were streetlights. The bulbs just hadn't been changed in ten years. There had been no regular garbage pickup, and the park had never been landscaped. As always, the media constantly presents people living in this neighborhood in such a way that the rest of America thinks they're asking for extra, they're asking for special consideration. No—they're asking for basic city services that were never there. What we could do as an arts festival was go to the L.A. City Council together with the neighborhood groups and say, "We're putting on an arts festival. The *New York Times* and *Time* magazine are going to show up. We need bulbs in the streetlights. We need the fountain turned on. We need the garbage picked up, and we need landscaping." And because of an arts festival, that neighborhood got basic city services. People now go back and do their Christmas shopping. Now the *L.A. Times,* whenever it wants a comment about anything, goes to that neighborhood and interviews Richard at Dick's Jazz Café, because now it's on the media map. So that's what I'm talking about: the arts as a social and economic player in the life of a city.

If I could just mention two more models around this question of memory. How do the arts contribute to memory? How is that actually a function?

I always remember going to the Soviet Union in the bad old days. One of the things that I remember from my fabulous experiences in Moscow was dodging my KGB colonel host and spending an afternoon with a poet in Moscow who would take me to a certain neighborhood and say, "You see the third window to the left in that apartment? That's where this painter lives. This apartment building over there—that's where that poet lives." All these people had become nonpeople, who had been airbrushed out of books and out of photographs, yet the actual history was still alive with people in the neighborhood who knew who lived in what building. This invisible history is, I think, very typical of most of our cities, and certainly of Los Angeles. The formal history of Los Angeles has nothing to do with who lives there. It has to do with three families and the water rights deals and then Hollywood. There is this unmarked history.

Of course, a work of art—a painting, a song, a poem—is an act of commemoration. It's the people who didn't make it into the newspaper: like painting right now in Zaire. You can't read in the paper in Kinshasa about all the people whom Mr. Mbutu just happens to rub out every time it looks like there's a democracy on the way. Somehow it just doesn't make it in. There are no photographs. Therefore painters would have to paint the massacre so that there will be a memory and there will be a record: the records that the media and that the powers that be choose to ignore for their reasons. So artists become actively engaged in the creation of alternative histories, and with the type of permanence that art has: the way a tune tends to live longer than lots of other things, the way poems are memorized and handed down on note paper, the way a memory lives, what it takes to keep something alive. That is, of course, the process of the arts.

So in the L.A. Festival, memory projects were one of our main things. You create a memory in a city about which Gertrude Stein could accurately have said, "There's no there there." Well, let's put some there there. So, for example, one memory project was created by a Salvadoran artist named Dagoberto Reyes. In the classic mode of a blind pig stumbling upon a truffle, I should emphasize that I became aware of the Salvadoran artists in Los Angeles through one spectacular gaffe. This is why I'm always in support of giant mistakes, because I make them all the time. In this case, in the 1990 L.A. Festival, we invited Latin American poets to come to Los Angeles. We had a committee of people who read lots of poetry books, picked their favorites, and then we invited ten marvelous poets including, from El Salvador, a fellow named David Escobar

Galindo, a lovely poet with very cultured works. In fact, he was the closest personal friend of Mr. Cristiani, and it was his signature that was on the evil false peace agreement. Indeed he was, in fact, the reason why Los Angeles has the largest population of Salvadorans outside of El Salvador. They can't live in their own country because of the death squads. So the fact that we were inviting the favorite poet of the death squads to come to Los Angeles was really not treated as a positive move within the El Salvadoran community. I arrived the day after an announcement in the newspaper that we were inviting David Escobar Galindo to find my office occupied by fifty angry Salvadoran artists, which is how I met the Salvadoran arts community in Los Angeles.

One of these artists, Dagoberto Reyes, then created a memory project for us in the next festival. He's a sculptor, but he had to leave El Salvador very rapidly. In fact, as his closest family members were killed, he escaped just with his life and nothing else. Sculpture is rather difficult to drag over the Mexican border at night. So he arrived with nothing to show that he was an artist. He began a new life here working in factories. For thirteen years he could not make any significant art because he was working so hard. We hired him in the L.A. Festival to create a bas-relief that he entitled *Why We Emigrate*. He made it over the course of a year, working three nights a week at the Salvadoran refugee center in the Pico Union district, which has probably the highest population density in North America: the highest crime rate, the highest murder rate, an intense drug economy because, of course, these immigrants from the Caribbean and from Central America can't get any other jobs, so they have to create their own economy. El Rescate is the main refugee center there. He was there three nights a week, and on those evenings people would bring photographs and mementos from their previous lives in El Salvador and bring objects of memory from their current life in the United States. Across six months they mounted rotating exhibits of these works, so the community could display to itself where it came from, its own mementos. People could compare notes on family members who were lost and on what this last period has meant for them. In the process he was absorbing that into his bas-relief. He created a bas-relief that was in two sections: one showing El Salvador with the death squads, open graves, people hanging from trees, prison cells, the families fleeing through the woods, and footprints everywhere. Then the center had a post representing the Mexican border with a woman climbing over the fence, and she was shot at the moment she was at the top of it. So it created a kind of crucifix with the impact of the bullet. Then on the other side of the fence was California, North America. The North American side showed, for example, a room full of kids watching a television because, of course, when they get here, because of La Migra, people are afraid to let their kids out on the street, much less go to school. So the kids are at home all day watching television. Another panel depicted factory work, showing the workers cleaning the machines because they're not allowed to work them. They can only get janitorial jobs. Another panel showed the traffic, the pollution. Another panel showed the field work, the migrant laborers, and the lettuce pickers.

The difference between the Salvadoran and the North American side was that on the Salvadoran side there were these faces with very intense emotions of what people were going through. On the American side you only saw the backs of people's heads, because once they're here, they're faceless. You don't know who they are. They don't know who they are. They're just someone you see across a street; blink, and you might not even see them.

This bas-relief we got past the L.A. City Council—the crucifix was a problem. It is now installed permanently in MacArthur Park, which is, of course, right in the center of the Pico Union area. It's the first permanent marker of the Salvadoran community in North America in the entire country. Installed underneath this sculpture is a time capsule filled with the exhibits of the six months at El Rescate. This is to be opened in a hundred years, so that their descendants will know one day why there are Salvadorans in North America: "Why we emigrate."

So it's a different model from an artist working alone in his studio and saying, "I am genius. The world must support me." It's a model of artists participating in ecology. We're moving on. As a sculptor, Dagoberto Reyes worked within the Salvadorian refugee center, and his sculpture, by the end, represented a wide range of things including and beyond his personal vision.

I would just mention quickly the World Arts and Cultures program at UCLA: I work a lot with Judy Baca, who, of course, is one of the heroes of the L.A. mural movement. For their spring assignment last year, her class created the world of a neighborhood clinic in East L.A. The project was really moving and beautiful. And so it was a question of what was on those walls. It had to do with the pregnant women who were waiting in that room every day. What types of thoughts did they have every day in that waiting room? What did that waiting room represent? It was about the engagement of the visual artists with that material and their response to it. They were working in a very collaborative way with people who used the room every day. I don't wish to understate how important solitude is from time to time in this life; I'm just trying to suggest that there is an arts ecology, that the arts can function not on the side or the way they're currently positioned as dessert, as something that's an extra, as something you can laugh off, or something that you didn't really need. I'm actually trying to position the arts at the center of society and social and economic discussion. Unless you have certain types of engagement in your life, you'll never have them in your art. That is, I think, one of the biggest tasks now for us and we need to include that in our understanding of education.

Let me just emphasize that we're in a period of mass hysteria, where every dopey little thing that comes out of Washington creates this really divisive, angry, vicious, pseudopublic debate because the real issues are never debated. It's just these strange symbols like burning the flag. The media has concocted nonissues that can be talked about endlessly, the way graffiti is portrayed, for example. I know we're in a zero-tolerant zone here in Berkeley, but I obviously have a very high regard for graffiti. All of which is just to say, how do you remain calm through this period of hysteria and churning that we're in right now? I really do look to the artists and to the arts for a zone of calm that is actually benign in a period where there's an open public hostility that greets you on every topic.

I'd like to mention, if I could, the work of another group of artists called Cornerstone Theater. This, again, is another very interesting model for me because it was founded by someone who was formerly my assistant at the Kennedy Center, working with the most famous actors in America, and the biggest budget, and my own "spectacular" productions—and he left. "That's not interesting," he said. Then, together with a group of his college friends—and I just mention that because we are at a college—instead of sending out eight-by-ten glossies of themselves to get work, they wrote to the mayors of towns across America with populations under five hundred, and they said, "We will come and be your arts presence for four months if you'll put us up. We will work with members of our company and people in your town to create a show." They did this for seven years. All across this country. Ranging from *Hay Fever* in Marco, Texas, performed by migrant laborers—you've never heard Noel Coward until you've heard it with a Mexican accent—to *The Oresteia* on a Hopi reservation; to Molière's *Tartuffe,* spelled "T-a-r-t-o-o-f" in Norcatur, Kansas; to *Hamlet* in South Dakota, where Hamlet was hotly debated in the pulpits of the town's two churches, for "how dare this young man question the existence of God?"

When they were in a small town in Wyoming, doing *The Good Person of Szechwan,* people would say, "I won't say that line." Someone else would say, "Oh, I will." Gradually, across four months, every single line in the Brecht play was discussed and debated by every person in the town. So by the time the actual performance shows up, it's not the usual consumer product. It has a whole set of layered meanings, and when the final blackout occurs, people can actually say their story was told. A mirror was held up.

Cornerstone now works in Los Angeles, which they're treating as a series of small towns. For the last two years they've been primarily headquartered in Watts, where high school students have a radius of ten blocks they're permitted to walk around in, and if you step over that, you'll be shot. So actually the containment nature of these small sectors of Watts becomes a really important place for theater to act as a zone of intervention. The zone of intervention, a demilitarized zone, which culture can provide in some way, is exemplified by the fact that in the 1990 L.A. Festival, which we announced on the first day of the Gulf War, central topics were Jewish and Arab art and the arts of the Diaspora. So to organize that festival took an enormous amount of care. The rule is don't surprise anyone. If you're going to have an evening of Palestinian and Jewish work on the same day at the same place, you'd better tell someone. Don't just spring it. What it means is lots of discussions with lots of people over a long period of time, since they're engaged in shaping the event. As soon as you permit that participation, then it turns out that the event is a lot more interesting than you would have made it. My favorite fascist empires on earth are in the arts. Artists are the least tolerant, most vicious individuals; they're the ones most anxious to kill another person's career because they're so angry that others got the grant and they didn't. Then there's the whole "who shall be first" mechanism, which is just maddening. Get over it. Live and let live.

In any case, what was interesting in planning this event was that we had the head of the Jewish National Congress in Los Angeles meeting with the head of the Arab Anti-Defamation League in Los Angeles. These two gentlemen had never met before, and there was a forty-five-minute protocol meeting scheduled, which lasted for four hours. They exchanged phone numbers, and now they do events together all the time. The point is they would never have met except through culture, except through this other zone which permitted contact.

Democracy needs to be cultivated. It's not something that happens naturally. It's something you have to work on just like dance, just like music. A voice must be cultivated. How you use your voice in public—this question of oratory, this question of how you can connect to something that you actually deeply believe and share that with other people, to have a more just, a more humane, society—is crucial, because basically none of us wants the situation that we're in now, which is Florence, Arizona. This university is struggling for funds while $13 billion are put aside for new prisons in the next five years. How did we get to that? Why can we not have an open and honest conversation about it? Surely it's common sense? How is it that in this polarized political environment that simple conversation can't happen?

Thomas Jefferson called it "declaring independence." What it means is that you stand up in public and you say "no" to something. You say, "We are independent of this." You express yourself elegantly, and that gives other people permission to reveal that they weren't for it either, that also in their hearts they have something else.

The key to the Declaration of Independence in eighteenth-century aesthetics is the phrase "We hold these truths to be self-evident." You have to proceed from a place where both Palestinians and Jews would say, "Actually, that's true." What are the truths that we hold to be self-evident and that we don't have to make a special case for? I would, for example, ask you to check out the self-evident truths at Mark Morris's show this weekend.

What does it mean that the arts can show you something, and it's not an essay in affirmative action, multiculturalism, or anything else? It's just human beings being how they are, self-evidently. But you don't have to make this a federal case because it's actually just normal, how the world has always been. So it doesn't have to be politicized in a completely reified way, that actually creates out of an infinitely flexible situation this horrible frozen rigid moment of multiculturalism, which then becomes, through objectification, the enemy. How can we create a way in which we're talking about process? In which we're talking about this ongoing engagement? And how can we get past this poverty mentality? We keep saying, "There's not enough to go around. There's not enough to go around." How can we get to the fact that wherever there's a human being on this planet, there is abundance, there is creativity, there is everything you haven't seen yet because that's why they're on the earth, to produce it. Of course, you haven't seen what we're about to do. We're creative beings. The world we're about to make isn't here yet. We're here to make it. The actual presence of art in the world is an activist statement. If there's too much red on one side of a painting, Picasso doesn't call the editor of a newspaper or his mother and complain. He doesn't get depressed and just sit down and do nothing for ten weeks. He picks up some blue paint and goes over and puts it where there's too much red. It's an activist thing. If there's a problem, solve it. If something needs to be done, do it. If you're looking for a job, find something that needs to happen and make it happen. In the process, you'll figure out how to get paid for it. But the first step is making yourself useful. It's really basic. Be a farmer at the same time as you're being an artist. Connect to people who have been under attack for a long time, who know what it means day to day.

There was a time when this country didn't just respond to the presence of lots of homeless people by building lots of new prisons to put them in. I'm referring, of course, to the Works Progress Administration, where for a moment in our history we took the fact that a lot of people were out of work, and we employed them. We employed them to build schools, libraries, post offices, roads, and bridges. We rebuilt the infrastructure of this country in the thirties. My personal attitude is that the only reason America could adopt a heroic posture in the 1940s was that finally in the 1930s it actually invested in itself. Those roads, those bridges, those libraries, and those post offices remain the most beautiful public spaces of our country's history. What it meant when you were just waiting to mail a letter, inspired by a beautiful work of art that places you and this post office in mythical surrounds, where you might be thinking in large terms about your country and who you are, and where we're going—and that's just waiting in line at the post office! Beautiful public space is created by artists, of course, so your imagination is ignited every time you go to the post office. Compare any post office built since the Reagan administration. Just look at new post offices. Mean, ugly, small, cramped, depressing public space that collapses while you look at it, that is offensive to set foot in. The developer made a killing, and while you're waiting to mail a letter, you're just getting more and more angry about everything in your life.

If I could return to theater for a moment, or rather Greek theater, where we're talking about music, dance, poetry. The Greeks, when they created this form of theater, were trying to prepare people for jury duty. That's why they made a form of theater that everyone in the society had to participate in. You didn't just watch it. As it went around, you were on stage with the chorus. It's a way of debating certain topics that were really difficult to talk about, like killing your mother, what it meant that dad sacrificed his daughter to have a better career, or how you treated prisoners in the last war. These were not pleasant topics. How do they have to be discussed? They can't just be discussed with a sociological spreadsheet: incidents of matricide from July through to August in comparative years. Isn't there another form of insight that's required in order to make public policy or to go into a courtroom and decide what would be just? The Greeks thought there was and subsidized any citizen who couldn't afford to go. It was part of the national identity and part of a democratic process. How do you vote? Learning to vote was a cultivation of democracy. What does it mean to create this famous garden, since we use the word "culture" all the time? Culture does mean to cultivate, to let something grow, to understand that you can't look at it the way it is now. You have to keep watering it, because it will change.

Let me tell you my favorite three rules for classical Chinese gardens of the Ming Dynasty. On the first section of the path you contract your range of vision. You are in close with little objects and enclosed spaces, and you can only see to get to the next place and not beyond. In the next section of the garden, as you pass through winding and indirect paths, you have to be willing to get lost. You have to be willing to let go of your ideas. You have to notice that you're not just going to get directly from here to there, but that in the process your ideas will change. The winding and indirect path: we're not just going to have the world the way we want to see it. This amazing, shocking thing happened where God created other human beings, and they have something to say. It's annoying, but there they are. And they're here to change your ideas. And, yes, there's the fact that you don't like them, and that you weren't even consulted. Not only do they not like you, they want to kill you, and you also have to live with them. The emblem of our age is one thing and one thing only: Nelson Mandela. You will take the people who for twenty-seven years tried to kill you and you will say, "Fine, let's form a government together." You will get over your enemy's rage. You will work with the very people you hate. Because until you do, no one is safe.

So you go through the passage of the winding and indirect path, and then there's the third step: you come out into a bright and spacious area. Then your vision is amplified. This path of a classical Chinese garden is, of course, the path of a democracy. You have to take an intricate path. You have to deal with micro details and what it takes to do community organizing one to one. It's not a media event. Mass communication, in my view, is a contradiction in terms.

I'd like to conclude by saying briefly why I'm here at Berkeley. First of all, because of my beautiful students, whom I adore, and I'm thrilled to teach. It is a privilege and honor, and I'm learning much more than I'm teaching. But I was attracted to come here this spring for several reasons: the Townsend Center for the Humanities has in place things that I view as really positive, vanguard activities. It is a humanities center which contains a human rights program where issues of political justice, exile and refugee issues, are discussed as humanities questions, not merely as politics. Here the humanities have a contribution to make toward understanding those realities which are usually reduced to "the news." How can we take the news and look back through the other end of the telescope and redeem it as history and as living people? That's a good path for the humanities in our period.

There's the ongoing program at the Townsend Center of discussions between physicians and humanities workers: that, in fact, the humanities have a role in how you die, in death and dying. Death is not just a technocratic, hyperscientific activity. There are larger issues about death that perhaps the humanities are in a position to address in a way that the scientific community cannot. Maybe a collaboration is required to provide a certain type of sensitivity and awareness for what it is we're dealing with. Because what the arts obviously specialize in is that which is unknowable, which is, of course, where the arts can begin to suggest that ethics are important. The minute you get to something that's beyond your own personal point of view, you have to open yourself to larger ethical laws and questions. The universe isn't just random; there are ethical considerations. For if this life is about a human being's moral progress, then utilitarian concerns are second to ethical questions. Talking about that in the high capitalist state is not often permitted.

Then, of course, there are some very exciting educational models for me here. Principally, I would just cite June Jordan's *Poetry for the People*, where poetry, which of course is usually imagined as a solitary event, is positioned as an active engagement within concentric communities. Here the students not only read poetry, not only learn to write poetry, but have to organize poetry readings all over the Bay Area. Part of their grade is awarded according to how many people come. So they have to learn how to fax radio stations. They have to learn how to get an audience.

June Jordan's *Poetry for the People* class, which lasts the entire year, is at Berkeley High School on Tuesdays, and on Wednesday nights at Glide Memorial Church. It has students out there actively engaging, actively using poetry as a way not just to get a job, but to make contact, and meanwhile to learn that if you're going to be a poet, you've got to learn how to talk to people. You've got to learn how to get an audience and how to engage with that audience. The class is very inspiring because it doesn't just turn out people who know how to put words on a page beautifully. It turns out people who know how to speak out for themselves, how to use their voice, articulate their situation, and advance a public discussion. Poetry is understood as a contribution to the public discussion of the kind of nation we want to have.

Finally, if I could just put forward for you a hope that I would have for the arts as a social and economic force in post-NEA America in the next century: how we're training young artists. The presence of the arts at a university is tremendously important, and I think, as Vice Chancellor Carol Christ has said, that probably in the next century the university will be the last patron of the arts in this society. We need to prepare for that.

I'm very pleased that the arts will have a presence in something that is not a conservatory. A conservatory has a limited technical function, and that is not enough to keep an artist alive. Right now the arts need to find their place in universities, in a broader discussion across cultures, across disciplines. This is our task for the next generation of artists. What I would like to see is a type of program that is project based, where a group of significant artists are brought together on campus to work on a project with a given subject matter. Say that subject matter is, as has come up earlier, prison reform. Right now, you can't read in the *New York Times* or *Time* magazine anything particularly informative about alternative approaches to prisons, and meanwhile the public keeps voting and voting and voting for the only thing they're told about. So I would like this program to gather not only a group of artists to create work on this topic, but actually to invite a group of scholars and activists to be in residence at the same time and the same place to engage with the artists every day and encourage accountability on both sides. People who are engaged in public policy need to be asked to take six months out of their lives to begin to reflect on issues they're working on as they're understood in the humanities, to suggest that maybe the humanities have something to contribute to a sociological or political or legal formulation. They also have to be there to help a lot of the people who are in the trenches to recover from burn-out. Give the artists real subject matter, something to talk about, something that demands action, subtlety and really profound strategic thinking.

I'd like to create a program that attracts students to engage with that process. During the course of creating the piece, the students are also engaged with the scholars and the social activists in creating high school curriculums and community intervention programs.

At the end of the one-year process, when we unveil the work, there is a miniature L.A. Festival that consists of poetry, dance, film, etc. around the topic. This says lots of people are thinking about this topic now, and here are a range of the points of view. At the same time, the university hosts a major national conference where the leading thinkers on prison reform are all here for four days, so that the response to the show, as it were, is not just "I didn't like the costumes in the second act," but a slightly larger issue presented against subject matter that is able to be foregrounded in the arts again. Meanwhile, *Time* magazine and the *New York Times* can actually publish six pages on prison reform because they can send a few people and get a real story. And the university and the arts are contributing to focusing the national discussion on the issues that have to be discussed, just as they did in Greece.

The second year of the program the students would tour with the work across the country, doing the high school curriculum and the community intervention programs in the cities. That to me is what it might take to prepare an artist to be alive and functional in our country.

I don't want to give the impression that any of the things that any of us are doing are easy. I'm assuming that I'm in a room of working artists and working people and working scholars who know that everything that any of us have done is really hard and up against a lot of opposition. That's why we're still alive. I hope that we don't have to show our medals to each other. I hope that we can just get to work.

We're talking about renewal. We're talking about social renewal. We're talking about spiritual renewal. We're talking about renewing people's energies in an entire period. My own hope would be that, instead of setting the year 2000 with all this apocalyptic art, we will remember that the year 2000 is about the fact that birth is miraculous.

Mike Davis

Golden Ruins / Dark Raptures: The Literary Destruction of Los Angeles

A SWELTERINGLY HOT DAY in Los Angeles, 1962. A pretty girl ("She reminded him of well water and farm breakfasts") is absentmindedly taking off her clothes at a bus stop. The corner newsboy gawks delightedly, but most passersby simply glance and continue on their way. A nerdish mathematician named Potiphar Breen comes to the rescue. As he wraps his coat around her, he explains that she is the victim of a strange epidemic of involuntary nudism known as the "Gypsy Rose" virus.

It is a small omen of approaching chaos; Breen has discovered that Los Angeles is the global epicenter of a sinister convergence of pathological trends and weird anomalies. All the warning lights are beginning to flash in unison: the mercury soars, skies darken, dams creak, faults strain, and politicians wave rockets. And, at the worst possible moment, the suburbs are gripped by a death wish to water their lawns:

> Billions in war bonds were now falling due; wartime marriages were reflected in the swollen peak of the Los Angeles school population. The Colorado River was at a record low and the towers in Lake Mead stood high out of the water. But Angelenos committed communal suicide by watering lawns

as usual. The Metropolitan Water District commissioners tried to stop it. It fell between the stools of the police powers of fifty sovereign cities. The taps remained open, trickling away the life blood of the desert paradise.[1]

Epic drought is quickly followed by flood, earthquake, nuclear war, plague, a Russian invasion, and the reemergence of Atlantis. It is the ultimate cascade of catastrophe. Breen hides out in the San Gabriel Mountains with his new girlfriend, amusing himself by shooting the odd Soviet paratrooper or two. Then, when the worst seems over, he notices an unusual sunspot. The sun has begun to die....

So ends Robert Heinlein's tongue-in-cheek novella, *The Year of the Jackpot* (1952). In coronating Los Angeles as disaster capital of the universe, Heinlein cannily anticipated the cornucopia of disaster to follow. According to my own incomplete bibliographic research, the destruction of Los Angeles is a central theme or image in at least 136 novels and films since 1909. More precisely, since Heinlein's heroine first took her skirt off, the city and its suburbs have been destroyed an average of three times per year, with the rate dramatically increasing in the 1990s.

TABLE 1. L.A. DISASTER FICTION: FREQUENCY

Pre-1920	2
1921–1930	5
1931–1940	7
1941–1950	8
1951–1960	16
1971–1970	21
1971–1980	29
1981–1990	31
1990–1996	19
Total	**136**

On the multiplex screen alone, during the grueling summer of 1996, Los Angeles was parboiled by aliens (*Independence Day*) and reduced to barbarism by major earthquakes (*The Crow, City of Angels,* and *Escape from L.A.*). Six months later, magma erupted near Farmer's Market and transformed the Westside into a postmodern Pompeii (*Volcano*), all to the sheer delight of millions of viewers. The City of Angels is unique, not simply in the frequency of its fictional destruction, but in the pleasure that such apocalypses provide to readers and movie audiences. The entire world seems to be rooting for Los Angeles to slide into the Pacific or be swallowed up by the San Andreas Fault.

Doom City

"This is so cool!"

—a typical Angeleno (*Independence Day,* 1996)

No other city seems to excite such dark rapture. The tidal waves, killer bees, H-bombs and viruses that occasionally annihilate Seattle, Houston, Chicago, and San Francisco produce a different kind of *frisson,* whose enjoyment is edged with horror and awe. Indeed, as one goes back further in the history of the urban disaster genre, the ghost of the romantic Sublime reappears. For example, the destruction of London—the metropolis most frequently decimated in fiction between 1885 and 1940—was a terrifying spectacle, equivalent to the death of Western civilization itself. The obliteration of Los Angeles, by contrast, is sometimes depicted as a victory for civilization.

Thus in *Independence Day,* the film that Bob Dole endorsed as a model of Hollywood patriotism, the alien holocaust is represented first as tragedy (New York), then as farce (Los Angeles). Although it could be argued, in an age of greedy suburbs and edge cities, that all traditional urban centers are equally expendable, the boiling tsunami of fire and brimstone that consumes Fifth Avenue is genuinely horrifying. When the aliens turn next to Los Angeles, however, it is a different story. The average film audience has little sympathy with the caricatured mob of local yokels—hippies, new agers, and gay men—dancing in idiot ecstasy on a skyscraper roof at the imminent arrival of the extraterrestrials. There is an obvious comic undertone of "good riddance" when kooks such as these are vaporized by their ill-mannered guests. (As one of Dole's senior advisors quipped: "Millions die, but they're all liberals.")[2]

The gleeful expendability of Los Angeles in the popular imagination has other manifestations as well. When Hollywood is not literally consumed in self-immolation, it is promoting its environs as the heart of darkness. No city, in fiction or film, is more likely to figure as the icon of a really bad future. Postapocalyptic Los Angeles, overrun by terminators, androids, and gangs, has become as cliché as Marlowe's mean streets or Gidget's beach party. The decay of the city's old glamour has been inverted by the entertainment industry into the new glamour of decay.

At the risk of sounding like a spoilsport (who doesn't enjoy a slapstick apocalypse now and then?), Los Angeles's reigning status as Doom City is a phenomenon that demands serious historical exegesis. Although the city's obvious propensity toward spectacular disaster—its "chief product," in the recent words of one critic—provides a quasi-realist context for its literary destruction, environmental exceptionalism does not explain why Los Angeles is the city we love to destroy. There is a deeper, Strangelovian logic to such happy holocausts. We must be recruited, first of all, to a dehumanized, antipathetic view of the city and its residents.

In the analysis that follows, I explore the underlying politics of the different subgenres and tropes of Los Angeles disaster fiction. If I appear heedless of Darko Suvin's strictures against using locale as a classificatory principle in science fiction, it is because I am interested in the representations of the city, not the debates about canon or genre per se.[3] My methodology, moreover, emulates the heroic example of jazz historian Gunther Schuller. In his magisterial survey of the Swing era, he committed himself "to hear *every recording* of any artist, orchestra, or group that would come under discussion—and to listen systematically/chronologically in order to trace accurately their development and achievements."[4] This entailed careful attention to some thirty thousand recordings and took Schuller more than twenty years to accomplish.

In my case, "comprehensive reading" has been a much more modest enterprise, involving only a hundred or so novels and a few dozen films.[5] Before I opened the first book, moreover, I searched for a vantage point that offered some vista of how imagined disaster fits into the larger landscape of Los Angeles writing. The bibliographic equivalent of Mulholland Drive is Baird and Greenwood's superb inventory of California fiction to 1970.[6] Out of 2,711 separate entries, I found 785 novels that obviously qualified as "Los Angeles based." Nearly two-thirds of this vast output is devoted either to murder (255 crime and detective novels) or to Hollywood (224 novels), with considerable overlap between the two categories.

Novels with disaster themes comprise 50 titles, or 6 percent of the total, just ahead of cult (39 titles) and citrus/ranching (30 titles) fiction, and just behind historical novels (66 titles).

These statistics, of course, are extremely crude indices of the relative popularity, let alone influence, of different themes and plot types. Chandlerian *Noir*, for example, continues to define the Los Angeles canon in the eyes of most critics, yet it is a tiny subset, possibly 20 or fewer examples, within the larger universe of regional fiction. Literary census methods, while indispensable for setting the stage, must quickly yield to qualitative and historical analysis. Thus, three simple theses, formulated midway in my "Schullerian" reading, structure my understanding of what Los Angeles disaster fiction is about.

First, there is a dramatic trend over time toward the identification of all Los Angeles fiction with disaster or survivalist narrative. Despite the one-sided obsession of formal literary criticism with Los Angeles as the home of hard-boiled detective fiction, the disaster novel is an equally characteristic, and culturally symptomatic, local export. It is true in the strict sense that, after 1980, a decisive quorum of the region's best young writers—including Octavia Butler, Carolyn See, Steve Erickson, Kim Stanley Robinson, and Cynthia Kadohata—routinely site their fiction in the golden ruins of Los Angeles's future. It is also true in the broader sense that disaster, as allusion, metaphor, or ambiance, saturates almost everything now written about Southern California.

Second, with surprisingly few exceptions, most of the work under consideration is easily mapped as coherent subgenres like "romantic disaster fiction" or "cult catastrophe." Although genre analysis is a notoriously subjective business, the repetition of basic thematic and plot patterns—e.g., women's redemptive role, inadvertent bio-catastrophe, the identification of cult with catastrophe, white survivalism in an alien city, disaster as creative alchemy, etc.—provides logical, if not exclusive, taxonomic guidelines. Eight major story types and their principal periods of popularity are listed in table 2, while an inventory of the diverse "means of destruction" is provided in table 3.

TABLE 2. L.A. DISASTER FICTION: STORY TYPES (PERIODS OF POPULARITY)

1.	HORDES	1900–40s
2.	ROMANTIC DISASTER	1920–30s
3.	CULT / CATASTROPHE	1930–50s
4.	THE BOMB	1940–80s
5.	ECOCATASTROPHE	1960–80s
6.	CINEMATIC DISASTER	1970s
7.	SURVIVALIST	1980–90s
8.	MAGICAL DYSTOPIA	1980–90s

Third, race ultimately unlocks the secret meaning of the genre. In spite of the rich diversity of leitmotifs, (white) racial fear is the dominant theme in disaster fiction over time, with the sardonic critique of cults and fringe culture a distant second. In pre-1970 novels, when Los Angeles was still the most WASPish of large American cities, racial hysteria was typically expressed as fear of invading hordes (variously yellow, brown, black, red, or their extraterrestrial metonyms). After 1970, with the rise of a non-Anglo majority in Los Angeles County, the plot is inverted and the city itself becomes the Alien. More than any other factor, racial difference is the distancing mechanism that provides the illicit pleasure in Los Angeles's destruction.

TABLE 3. L.A. DISASTER FICTION: MEANS OF DESTRUCTION (NOVELS & FILMS)

1.	NUKES	49
2.	EARTHQUAKE	28
3.	HORDES (INVASION)	10
4.	MONSTERS	10
5.	POLLUTION	7
6.	GANGS / TERRORISM	6
7.	FLOODS	6
8.	PLAGUES	6
9.	COMETS / TSUNAMI	5
10.	CULTS	3
11.	VOLCANOES	2
12.	FIRESTORMS	2
13.	DROUGHT	1
14.	BLIZZARD	1
15.	DEVIL	1
16.	FREEWAYS	1
17.	RIOT	1
18.	FOG	1

Because this last hypothesis is apt to be controversial (political correctness again runs amuck...), it is best to begin by putting Los Angeles disaster fiction in its larger context: the genealogy of the modern fascination with dead cities.

Urban Eschatology (a Brief Digression)

Lo! Death has reared himself a throne
In a strange city lying alone
Far down within the dim West
—Edgar Allan Poe, "The City in the Sea"

A starting point: Lisbon was the Hiroshima of the Age of Reason. Goethe, who was six at the time of the destruction of the Portuguese capital by earthquake and fire in 1755, later recalled the "Demon of Fright" that undermined belief in the rational deity of the *philosophes*. "God, said to be omniscient and merciful, had shown himself to be a very poor sort of father, for he had struck down equally the just and the unjust."[7]

The Lisbon holocaust, together with the rediscovery of Pompeii and Herculaneum a few years earlier, were profound shocks to the philosophical "optimism" (a word coined in 1737) that had infused the early Enlightenment under the influence of Newton, Leibniz, and Pope. The "best of all possible worlds," it seemed, was subject to inexplicable and horrifying disasters that challenged the very foundations of reason. Following the famous debate with Rousseau that led Voltaire to produce his skeptical masterpiece *Candide*, Lisbon and Pompeii—and, later, the Terror of 1791—became the chief icons of a fundamentally modern pessimism that found its inspiration in historical cataclysm rather than the Book of Revelations.[8]

An influential literary template for this anti-utopian sensibility was Jean-Baptiste Cousin de Grainville's *Le dernier homme*. Written in 1805 at the apogee of Napoleonic power, this strange novel by a bitter enemy of the *philosophes* depicted mankind's disappearance as the result of soil exhaustion, human sterility, and a slowly dying sun. Although religious motifs do appear (de Grainville was a cleric of the *ancien régime*), it is likely the first book in any language to sketch a realistic scenario of human extinction. Moreover, it provided the dramatic conception for Mary Shelley's three-volume epic of despair, *The Last Man* (1826), which chronicles how a utopian age of peace and prosperity in the late twenty-first century is transformed, by plague and religious fundamentalism, into a terrifying End Time whose sole survivor—the Englishman Lionel Verney—is left alone in the howling ruins of the Roman Colosseum. As various critics have appreciated, *The Last Man*, although a bad novel, was an intellectual watershed, the first consistently secular apocalypse.[9]

From the dandified fringe of Shelley's circle also came the most popular urban disaster novel of all time, Edward Bulwer Lytton's *The Last Days of Pompeii* (1834). Bulwer Lytton, who started as a Godwin radical and ended as minister for the colonies, eulogized the cultured and cosmopolitan decadence of the doomed Roman summer resort under the shadow of Vesuvius. In its immediate context (the passage of the first Reform Bill in 1832 and the rise of Chartism), it can also be read as a premature elegy for the equally decadent British upper classes, whom Bulwer Lytton saw as threatened by their own volcanic catastrophe: the gradual advent of universal suffrage. In the century-long run of its popularity, however, *The Last Days of Pompeii* simply offered the typically Victorian titillations of orientalized sensual splendor followed by sublime, all-consuming disaster. With the advent of cinema, it immediately became the most filmed novel, with at least four movie versions made between 1903 and 1913 alone.[10]

In American literature, with its notorious "apocalyptic temper," the city of doom was already a potent image in such early novels as Charles Brockden Brown's *Arthur Mervyn* (1799) and a "Lady of Philadelphia"'s *Laura* (1809), both of which portray the horror of the "yellow plague" (yellow fever) in Philadelphia.[11] In succeeding decades, the great city, with its teeming masses of immigrants and papists, is routinely demonized as the internal antipode of the republican homestead and small town. This plebeian-nativist anti-urbanism reaches its hallucinatory crescendo in George Lippard's gothic tale of oligarchy and corruption, *The Quaker City* (1844).[12] Philadelphia is depicted as a nocturnal labyrinth of temptation and crime, whose evil center is the mysterious Monk Hall guarded by the monstrous "Devil Bug." As Janis Stout points out, Lippard may be the first literary portraitist of the American city to move beyond "simple terror of place" to the "explosion of reason" and metaphysical catastrophe. "At the end of the book, in an apocalypse which the reader scarcely knows how to accept, 'Death-Angels,' 'forms of mist and shadow,' hover over the city."[13]

Although Edgar Allan Poe continued to add his own amazing glosses to the Last Days, secular doom fiction virtually disappeared during the long sunny afternoon of mid-Victorian expansion, between 1850 and 1880. In their different ways, the Crystal Palace and Jules Verne's novels exemplified the bourgeois optimism of the Age of Capital. After Sedan, the Paris Commune, and the depression of 1876, however, the spell was broken. An explosion of copycat novels speculatively explored the possibilities of a mechanized world war between the great powers, usually with an invasion of Britain and the sacking of London. More intrepidly, a few writers, influenced by vulgar Darwinism, questioned the long-term survival of Victorian civilization in the face of growing revolts by the lower classes and "lower races."[14]

Significantly, one of the earliest of these social apocalypses was published by a California populist, Pierton Dooner, in 1880. His *The Last Days of the Republic* describes the conquest and destruction of the United States by a "human ant-colony" of Chinese coolies.[15] The novel begins in San Francisco, where selfish plutocrats have encouraged unrestricted Chinese immigration to depress wages. Desperate white workingmen attempt to massacre the Chinese but are shot in the back by militia under the command of the oligarchs. The Chinese are then given the franchise, which they use to enlarge their political and economic beachhead, ultimately producing a civil war which the coolies win by virtue of their superior numbers and insectlike capacity for self-sacrifice. The banner of the Celestial Empire is raised over the smoking ruins of Washington, DC:

> The very name of the United States of America was thus blotted from the record of nations.... The Temple of Liberty had crumbled; and above its ruins was reared the colossal fabric of barbaric splendor known as the Western Empire of His August Majesty, the Emperor of China and Ruler of All Lands. (p. 257)

Dooner's novel created a sensation in English-speaking countries and provided a plot outline—alien invasion/yellow hordes—that, like the "last man" narrative, has been copied right down to the present. It was followed the next year (1880–81) by four emblematic visions of future cataclysms. In Park Benjamin's satirical short story "The End of New York," an invading Spanish armada uses balloon-borne nitroglycerine bombs to destroy Manhattan from the air. Total American capitulation is only avoided by the fortuitous appearance of a friendly Chilean fleet (!), as Benjamin denounces "the weakness of our navy and the unprotected position of our seaports."[16]

Mary Lane's *Mizora: A Prophecy* describes an elite, subterranean society of women living in a lush paradise under the North Pole. As Naomi Jacobs points out, however, this parthenogenetic utopia is premised on a genocidal eugenics:

> At the very foundation of Mizoran perfection is the racial purity of its inhabitants, who are all blond-haired and fair-skinned—emphatically the "cool" type of beauty. Dark-haired Vera objects only silently to the Preceptress's argument that "the highest excellence of moral and mental character is alone attainable by a fair race. The elements of evil belong to the dark race." For these reasons, dark complexions have been "eliminated." Gender is also considered a racial category by the

> Mizorans, and Vera eventually learns that the first step in the eugenic campaign to purify the race had been the elimination of men some 3000 years earlier.[17]

Meanwhile, the popular English writer and advocate of "Anglo-Saxon union," W. Delisle Hay, published back-to-back novels, *The Doom of the Great City* and *Three Hundred Years Hence*, portraying alternative futures. In the first, London is choked to death by its poisonous fogs and toxic wastes. In the second, white civilization is on the verge of transforming the world into a superindustrial utopia that includes greenbelts in the Sahara, flying machines, and television. The major obstacle to progress, however, is the continued existence of "worthless Inferior Races but a step above beasts." The "Teutons" solve this problem by sending air armadas which unleash "a rain of death to every breathing thing, a rain that exterminates the hopeless race, whose long presumption it had been that it existed in passive prejudice to the advance of United Man."

As I. F. Clarke has emphasized, Hay's chapter on "The Fate of the Inferior Races" ("a billion human beings will die") was an eerie anticipation of *Mein Kampf* (and, more recently, *The Turner Diaries*).[18]

These tales, those by Dooner and Hay especially, opened the door to a flood of apocalyptic fiction after 1885.[19] Overwhelmingly it was a literature written and consumed by the anxiety-ridden urban middle classes. It depicted the nightmare side of rampant Social Darwinism. Growing fear of violent social revolution and the "rising tide of color" was matched by increasing anxiety over the inevitability of world war between the imperialist powers. Microbes, radioactivity, poison gases, and flying machines provided new means of mass destruction, while Schiaparelli and Lowell's "discovery" of canals on Mars gave temporary plausibility to an extraterrestrial threat. The result, as W. Warren Wagar has shown, was a proliferation of doom fiction that established virtually all the genre conventions still in use today.

> Between 1890 and 1914 alone, almost every sort of world's end story that one finds in later years was written, published, and accepted by a wide reading public. Great world wars that devastated civilization were fought in the skies and on imaginary battlefields dwarfing those of Verdun and Stalingrad. Fascist dictatorships led to a new Dark Age, class and race struggles plunged civilization into Neolithic savagery, terrorists armed with superweapons menaced global peace. Floods, volcanic eruptions, plagues, epochs of ice, colliding comets, exploding or cooling suns, and alien invaders laid waste to the world.[20]

In the United States this genre remained immovably fixated upon the specter of subversive immigrants and nonwhites. The Irish-led "Draft Riots" of 1863, suppressed with great difficulty by the regular army, provided a precedent for nativist fears. Thus, in John Ames Mitchell's *The Last American* (1889), the alien hordes turn green and destroy New York after massacring its Protestant bourgeoisie. A Persian expedition, reconnoitering the wasteland of Manhattan in the year 2951, excavates dramatic numismatic evidence of this Irish-led insurrection: a 1937 half-dollar (illustrated in the book) with the bulldog image of "Dennis Murphy Imperator," "the last of the Hy-Burnyan dictators." The explorers also discover the rusting hulk of the Statue of Liberty, Delmonicos, Astor House, and a moldering thousand-year-old blonde in her bed. In a side trip to Washington, DC, they encounter the "last American" of the title sulking in the ruins. He is slain in a brief scuffle and his skull taken back to Persia to be displayed in a museum.[21]

Late twentieth-century New York is consumed by an even more terrible revolutionary holocaust (again led by the immigrant proletariat) in Ignatius Donnelly's *Caesar's Column: A Story of the Twentieth Century* (1890). Inverting the utopian plot of Edward Bellamy's *Looking Backward* (1888), Minnesota populist Donnelly portrays the historical alternative to the Peoples' Party moderate platform, a genocidal final conflict between a debased, polyglot proletariat and a Jewish-dominated financial oligarchy. With the aid of mercenary airmen (the "Demons") who drop poison gas on New York's wealthy neighborhoods, the slum hordes, led by the ogre-like Italian giant Caesar Lomellini, ruthlessly annihilate bourgeois society. A quarter-million well-dressed corpses form the pedestal for Lomellini's grotesque column commemorating "the Death and Burial of Modern Civilization."[22]

Racial cataclysm meanwhile also remained a popular theme in Gilded Age catastrophe fiction. While the annihilation of Native Americans was almost universally accepted as a necessary cost of progress, some Social Darwinists experimented with other genocides. In *The Last Days of the Republic*, for instance, Dooner already had disposed of the entire ex-slave population in a single, enigmatic line. African Americans, he claimed, "rapidly and noiselessly disappeared, perished, it seemed, by the very act of contact" (with Chinese conquerors) (p. 127).

A decade later, in the Jim Crow novel *The Next War* (1892), King Wallace openly exulted in the biological extinction of black America. Northern and Southern whites, finally overcoming their Civil War animosities, unite in a war of extermination against a rebellious black population. After a failed attempt to poison all whites on the first day of the twentieth century, thirty million blacks flee into the southern mountains where, completely surrounded by the white armies, they die of exposure and starvation. With cool matter-of-factness, Wallace describes the "continuous and unbroken line of dead infants, none of whom were older than six or seven years old."[23]

Dooner's and Hay's yellow hordes, meanwhile, returned in a bloodthirsty trilogy by M. P. Shiel (*The Yellow Danger* [1899], *The Yellow Wave* [1905], and *The Dragon* [1913]) in which hundreds of millions of fiendish Chinese are slaughtered by British naval heroes who, when firepower alone fails, resort to the bubonic plague. Shiel was widely imitated by other writers, including Jack London, whose 1906 short story "The Unparalleled Invasion" also solves the "Chinese problem" with all-out germ warfare followed by the massacre of survivors. "For that billion of people there was no hope. Pent in their vast and festering charnel house, all organization and cohesion was lost, they could do naught but die" (p. 119). As the white races recolonize China, "according to the democratic American program," "all nations solemnly pledged themselves never to use against one another the laboratory methods of warfare they had employed in the invasion of China" (p. 120).[24]

Some petit-bourgeois phobias, of course, were quite fantastic. A rather quaint obsession of the *fin de siècle*, for example, was the specter of anarchists in airships, like Donnelly's "Demons," raining death upon the bourgeoisie. In addition to *Caesar's Column*, this is also the common plot of E. Douglas Fawcett's *Hartmann, the Anarchist: or, The Doom of the Great City* (1893), George Griffith's *The Angel of the Revolution: A Tale of Coming Terror* (1893), and T. Mullett Ellis's *Zalma* (1895). The fictional aircraft described in these novels—dark dreadnaughts of the skies with names like Attila (Hartmann)—helped excite the first worldwide wave of "UFO" sightings in 1896–97, six years before Kitty Hawk and a half-century before Roswell. Anarchists and Martians were equally popular explanations.[25]

Griffith, who rivaled H. G. Wells in popularity, was the world's most prolific writer of chauvinist science fiction. He thrilled and terrified his reading public of clerks and shopkeepers with a virtually annual production of doom-laden tales: *Olga Romanoff* (1894), *The Outlaws of the Air* (1895), *Briton or Boer?* (1897), *The Great Pirate Syndicate* (1899), *The World Masters* (1903), *The Stolen Submarine* (1904), *The Great Weather Syndicate* (1906), and *The World Peril of 1910* (1907). Like Hay earlier, he preached Anglo-Saxon racial unity against the twin evils of urban anarchy and colonial revolt.

Within this emergent genre of apocalyptic futurism, only two important English-language novels broke ranks with reigning xenophobic obsessions. One was naturalist Richard Jeffries's influential *After London, or Wild England* (1885), which anticipated the environmental collapse of the unsustainable industrial metropolis. As Suvin points out, Jeffries was the only major writer of British catastrophe fiction before Wells "to spring from the working people," in his case, the yeomanry. Like Donnelly, he despised the urban financial oligarchy that had starved the countryside of credit and ruined the small farmer. The miasmatic ruins of London express "a loathing ... of upper-class pride and prejudice based on money power."[26] Although Jeffries helped pave the way for the Gothic socialist vision of William Morris (whose *News from Nowhere* is a utopian reworking of *After London*), the sheer ferocity of his anti-urbanism put him in a category apart, as a kind of Victorian Edward Abbey.[27]

The other novel, of course, was H. G. Wells's great anti-imperialist allegory, *The War of the Worlds* (1898), which stood white supremacy on its head by depicting the English as helpless natives being colonized and slaughtered by technologically invincible Martians. His description of the Martian destruction of London ("It was the beginning of the rout of civilization, of the massacre of mankind") stunned readers who were forced to confront, for the first time, what it might be like to be on the receiving end of imperial conquest.[28] The novel, in fact, had grown out of a conversation with Wells's brother Frank about the recent extinction of native Tasmanians by English settlers.[29] Within a year of its serialization in *Cosmopolitan*, moreover, American newspapers had already plagiarized the story and printed terrifying accounts of Martian attacks on New York and Boston. (Los Angeles, thanks to Paramount Films and director Byron Haskin, was to follow in 1953.)[30]

Yet even Wells, who ends *The War of the Worlds* with a powerful call for a "commonweal of mankind," was obsessed with race, and in his most radical early novel, *The Sleeper Awakes* (1910), did not shrink from depicting a cataclysmic race war between the London poor and the African police sent to suppress them. Previously, in *The Island of Dr. Moreau* (1896), he had horrified readers with the image of animals transformed into humanoid monsters (analogues of mutant, inferior races), while in *The Time Machine* (1895) he forecast the evolutionary divergence of the human race into the antagonistic species represented by the gentle, retarded Eloi and the hideous, troglodytic Morlocks.

The Yellow Peril, moreover, makes a sinister appearance in *The War in the Air* (1908), Wells's extraordinary "fantasy of possibility" about Armageddon in the skies over New York, which Patrick Parrinder has described as science fiction's first analogue to Gibbon's epic of imperial decline and fall.[31] Hungry for New World colonies but blocked by the Monroe Doctrine, Wilhelmine Germany unleashes its secret zeppelin armada against the United States. After sinking the American Atlantic fleet in a surprise attack, the great airships, emblazoned with black iron crosses, punish New York City's refusal to surrender with a merciless bombardment of the congested neighborhoods of lower Manhattan. Prefiguring the Martian attack in *Independence Day*, Broadway is turned into a "hideous red scar of flames" (p. 213). Wells pointedly compares this first "scientific massacre" of a great metropolitan center to routinized imperialist atrocities:

> As the airships sailed along they smashed up the city as a child will scatter its cities of brick and card. Below, they left ruins and blazing conflagrations and heaped and scattered dead; men, women, and children mixed together as though they had been no more than Moors, or Zulus, or Chinese. (p. 211)

The victorious Germans, however, have fatally underestimated the other powers' equally clandestine and fanatical preparations for strategic air war. As the enraged Americans strike back at the Germans with their own secret weapons, France and England unveil huge fleets of deadly long-range airships. In short order Berlin, London, and Paris all suffer the fate of New York City. Finally, while the Americans and Europeans are preoccupied with an attack on the German "aerial Gibraltar" at Niagara Falls, thousands of Japanese and Chinese airships suddenly darken the sky.

> The Japanese and Chinese have joined in. That's the supreme fact. They've pounced into our little quarrels.... The Yellow Peril was a peril after all! (p. 240)

The modern integration of science into warfare, Wells warns, will inevitably erase arrogant Victorian distinctions between Europe and Asia, civilization and barbarism. Yet the threat of a new "dark age" is precisely what provides a romantic plot for the most popular American end-of-the-city novel from the Edwardian era: George England's *Darkness and Dawn* (1914).[32] England's story (actually a trilogy serialized in *Cavalier* magazine during 1912–13) is a rather banal specimen of the renewed interest in the catastrophic that preceded, and in eerie ways, prefigured the holocaust of the First World War. (In Europe, the shrieking urban apocalypses of Ludwig Meidner's 1912–13 paintings and Georg Heym's poems were incomparably more oracular; terminal points of prophetic despair after the successive omens of the first Russian Revolution (1905–6), the San Francisco and Messina earthquakes (1906 and 1908), Halley's Comet (1910), and the sinking of the Titanic (1912).[33]

The chief novelty of *Darkness and Dawn* is in the opening pages, where England depicts the destruction of New York's newly built skyline. Allan and Beatrice (a handsome engineer and his beautiful secretary) awake from a century of suspended animation on the forty-eighth floor of the ruined Metropolitan Tower (tallest building in the world in 1912) overlooking Union Square. From their high perch, they survey a scene of unprecedented devastation. The great Flatiron Building is a "hideous wreck" (p. 23) while the Brooklyn Bridge has collapsed and the Statue of Liberty is just "a black, misshapen mass protruding through the tree-tops" (p. 20). Manhattan has become the first skyscraper ghost town.

They quickly leave this "city of death" (translate: "dead immigrants") to search for other Anglo-Saxon survivors of the unexplained holocaust. England, like Jack London, was both a socialist and Aryanist.[34] Inevitably, on the road to rebuilding civilization, his "white barbarians" must fight a pitiless war of extermination against the "Horde," a species of cannibal ape-men whom the reader is led to assume are the devolved offspring of inferior races. Once the ape-men are annihilated, progress is rapid because "labor reaps its full reward" (p. 672) in the cooperative commonwealth established by the survivors. In the last scene, Allan points to a swift-moving light in the sky: "Look Beatrice! The West Coast Mail...!" (p. 670). It is a biplane bearing the hope of a new age from Southern California.

Endnotes

1 Robert Heinlein, *The Year of the Jackpot* (1952), reprinted in Donald Wollheim, ed., *The End of the World* (New York, 1956), p. 29.

2 For Dole's reaction to a screening of *Independence Day*, see *Los Angeles Times*, 20 July 1996, p. A19.

3 Discussing the subgenre of "Victorian Alternative History," Suvin argues that "fictional locus is more vehicle than tenor; hence, it is not a narratively dominant element and cannot serve as a meaningful basis for classification with SF. To constitute a class of 'Martian stories,' or, say 'Symmes' hole' stories would make as much sense as allotting the biblical parable of the mustard seed to 'agricultural stories' or Brecht's *The Good Person of Setzuan* to 'Chinese stories.' Darko Suvin, "Victorian Science Fiction, 1871–85: The Rise of the Alternative History Sub-Genre," *Science Fiction Studies* 10 (1983): p. 150.

4 Gunther Schuller, *The Swing Era: The Development of Jazz, 1930–1945* (New York, 1989), p. x.

5 In order to view the whole landscape of imagined disaster, I have purposefully sought out ephemera—religious rants, privately printed tracts, occult speculations, soft-core pornography and B movies—as well as pulp fiction and "serious" literature. The eccentric works offer uncensored access to the secret sexual and racial fantasies that rule the genre's unconscious.

6 Newton Baird and Robert Greenwood, *An Annotated Bibliography of California Fiction, 1664–1970* (Georgetown, CA, 1971).

7 Quoted in T. D. Kendrick, *The Lisbon Earthquake* (Philadelphia, 1955), pp. 222–23.

8 Cf. chapter 7, "Optimism Attacked," in ibid; and Otto Friedrich, *The End of the World: A History* (New York, 1982), pp. 179–212.

9 "The Last Man is an anti-Crusoe, conquered rather than conquering, crushed by his solitude, and sure of his defeat." See W. Warren Wagar, *Terminal Visions: The Literature of Last Things* (Bloomington, 1982), p. 13.

10 On its film history, see Mick Broderick, *Nuclear Movies* (Jefferson, NC, 1988), p. 2.

11 Charles Brockden Brown, *Arthur Mervyn* (Philadelphia, 1799), and *Laural by a Lady of Philadelphia* (Philadelphia, 1809).

12 George Lippard, *The Quaker City: or, The Monks of Monk Hall* (Philadelphia, 1844).

13 Janis Stout, *Sodoms in Eden: The City in American Fiction before 1860* (Westport, CT, 1976), pp. 50–54.

[14] For 1871 as the literary birthday for UK science fiction, see Suvin, "Victorian Science Fiction," p. 148.

[15] Pierton Dooner, *The Last Days of the Republic* (San Francisco, 1880). In the same vein, see also Robert Woltor, *A Short and Truthful History of the Taking of California and Oregon by the Chinese in the Year A.D. 1899* (San Francisco, 1882).

[16] Benjamin Park, "The End of New York," *Fiction Magazine* (31 October 1881).

[17] Naomi Jacobs, "The Frozen Landscape," in Jane Donawerth and Carol Kolmerten, eds., *Utopian and Science Fiction by Women: Worlds of Difference* (Ithaca, 1991), pp. 194–95.

[18] I. F. Clarke, *The Pattern of Expectation, 1664–2001* (London, 1979), pp. 158–60.

[19] The best, although by no means exhaustive, discussion of American futuristic novels from this period remains Thomas Clareson, "The Emergence of American Science Fiction: 1880–1915" (PhD diss., University of Pennsylvania, 1956). See also Roberta Scott and Jon Thiem, "Catastrophe Fiction, 1870–1914: An Annotated Bibliography of Selected Works in English," *Extrapolation* 24, no. 2 (Summer 1983).

[20] Wagar, *Terminal Visions*, p. 20.

[21] J. A. Mitchell, *The Last American: A Fragment from the Journal of Khan-Li, Prince of Dimph-Yoo-Chur and Admiral in the Persian Navy* (New York, 1889), pp. 32–33. The illustrations are spectacular.

[22] Ignatius Donnelly, *Caesar's Column: A Story of the Twentieth Century* (Chicago, 1890). See also David Anderson, *Ignatius Donnelly* (Boston, 1980), pp. 67–80.

[23] Wallace King, *The Next War: A Prediction* (Washington, DC, 1892), pp. 204–5. Wallace claimed that the absurd black conspiracy in his novel is "based on the facts already firmly established" and that "the very day fixed for exterminating the white race, December 31, 1900, as given in the story of 'The Next War,' is the identical date fixed upon by the (actual) conspirators" (p. 15).

[24] Jack London, "The Unparalleled Invasion," in Dale Walker, *Curious Fragments: Jack London's Tales of Fantasy Fiction* (Port Washington, NY, 1975). Written at the end of 1906, this "freak short story," as London described it, was published in July 1910. See Earle Labor, Robert Leitz, and I. Milo Shepard, eds., *The Letters of Jack London*, vol. 2, *1906–1912* (Stanford, 1988), p. 680 (letter of 28 March 1907 to Robert McKay).

[25] See the fascinating description in Dave Jacobs, *The UFO Controversy in America* (Bloomington, 1975), p. 29.

[26] Suvin, "Victorian Science Fiction," pp. 164–65.

[27] Jeffries imitators have been legion. Aside from the Mitchell novel already mentioned, Van Tassel Sutphen's *The Doomsman* (1906) freely purloined scenes from *After London* to tell a tale of romance and knightly derring-do in a ruined and medievalized New York.

[28] H. G. Wells, *War of the Worlds: A Critical Text of the 1898 London First Edition*, ed. Leon Stover (Jefferson, NC, 2001), p. 167.

[29] It is important to reemphasize that *War of the Worlds* was originally read within a context of widespread popular acceptance that intelligent life, as evinced by the "canals," existed on Mars. For a fascinating discussion of the imperialist nations as "cosmic savages" in light of extraterrestrial civilizations see Karl S. Guthke, *The Last Frontier: Imagining Other Worlds, from the Copernican Revolution to Modern Science Fiction* (Ithaca, 1990), pp. 358 and 386–89.

[30] *New York Evening Journal* writer Garrett Serviss in 1898 serialized a pro-imperialist sequel which depicted the Great Inventor invading the red planet and exterminating all of its inhabitants. In a climax of vulgar Darwinism, "it was the evolution of the earth against the evolution of Mars. It was a planet in the heyday of its strength matched against an aged and decrepit world." Garrett Serviss, *Edison's Conquest of Mars* (Los Angeles, 1947), p. 35.

[31] H. G. Wells, *The War in the Air* (New York, 1908). For the Gibbon analogy, see Patrick Parrinder, *Shadows of the Future: H. G. Wells, Science Fiction, and Prophecy* (Syracuse, 1995), pp. 78–79.

[32] George Allan England, *Darkness and Dawn* (Boston, 1914).

[33] What darker epiphany is there of the rest of the twentieth century than Meidner's 1913 canvas *Burning City*? See Carol Eliel, *The Apocalyptic Landscapes of Ludwig Meidner* (Munich, 1989).

[34] His most explicitly anticapitalist novel is *The Air Trust* (1915).

Arthur Danto

The Work of Art and the Historical Future

I

GIORGIO VASARI OPENS HIS LIFE of Michelangelo with a prophetic exordium, in which the Tuscans are pictured as a kind of chosen people and Michelangelo himself as a redeemer, sent by God, yielding through his example a knowledge to which the Tuscans aspire, but which otherwise would lie beyond their powers to achieve. Here is the passage:

> While the best and most industrious artists were labouring, by the light of Giotto and his followers, to give the world examples of such power as the benignity of their stars and the varied character of their fantasies enabled them to command, and while desirous of imitating the perfection of Nature by the excellence of Art, they were struggling to attain that high comprehension which many call intelligence, and were universally toiling, but for the most part in vain, the Ruler of Heaven was pleased to turn the eyes of his clemency towards earth, and perceiving the fruitlessness of so many labours, the ardent studies pursued without any result, and the presumptuous self-sufficiency of men, which is farther from the truth than is darkness from light, he resolved, by way of delivering us from such great errors, to send to the world a spirit endowed

> with universality of power in each art...capable of showing by himself alone what is the perfection of art....
>
> ...The Tuscan genius has ever been raised high above all others, the men of that country displaying more zeal in study, and more constancy in labour, than any other people of Italy, so did he resolve to confer the privilege of his birth on Florence ...as justly meriting that the perfections of every art should be exhibited to the world by means of one who should be her citizen.[1]

Clearly modeled on the Christian epic, this passage stipulated the end of a history, defined by the cumulative effort to achieve a perfection artists are incapable of without the revelation through example of a divine intercessor, born, like a savior, in Florentine precincts: a Florentine among Florentines, as Christ was a human among humans. I employ the term "revelation" here as implying knowledge of the highest importance which we would be incapable of attaining through the common cognitive routines—induction, deduction, observation, testimony, experimentation, or, in the specific case of the visual arts, "making and matching," to use Gombrich's expression. Artists now know what *perfection* is, and need no longer blindly seek it. Rather, they can, by emulating Michelangelo's example, achieve perfection in their own work. The history of art, conceived of as the seeking of representational perfection, has concluded through divine intercession.

Imagine, on the model of revelation, a vision granted to Giotto of Michelangelo's *Last Judgment*. A voice calls out: "Is this what you are trying to do?" Vasari's account assumes that Giotto's answer would unequivocally be "Yes"—that he would instantly see not only that Michelangelo had achieved what Giotto himself aspired to, but that, in point of an art criticism that belonged to that project, Giotto's personages were revealed as wooden, disproportionate to their architectural settings, and visually unconvincing. Of course, it is thinkable that Giotto would have thought differently, and if we could then imagine on what grounds he might have rejected the model of Michelangelo, we would have a very different understanding of Giotto's art than we now have, which depends upon seeing him and Michelangelo as belonging to the same developmental history. Suppose, however, he were granted a vision of *Les demoiselles d'Avignon*, or Matisse's *Luxe, Calme, et Volupté*. My counterfactual opinion is that Giotto would not have viewed these as art, or, if as art, then it must have been done by savages or madmen, or vastly earlier in the same history his work belonged to: these were to become the fallback positions when Modernism challenged received views of art with precisely these works. Giotto would have had no impulse to emulate, to learn how to do what Matisse and Picasso were revealed to have done. Rather, he would see himself as having made immense progress beyond them, whoever they were and whenever they worked. It would be like Chinese art, were he to have had a vision of that. In his *Lectures on the Philosophy of History*, Hegel writes: The Chinese "have not yet succeeded in representing the beautiful as beautiful; for in their painting perspective and shadow are wanting."[2] With qualification, Giotto had both.

I think we might use this counterfactual story to make plain what *belonging to the same history* means, and at the same time what it would mean not to belong to the same history. So I would assume that while Giotto and Michelangelo belong to the same history, neither of them belongs with Matisse or Picasso, and that, if this were true, then we would have an intuitive grasp of historical discontinuity. To belong to the same history would mean that earlier artists could achieve what later artists achieved, without the labor of searching for it, once they had the example. Vasari's image is that artists would have stumbled forever in the dark, without finding what they were looking for, and that Michelangelo showed them what it was. One might argue that Michelangelo appeared when the Tuscan art world was ready for him, and that he had in some measure internalized the history that intervened between Giotto and himself. Certainly we could not imagine him as a contemporary of Giotto, nor as coming immediately after Giotto in a historical sequence instead of the artists who did, like Masaccio. But we could imagine a counterfactual history in which artists were spared the search, and could move directly and immediately to their goal as embodied in Michelangelo's towering work. Of course, a lot would have had to change for this to happen: were there actually walls high enough to execute something like *The Last Judgment* in Giotto's time?

In any case, art after Michelangelo would be posthistorical with respect to a history whose terminus is the Sistine Ceiling and *The Last Judgment*. There was a great deal of art made after that, so it was not as though the history of art had stopped, but rather had come to an internally defined end. It had moved from search to application, from looking for representational truth to working in the light of that truth. Beyond the figure of Jonah in the Sistine Ceiling, it was impossible to advance. Of course artists were to become more adept than Michelangelo in certain ways: Tiepolo handled foreshortening with an ease and certitude Michelangelo would have envied, had he been granted a vision of Tiepolo's ceiling painting for *Der Rezidens* in Würzberg. But he would in no further sense have seen it as diminishing his achievement—and in any case he always complained that he was, after all, not a painter. Tiepolo would be entirely a posthistorical artist with regard to that history, though three centuries further along: Michelangelo died in 1564—the year of Shakespeare's birth; and Tiepolo in 1770—six years before the American Revolution.

In that long posthistorical evening, there were a great many changes in what artists were asked to do, so that in a way the history of art was the history of patronage. Mannerist art was a response to one set of briefs, the Baroque to another, Rococo to yet a third, and Neo-Classicism to a fourth. It would be inconceivable that these varying briefs could have been imposed on art if it were as it had been at the time of Giotto. Rather, this variety was a possibility only because the use of perspective, chiaroscuro, foreshortening, and the like no longer had to be struggled with. They could be mastered and used by everyone, and they defined what the curriculum of the workshop as art school should be. This merits a further observation. Multiculturalism in art is today very much a political ideal, but it is an artistic ideal just because there is no such curriculum—nothing which qualifies artists to enter the world of commissions. Today, a Chinese artist might respond to Hegel that he has exceedingly provincial ideas of beauty as beauty. In the seventeenth century, on the other hand, mandarins could see, as immediately and intuitively as Giotto is imagined here seeing Michelangelo, that the way a Western artist used perspective was correct, and that their own history would have been different had the ancients the luck to see such models. But in their case, art was too embedded in practices they could not change in order to assimilate the perspective they now knew. That knowledge represented what they freely admitted they should have done, but which (unlike the case of Giotto and Michelangelo) it was too late to do. Art was differently implicated in their life and culture, and a deep transformation in the whole of their society would be required if it were to be accepted. They belonged to a different history entirely. But today the "should" would drop out of consideration: There is no art-educational curriculum. That is why multiculturalism is a valid ideal as it would or could not have been in 1770, or until the advent of Modernism, however we date that.

To the degree that anyone thought about the future of art, it would not have the form "Someday artists will ... "—on the model of "Someday medicine will find a cure for cancer" or "Someday man will walk on the Moon"—but rather the form that the future would be in essential respects like the past, except perfect where it is now deficient. One could learn the meaning of the term "art" through induction over known instances and could rank artworks in terms of their distance from Vasari's paradigms. In a way, the class of artworks had the structure of a species, with all conspecifics sharing the defining features, but with enough variation that connoisseurs could single the best out from the better, the way dog or pigeon breeders do in Darwin's best examples of artificial as against natural selection. These views loosely defined the visual arts through the long interval from Michelangelo and his peers—Raphael, Leonardo, and Titian—until the dawn of Modernism, at which time, for reasons it would be fascinating to discover, a discontinuity emerged in the class of artworks so sharp that even connoisseurs were uncertain whether it was art at all. The historically important painting of the mid- to late nineteenth century did not seem to belong to the future of art as that conception would have been intelligible to someone at home in the Vasarian posthistory. It was at times so discontinuous that one could not easily explain it with reference to the kind of grading which went with species-like variations. Modernist works seemed entirely off the scale. Nor could it be explained with respect to the principles of perfection it in fact counterexemplified. One would rather have explanatory recourse to hoaxes or insanity, to mischief and mockery. This, as in science, was a way of saving the appearances, enabling the concept of art, together with the apparatus of connoisseurship, to remain intact. It was a way of "explaining away" whatever seemed to threaten the concept—an entirely creditable defensive measure, since the new work, if admitted under the concept, would inevitably entail revisions in the tacit schedule of necessary and sufficient conditions for something being an artwork. This of course is not to explain the need to preserve appearances in the case of art, or why, nearly a century after Matisse and Picasso, Modernist art has still to be explained away. Perhaps it is because we are supposed to be made in God's image, and God could not look like one of the *Demoiselles*. Or, if he could, we were not his images at all.

II

In 1873, Henry James published "The Madonna of the Future," a story about an artist I—but hardly James—would describe as posthistorical. This is Theobald, an American working in Florence, consumed by the ambition to paint a Madonna which will equal Raphael's *Madonna della Seggiola*. He had found a model, a beautiful young mother who embodied the qualities of feminine grace Raphael shows, and which Theobald wished his own Madonna to have. But instead of painting this woman, he devotes himself to the prolonged study of the painting he hoped to rival, seeking to discover what he refers to as "the secrets of the masters." These secrets would at best have a historical interest today, and would have been of incidental use in the history which succeeded the Vasarian history. James sees Theobald as ridiculous and at the same time tragic. He nevertheless entirely accepts Theobald's project of painting what the narrator refers to as *The Madonna of the Future*, giving James his title. That meant that James and Theobald belonged to the same moment of the same history: one could make valid art by recreating valid art. So James could say that, if successful, Theobald's picture would embody the qualities that Raphael's painting embodied and hence he would be as good a painter as Raphael was. (Precisely such an inference governed Han van Meegeren's decision to paint what everyone would believe was done by Vermeer.) Theobald once drew a picture of a child which could have passed for a Correggio, and it is striking to speculate that he would not have made a drawing which could have passed for a Giotto—that would have either have been a deliberate archaism or a mark of not having learned properly to draw. So Theobald and Raphael belong to the same prolonged historical moment. The story now takes a turn: James's narrator is introduced to the woman in whom Theobald saw his Madonna inscribed, and is shocked to discover she has grown coarse and stout and sexual, though what James calls *les beaux restes* can still be made out. Theobald has waited too long—waited twenty years in fact, in which his model went from youth to thickened middle age. He had studied painting too long to the detriment of depicting life. Stunned by this truth, he resolves to paint his masterpiece, which, he says, pointing to his head, is already created, needing only to be transcribed. In fact transcription is more of a problem than he envisioned, and when the narrator seeks him out, Theobald is sitting before a blank canvas. Not long afterward he dies an operatic death, which is the only way to end a story like that.

Let us conduct the same kind of historical experiment with Theobald as we did with Giotto. We might imagine someone appointed in 1973 as chief curator of the Museum of Monochromy, in, let us say, Cincinnati. He enters Theobald's studio at the moment when, all passion spent, the artist sits listlessly before a canvas which James describes as "a mere dead blank, cracked and discolored by time"—an object which emblematizes as dramatic a failure as Fremincourt's painting in Balzac's *Le chef d'oeuvre inconnu*. And indeed the canvas is to the curator's eyes a *chef d'oeuvre inconnu*. "It is," he tells Theobald, "a masterpiece." And he assures him that he is ahead of his time. That the history of the all-white painting, which includes Rodchenko, Malevich, Rauschenberg, and Ryman, begins with him. "Has it a title?" he asks. Theobald replies: "It has been referred to as 'The Madonna of the Future.'" "Brilliant!" the curator responds. "What a comment the dust and cracks make on the future of religion! It belongs in my monograph—it belongs in my museum! You will be celebrated!" This "Ghost of Art Worlds Future," as a curator, will have some slides—of Malevich, Rodchenko, Rauschenberg, Ryman. The slides are pretty much all alike, and each resembles Theobald's blank canvas about as much as they resemble one another. Theobald would have no choice but to regard the curator as mad. But if he has a philosophical imagination, he might think this: It does not follow from those blank canvases being artworks, despite the resemblance between their work and my blank canvas, that my blank canvas is an artwork. And it will occur to him that it almost immediately must follow that one cannot tell artworks from other things on the basis of observation, induction, and like cognitive practices which served in the art world he knew. At a more human level, he would continue to count himself a failure, even if the site of his failure would be regarded in the future as an artwork. That would not be a future he would wish to be part of: he wants to be the Raphael of the future, and achieve a work in every particular the peer of the *Madonna della Seggiola*. It is no consolation that there will be works which resemble something he has not relevantly touched. Still, the Ghost of Art Worlds Future will have planted a question. The question is: What is an artwork? That is not a question which could interestingly arise in the reign of Vasari.

"What is an artwork?" became part of every artwork belonging to the Modernist era, and each such artwork advanced itself as a kind of answer: *Anch'io sono pittore*. It is because artworks could be enfranchised only through an analysis of art that it would be correct to say, as Clement Greenberg famously did, that the mark of Modernist painting was self-critique: "The essence of Modernism lies, as I see it, in the use of the characteristic methods of a discipline to criticize the discipline itself."[3] Greenberg saw this as a search for what was "unique and irreducible in each particular art," and hence for a perfection quite different from what Vasari imagined. Modernism, in virtue of this ascent to self-consciousness, marks a new kind of historical reality, and not just a new historical reality. Modernism contrasts, in virtue of this self-consciousness, with everything that went before, and does so, in virtue of self-consciousness, in ways in which the various stages and movements of the tradition did not differ one from another. In some way paintings themselves became objects rather than ways of showing objects. It is not surprising—it was to have been expected—that as Modernism advanced, more and more of the art that had not been considered part of the history of art was admitted as art—folk art, primitive art, oriental art, the art of outsiders—simply because it was no longer considered important that these arts look as if they fit into the Vasarian narrative. This induced an increasingly radical heterogeneity into the *extension* of the term "artwork." And it raised questions for each tentative definition of art, just because none of the ways in which these objects differed from one another could belong to the definition. If it belonged to the definition, one or the other of the differing works could not belong to the term's extension. So the answer had to be universal and complete, which is by and large what Hegel meant by Absolute Knowledge. And, in a singularly important way, the answer had to lie outside history, as having to be compatible with whatever art there was or would be, in any possible world in which there was art at all. It would in particular have to explain why a blank canvas from 1873 and a blank canvas from 1973, otherwise entirely alike, differed in that one could not be an artwork, though the other is one. This I regard as the central question of the philosophy of art. It is scarcely a question that could have arisen for the doomed Neo-Raphaelian painter Theobald. It is after all the mark of history that the future is not disclosed in the present. One might have been able to imagine, at some earlier moment in Vasarian history, that there would be a time in the future when artists would be able to create works so like reality that no one could tell the difference. But they would not know how to generalize upon their own representational strategies to know how—which is why Vasari counted Michelangelo's coming as a revelation.

III

There were, of course, the first stirrings of Modernism by 1873. If we think of the consignment of Manet's *Déjeuner sur l'herbe* to the Salon des refusés as the first event in Modernism's history, that history was but ten years old when James published his story. The First Impressionist Exhibition was held in (*nota bene*) the studio of the photographer Nadar in 1874. In 1876 there was a famous encounter between the critic Ruskin and the painter Whistler (which James reported on in the *Nation*). Whistler insisted that *Nocturne in Black and Gold: The Falling Rocket* was a painting, while Ruskin dismissed it as a paint box flung in the public's face. Compared to what Ruskin admired, it could hardly have been accepted as art. Compared to Pollock—or even to Bacon, who talked about throwing paint at the canvas—it was pretty tame. But it was a quarrel over what everyone thought they knew. The history of Modernism was the history of scandals, as, one after the other, works of art bumped some cherished criterion out of the definition of art. The first two-thirds of the twentieth century saw the end of this history, when works of art began to appear which resembled quite ordinary things—like soup cans and Brillo boxes—far more than they resembled what would have been counted works of art in the age of Giotto or of Theobald.

It is this moment of closure that I refer to as The End of Art. As with Michelangelo, beyond whom one could not advance, on the Vasarian narrative, there would be no going beyond the Brillo box in the history of artistic self-consciousness, since the class of artworks includes *Brillo Box* but excluded Brillo boxes which look exactly like them, so that we cannot base a definition of art on what meets the eye. It does not mean that art will not be made. It means the closure of a history, not the termination of a practice.

I want to pause and reflect upon the kind of concept the concept of art is. Logicians distinguish between what they term the *intension* of a concept, and the concept's *extension*. The extension of a concept (or a term) will be all and only those things which fall under the concept—robins and sparrows and ducks if the concept is "bird." The intension comprises all the conditions deemed necessary for something to be classed as a bird—wingedness, oviperousness, and the like. Everything in the extension has, through meeting these criteria, to resemble the rest. Whatever the difference between ducks and sparrows, both of them are birds. The history of Modernism, by adding disjunctively to the extension of the concept "artwork," tended to bump from the intension one or another condition—and when that happened, things became candidates for art that would not have been before. The intension of "artwork" is transhistorical: it specifies the invariant condition for something being art in every world in which there is art at all. But the extension of the concept is entirely historical in the sense that Theobald's canvas could not have been an artwork in 1873, though something just like it could already have precedents a century later. Indeed, the possibility was realized a few years after Theobald's death, albeit as a spoof by the artist Alphonse Allais, who, in 1879, printed a blank white rectangle with the jokey title *Première communion de jeunes filles chlorotiques par un temps de neige*. Chlorosis is a disease due to iron deficiency, leaving the skin greenish (it is called "greensickness" in the vernacular), and "chlor" means "green"—think of chlorophyll. "Albino" would have served Allais's purpose better, since he clearly intended a picture of abnormally white-skinned girls in white communion frocks in white snow. He did an all-black picture as well: *Combat de nègres dans une cave pendant la nuit*. Both, however, are *pictures*, and though the difference between one of them and Theobald's blank canvas could have been invisible, it is no less profound for that. It is a picture of an all-white world, whereas the blank canvas is not a picture at all (not even a picture of nothing), however great the resemblances (let them be arbitrarily close). The blank canvas can become an artwork only with the advent of abstraction, which bumped "is a picture" from the concept of the visual arts. And in that, startling as it may seem, the concept of visuality itself was bumped from the concept of the visual arts, even if the extension of the concept was filled with objects of visual beauty and interest. What delayed the advent of Absolute Knowledge in the case of art is that, for historical reasons, certain features of objects in extension were believed to form part of the intension of the concept, when in fact they lay outside the essence of art entirely.[4] Even if there were no conceptual analog, it is valuable to see in what ways the concept of art is different from such concepts as "bird," with which the old logic texts concerned themselves. This would explain why the history of Modernism differs from the Vasarian history as well. Giotto could have made great strides in approaching Michelangelo by studying the future great man's secrets, just as Theobald did in studying the secrets of Raphael. But Modernism is conceptual. Its history is the history of adding to the extension of art and at the same time modifying its intension until it becomes plain with the fullness of self-consciousness that there is no way a work of art cannot appear—that anything can be a work of art, the question now being what must be true of it for this to be true.

This way of seeing the problem did not disclose itself all at once. But there is a marked difference between Modernism's approach and that of the art which in a way put an end to Modernism. Modernism's was a pursuit of essence, of what art solely and truly is, hence of a kind of pure art, very much as if the art which resulted was like an alchemical precipitate, from which impurities had all been purged. This suggests a Grail-like narrative, in the framework of which the all-white painting might have been regarded as the climax—the work beyond which it was impossible to go. I heard Robert Colescott explain his reasons for making comic paintings of blacks, namely, that Ryman had gone as far as one could go with his all-white paintings, and that in consequence a history was over with. There is, I think, a logical flaw in this agenda, namely, that though the all-white painting could be considered art and be considered pure—it would not follow that it was pure art—art in a pure state. That is because white is at best a metaphor for purity. The essence of art must be possessed by every work of art, even the least pure—like Colescott's cartoon masterpieces.

The other and succeeding strategy was to put pressure on the intension of the concept by advancing something as art which violated some accepted criterion, and to see what then happened. Wittgenstein talks about a chess player who puts a paper hat on a king, which of course, whatever meaning it has for him, means nothing under the rules of chess. So you can really take it off without anything happening. In the sixties and beyond, it was discovered how many paper hats there were in art. They were thought to be part of the meaning of art when in fact they were subsidiary properties of certain works of art of surprisingly local interest. I think of Warhol as having followed this line of investigation with greater conceptual imagination than anyone else, erasing false criteria at every step, until it began to be appreciated that there was nothing that could not be art. But that was happening everywhere at that time in the arts—in dance, in theater, in music. Since anything could be art, the question arose why everything wasn't art: what made the difference between what was and what was not? A number of fairly bad answers were given. One would be that whatever an artist says is a work of art is, through that fact, a work of art, period. Or—this is the Institutional Theory of Art—whatever an art world decrees is a work of art is one through that declaration. This makes the history of art a series of proclamations, which leaves the problem of why Theobald's blank canvas was not an artwork in 1873 a mere matter of his not declaring it to be one. And that seems to leave a great deal out of the picture. It seems simply unacceptable that the members of the class of artworks have only the fact that someone called them art to license their being in the class at all. But what then can they have in common if there are no limits on what can be an artwork, especially if two things can look entirely alike but only one of them be an artwork? That question is philosophical, and when I speak of the end of art I mean specifically that progress from this point is philosophical progress, progress in the analysis of the concept. It is not that art has turned into philosophy but that the history of art has moved onto a philosophical plane. Art making may go on and on. But so far as self-understanding is concerned, it cannot take us further.

I might only add that the history could not have attained this point by philosophical reflection alone. It has been entirely internal to the history of art, and the progress to artistic self-consciousness has emerged through the kind of philosophy in action which the history of Modernism has been. Philosophers could not have imagined a situation like the present one in which, with qualification, anything goes.

IV

So what does it take to be an artwork in what I term posthistory? I want to concentrate on an interesting example which should make the problem vivid, and which shows to what degree art making has been penetrated by philosophy. This was an installation by an artist with the surprising name (in fact a pseudonym) L. A. Angelmaker, in the Momenta Art gallery in Brooklyn, New York, in Spring of 1997. The work has a title—"Bad Penny: For Museum Purchase Only." And it consists of articles of antique furniture which were either not works of art, because they were instead works of craft, or were works of art only because they were made at a time when the line between art and craft was not considered firm. These articles in any case had once been in the decorative arts galleries of museums and had subsequently been deaccessioned. But through Angelmaker's intervention they constitute works of contemporary art, or are in any case integral to a work of art which would not have been possible as art in an earlier moment, and certainly not under Modernism. Whatever else we can say about them, their being art now has nothing greatly to do with an artist or a group of artworlders transforming them into art by saying simply, "Be thou art." One of Angelmaker's objects is a French Henry II–style walnut extension table incorporating renaissance elements. It was given to the Metropolitan Museum of Art by J. P. Morgan in 1916. The other object is described as "A French Provincial Late Renaissance Walnut Armoire, early 17th Century." Both are handsome pieces of furniture which anyone would love to live with, but I am interested in them through the fact that they are offered as art today in a different way from any perspective under which they might have been viewed as art before. The items of furniture were, as said, "deaccessioned" by museums and offered at auction to a public which doubtless bid on them as luxurious articles of use. Angelmaker "is offering to resell the furniture to museums as contemporary works by dint of their participation in his project." So the seventeenth-century armoire is transformed into a late twentieth-century piece of art as part of a complex performance. The artist is attempting "to disrupt the flow of objects from public collections into private ownership." In any case, the art criticism of Angelmaker's project is obviously vastly different from the art criticism of the pieces of furniture as such, with reference to the patina of the wood, the design of doors, the cabinetry. In becoming art, the articles of furniture retain those now irrelevant properties, which form no part of their status as art in the late twentieth century.

I regard this work as a deeply posthistorical object in that it could not, unlike Michelangelo's work—or a blank canvas—be imagined as of use in showing what earlier artists in their respective histories were trying to do, since they culminated those histories. Nor can we imagine some later work showing what Angelmaker really aspired to achieve. Angelmaker's work develops no history, nor will it develop into further history, at least not as art. This is the mark of contemporary art, in which each work has only its own history. But that is to say that contemporary art has no mark, which is the external side of the slogan that anything can be art. Beyond that, it is clear that *Bad Penny*'s status as art has nothing to do with its maker merely declaring it to be art. Its being art instead is implicated in its conceptual complexity, its purpose, and its means. One might notice in passing that one would have to view antique furniture as part of the material of the artist, like paint and plaster. The materials of the artist are as diverse as the class of artworks themselves, since anything is subject to having its identity transformed by someone who sees how to use it in a work. The art supply store would then have to carry *everything*. Their inventory would have to be as rich as the inventory of life.

I want to conclude with one further example. The sculptor Tom McAnulty recently completed a commission he had received from a monastic order in Indiana, to make an altar for their church. The brothers had been struck by the magnificent altar in Aachen, from the time of Charlemagne, and wanted something exactly like that, though not an imitation of it. This left the artist a great deal of room when it came to the gilded bronze panels, which decorated the four sides of the altar (the frame would be built by a monk gifted in cabinetry). It was a wonderful commission, and involved a great deal of discussion as well as reading the Bible carefully, but at the same time it left McAnulty uncomfortable. What business, he wanted to know, has a modern sculptor working on a Carolingian altar? I told him that a *modern* sculptor would have had no business producing such a work. But it was perfectly all right for a *contemporary* artist to do. For an object not deeply different from an eighth-century AD altar can be a work of contemporary art. His work may enter into subsequent history in many ways: he may go on to execute other liturgical commissions; he may start a trend in which nonliturgical artists find satisfaction in liturgical art. But this is not a master narrative. To say that the work is posthistorical is merely to stress that. If we think laterally of everything actual and possible as art—that is, the art being made all across the art world at a given time—then it must be clear that the heterogeneity today is of so high a degree, the media so interpenetrate one another, and the purposes are so diffuse, that a next lateral cut will be strictly unpredictable. All that one can predict is that there will be no narrative direction. And that is what I mean by the end of art.

When I first wrote about this concept, I was somewhat depressed. I concluded my text by saying that it had been an immense privilege to have lived in history. I wrote that as a New Yorker who had lived through many changes, each surprising and yet each developing what went before. So one went to exhibitions to try to determine where art was heading. I felt about that history, in truth, as I did about analytical philosophy, which also seemed to be moving inevitably toward certain ends. But now I have grown reconciled to the unlimited lateral diversity of art. I marvel at the imaginativeness of artists in finding ways to convey meanings by the most untraditional of means. The art world is a model of a pluralistic society, in which all disfiguring barriers and boundaries have been thrown down. (For what it is worth, I have no use for pluralism in philosophy.)

Hegel's final speech in the course of lectures he delivered at Jena in 1806 could be describing this moment in the history of art:

> We find ourselves in an important epoch, in a fermentation, in which Spirit has made a leap forward, has gone beyond its previous concrete form and acquired a new one. The whole mass of ideas and concepts that have been current until now, the very bonds of the world, are dissolved and collapsing into themselves like a vision in a dream. A new emergence of Spirit is at hand; philosophy must be the first to ... recognize it, while others, resisting impotently, adhere to the past.... But philosophy, in recognizing it as what is eternal, must pay homage to it.[5]

From that tremendous perspective, the liberation of a life beyond history might be experienced as exhilarating.

Endnotes

1 Giorgio Vasari, "Life of Michelangelo," in *Lives of the Most Eminent Painters*, trans. Mrs. Jonathan Foster (New York, 1967), 2:p. 107.

2 G. W. F. Hegel, *Lectures on the Philosophy of History*, trans. J. Sibree (London, 1914), p. 144.

3 Clement Greenberg, "Modernist Painting," in *Forum Lectures* (Washington, DC, 1960).

4 It would be fascinating to find some other concept of which something like this is true. It has at times seemed to me that the concept of number, which has its own history, beginning with the whole numbers, the integers with zero, the rationals, the reals, and so on has something like the structure of the concept of art, but I do not wish to develop that comparison here.

5 G. W. F. Hegel, Jena lecture on the "philosophy of spirit" (1806), as cited in Alexandre Kojève, *Introduction to the Reading of Hegel*, assembled by Raymond Queneau, ed. Allan Bloom; trans. James H. Nichols Jr. (Ithaca, 1969), p. vi.

Ivan Klíma

Living in Fiction and History

WHEN I WAS STILL A STUDENT—and unfortunately I studied in the not very favorable time of the 1950s—we were made virtually to memorize Engels's definition of realism and rendition of Balzac. Realism, according to Engels, meant, "besides truth of detail, the truthful reproduction of typical characters under typical circumstances."[1] Whenever an author does precisely this, he achieves a truthful image of history, and this frequently even against his will. In the *Human Comedy*, at least, that is what Engels claimed. Balzac set out the entire native history of French society, from which, Engels went on, he had learned more even in economic details (for example, a new arrangement of movable assets and reality after the revolution) than from all the professional historians, economists, and statisticians of that period.[2] On the basis of this statement—which reveals a remarkable lack of understanding of the specific qualities of prose—writers in the Soviet empire were assessed according to the way they depicted typical characters under typical circumstances and the way they described everything the party regarded as social and economic conditions and historical realities. But even Milan Kundera argues in his stimulating *Art of the Novel*: "Since Balzac, the world of our being has a historical nature, and characters' lives unfold in a realm of time marked by dates. The novel can never rid itself of that legacy from Balzac."[3] It would be futile to argue against the fact that practically every novel, every plot, takes place in a time of its own. This was true even long before Balzac. As we know, Boccaccio's *Decameron* is played out right from the start in the year "one thousand three hundred and forty eight, when the deadly plague swept the magnificent city of Florence, more beautiful than all other Italian cities." The famous *Robinson Crusoe* not only takes place in a specific time, but the hero makes an effort to give an accurate account of the time of his stay on the island.

As an author who attempts to write about people living in the world of today, about their relations, their problems, I am interested to what extent historical events are meant to, are allowed to, or even have to become components of the composition of the novel. Is it at all possible to determine some permitted or recommended measure?

More than one critic has tried to compare two contemporaries who simultaneously lived their short lives in Prague and, among other things, experienced the time of the First World War: Franz Kafka and Jaroslav Hašek.

As we know, the work which made Jaroslav Hašek famous is closely connected with the history of the First World War. Even the famous first sentence of the novel *The Good Soldier Schweik*, "So they've killed our Ferdinand," directly refers to the Sarajevo assassination and no longer means very much for most contemporary readers. At a time when a recent opinion poll reveals that half of all English schoolchildren do not know where London is and what language is spoken in Tokyo, would anyone have the slightest idea that this was Ferdinand, the crown prince on the Hapsburg throne?

In contrast, Franz Kafka's note that Germany had entered the war is well known. "August 2. Germany has declared war on Russia. —Swimming in the afternoon."[4] The second sentence totally destroys the historical significance of the first sentence. It is worth noting that in the dialogue between Schweik and his landlady, even Hašek disparages that which was seen as a historical event. Schweik asks which Ferdinand had been killed—He knew two: one was an attendant in the chemist's store; the other one collected dog excrement. However, the course of events of the war form an inseparable background to Hašek's novel, whereas war, which seemed to form the lives, destinies, and thinking of at least two generations, rarely entered Kafka's work. I am convinced that this in no way weakens the impact of his work. What is more, I maintain that when reading Hašek's brilliant work today we perceive all that refers to the knowledge of history, to individual battles or transfer of troops almost as a superfluous burden, something that might be omitted. Nonetheless, I am convinced that an attempt at determining the extent to which the author ought to incorporate historical facts in his work would be a waste of time.

Let us formulate the question in greater detail: Should the author of a novel expect the reader to be familiar with a historical event which the author regards to be of vital significance and with which he is working, in brief, to refer to something that exists outside his work but which nevertheless shifts the destinies of his heroes and which very frequently is presented as destiny?

I would say that most contemporary novels give a negative answer to this question. There are few things in this world which are as transient as a historic event. Milan Kundera notes: "Of the historical circumstances, I keep only those that create a revelatory existential situation for my characters." Further on he outlines the difference between historiography and the art of the novelist: "Historiography writes the history of society, not of man" (37).

Unless the author intends to address only his contemporaries and, what is more, only those in his own country, he ought to refer to historical events outside his work as little as possible. This does not mean that he should not be able to portray how this or that event, whether large or small, has been reflected in the life of his heroes. This does not mean that his characters could or should exist outside time. After all, all of Kafka's major works, since we have mentioned him, are anchored in time. Few works reflect the emotions of a human being who has been isolated in the modern world as well as his *Metamorphosis, The Trial,* or *The Castle.*

With some exceptions, the significance of historical events is generally transient. All that generations of contemporaries see as having a great impact on world history shrinks into an insignificant episode in the life of later generations. This applies to most battles, revolutions, the fate of dictators—I do not share the view that we find ourselves at the end of history but am rather convinced of something else, most substantial for an author. Each historic event was—and remains—hard to understand. It does not resemble a rock to which we are able to give a precise definition and description of its degree of hardness, its composition as well as its height above sea level. Each historic event is subject to countless interpretations, and it can be said that it is at all times merely a variety. In addition to some event which has really taken place, this variety comprises a multitude of personal views, renditions, and attitudes. Even that which appears to be beyond doubt, such as the time when it has occurred, could be inaccurate. I remember that we used to deride the so-called Great October Revolution—saying that it was not great, that it took place not in October but in November, and that it was not a true revolution. But regardless of whether this seizure of power occurred in October or in November, it is undisputed that for some it represented a supreme event in history, while for others it was an event in which Dostoyevsky's gloomiest forecasts came true, the demons which terrified him spread out their clutches and tyrannized mankind. If we compare Babel's work with those which, for example, Merezhkovsky wrote, we cannot but have our doubts that they attempted to portray the same historic event.

Everyone writing about a historic event introduces into his own image his own experience, his own way of looking at things. While the historian does his utmost (and generally in vain) to suppress this personal way of seeing things, the writer, on the contrary, uses it as his foundation.

Tolstoy's Napoleon, in one of the greatest works of world literature, is rather a projection of Lev Nikolaevich Tolstoy than an image of the actual Napoleon. His portrayal is such that it should bring out the character of the Russian warrior Kutuzov; but even Kutuzov is more than likely only a projection of Tolstoy's conception of a great patriot who personified the genius of the Russian people. And both warriors confirm his theory that great personalities do only that for which they are predestined. "There are," he wrote, "two aspects to the life of every man: the personal life, which is free in proportion as its interests are abstract, and the elemental life of the swarm, in which a man must inevitably follow the laws laid down for him."[5] Napoleon suffers defeat because he fails to understand that which Tolstoy considers the fundamental law of history.

Reflections on the Russian national character and on the demons hiding in the Russian soul very often proceed from the works of Dostoyevsky. As the eminent modern Czech literary critic and historian Václav Černý wrote, "Masaryk... based the entirety of his famous book *Russia and Europe (1913–1919)* on the thesis that analyzing Dostoevsky is the best means of understanding the complete historical, spiritual, and political development of the Russian people." Černý then analyzes the various characters in Dostoyevsky's work and notes that their portrayal shows signs of the author's sadism: "This could only be invented by completely overwrought nerves and a perverted imagination intoxicated with delirious vengeance!"[6] In analyzing any major literary work, we always discover a great deal about the author and less about history. Or, to be more exact, at best we are able to form a picture of his view of history.

Let us complete Kundera's definition: the novelist does not discuss history but the personal experience of man in history. His image of the world is essentially influenced by his manner of seeing and perceiving—in other words, by his personal characteristics, by his convictions. The novel provides a picture of the world as seen by the individual even when the author attempts to create the impression of giving an objective account of the world, of conditions, people, the lifestyle, the morality, and immorality of a given era. Great literature originates precisely because there is a fragile balance between the subjective and the objective in a novel. The more there is of the objective, the more of the subjective is added. Whenever there is an absence of the subjective, the result is a boring pamphlet; where the objective is missing, the result is a fairy tale or dream about the world.

This is an important point because a reader—even an educated reader such as Masaryk and before him Engels—is inclined to analyze a literary work as a sociological study and present it as the portrayal of an era.

In 1990 Philip Roth wrote: "When I returned to the US from Prague after my first visit in the early seventies, I compared the Czech writers' situation to ours in America by saying, 'there nothing goes and everything matters—here everything goes and nothing matters.'"[7] With these words he expressed a view I had heard expressed in my lifetime many times by my colleagues in the free world: namely, that history had "passed on" to us more significant experiences and thus had made our work easier. We do not have to invent things. All we have to do is to live and record events. It was this view that motivated the question repeated time and again after the November revolution: And what are you going to write about now?

To my generation, in my country life has indeed been most generous with regard to events which we considered to be revolutionary. We spent our childhood in the democratic republic of Masaryk. Then came Munich, two mobilizations, capitulation, the Nazi occupation and war. The enraptured experience of the defeat of Nazism and the restoration of peace. Less than three years of relative freedom, and then the Communist coup. On the one hand, the enthusiasm of the builders of socialism; on the other hand, hundreds of thousands of those whom the new regime deprived of their employment, property, and freedom.

Trials. Concentration camps. The first wave of emigration. The immediate sealing of the border. Censored libraries, a press forced into conformity. Massive brainwashing. Then the thaw in the 1960s, the Prague Spring, and again an occupation, this time a Soviet one. Again, hundreds of thousands stripped of their jobs, again political trials. A new wave of emigration and again sealed borders. Then came the Velvet Revolution—My generation has lived through so many historical transformations, people had to adapt so many times, that it could not fail to influence their character. What more can an author wish for than a world where the characters of people, including those of the authors themselves, are repeatedly exposed to such trials?

From a social and economic point of view, the majority of my colleagues, like me, were hurled to the very bottom social strata, at least during some part of their lifetime. We were definitely not threatened by that which Thornton Wilder wrote about American writers: "One of the dangers of the American artist is that he finds himself almost exclusively thrown in with persons more or less in the arts. He lives among them, eats among them, quarrels with them, marries them."[8] Almost all of us had more than one job: as janitor, watchman. Several of my colleagues cleaned windows or spent their time in caravans measuring water wells. All that which for a normal citizen would be the cause of humiliation, strife, and poverty is figured as a source of inspiration for a writer.

When history affects a writer and draws him into its net, this might serve as an inspiration. I said *might* serve, with emphasis on the word "might," because reality proves that only a few will take advantage of this opportunity. Some become so entangled in the net that they cannot disentangle their hands sufficiently to take up a pen. Others try to become disentangled even when it means forfeiting their souls to the devil. This "devil" might take upon himself the form of money, a career, or willingness to accept a foreign ideological image of the world. Historical changes appear more attractive from outside than from inside. From within they are able to crush or, on the contrary, to blind—to the extent of depriving a person of his good judgment.

At the outset I put forward a rather massive rhetorical question in order to discover to what extent historic events can become a component in the construction of a novel. It is, of course, senseless to look for an answer to a question of that scale. I think it makes more sense to ask in what way an author is able to allow history to enter his work, make it part of its structure, without jeopardizing its credibility, its impact.

Something has changed substantially since the time of Balzac, the time of Tolstoy, or Dostoyevsky. Mountains of work permeated with ideology have been created which distort history along an *a priori* pattern as determined, for example, by so-called socialist realism. But what is more important, a "mass media" has emerged, treating historical facts in the same way they treat everything else, including language—they change everything into a cliché, and what is worse, often into a cliché with an ideological blemish. As presented by the mass media, historic events become a collection of prepared symbolic images which frequently have nothing in common with any real event. The entire agonizing history of the end of Czechoslovak independence was transformed into a picture of Hitler and Chamberlain signing a scrap of paper; the end of the war into a meeting of the soldiers of the victorious Allies on the River Elbe, a soldier hoisting the Soviet flag on the roof of the Reichstag. In Communist Czechoslovakia, some thousand political trials were held; more than two thousand people were executed. A quarter of a million innocent persons were imprisoned while the general secretary of the Communist Party, Slansky, became the symbol of the utterly absurd game of justice. In a trumped-up trial he was condemned to death and executed. Czech television screens over and again showed the brief shot where he stood face to face with the fuming prosecutor. The occupation and revolution in my country were accompanied by battles for the building of the broadcasting station. Tanks in flames. Each one of us has seen these shots on innumerable occasions. Kundera recalls Dubček virtually in tears on his return from Moscow. These shots, too, were seen by millions of viewers throughout the world, in the same way that the crumbling wall which for decades divided Berlin and was the symbol of the Cold War was viewed globally. The mass media make a cliché of everything that is shocking, everything we might consider to be substantial in our history, everything that in the past might have been the skeleton of a literary work: starving children, raped women, executions of the innocent, torture, people perishing in flames, funerals of famous persons, cheering crowds, demonstrations, police officers beating the innocent, phony embraces of statesmen, shots fired from the rear, crashed aircraft, sinking ships, derailed trains, bereaved families.

The most tragic thing in all this is that the audience accepts these clichés as the only image of the history of mankind. A cliché facilitates communication and helps to reduce a complicated reality into simple and understandable elements. A cliché makes genuine communication impossible, just as it makes it impossible to grasp the complexity of each historic event.

Many writers—in Czech literature, almost the entire postwar generation—have concluded from this that literature should turn away as much as possible from a world contaminated by the cliché, in other words, from life as it is perceived by the ordinary citizen. Literature should create its own world which has its own laws or has no laws whatsoever, but rather is no more than a succession of images, ideas, absurdities, shouts, sighs, and intimacies which until now have been taboo.

However, several works in Czech literature about which I now want to speak, which did not embark along this road, but rather attempted to capture historical changes, were also created. The authors of these works mostly belonged to a generation which experienced the Second World War as well as the Communist coup. The way these authors attempt to reflect history deserves a close examination.

I remember how my generation was affected after the war by Salinger's novel *Catcher in the Rye*. The novel, like Hemingway's prose, unquestionably influenced the young Czech author Josef Škvorecký, who, less than five years after the war, at the age of twenty-five, completed a remarkable novel about the revolution set in a small town during the last few days of the war: *The Cowards*. The plot spans the time of the revolution between May 4 and 11, 1945.

Škvorecký, like Salinger, chose a teenager to be the narrator, a keen jazz fan. His hero, if for no other than generational reasons, sees the entire attempt at an uprising against the already essentially defeated German army as an incompetent farce, an escapade. Although he takes part in the revolution and is even taken prisoner, then liberated, whereupon he destroys a German tank, his unfulfilled longing for love is more important for him. Events which were officially or in general presented as being among the principal moments in modern Czech history thus lose all their glory. This vision of the young hero deprives these events of their pathos by giving priority to his amorous longing. An ironic distance; long, jabbering enamored dialogues; and a seemingly cynical view of all that is sacrosanct helped Škvorecký use dramatic historic events in the fiber of the novel in such a way as to avoid cliché. (In its time the novel was so unconventional that for political reasons it could only be published seven years after it was written, and even then it triggered a wave of hostile reaction among official reviewers and among party writers.) Škvorecký again used a similar method of belittling historic events in his other great novel, *Mirakl,* where he attempts to capture the contradictory character of the Prague Spring as well as the brutality of the Soviet occupation.

Since I mentioned Salinger, I cannot but remember how fascinated I was by his short story "A Perfect Day for Bananafish." It came out roughly at the time major wartime novels such as *Catch 22* or *The Naked and the Dead* were published. Salinger's plot also centered on a defect suffered by the hero during the war. But the fact that he was in the war is mentioned merely in two brief remarks, while the entire story takes place at a level which has nothing in common with the war. There remains only the wound in the soul resulting in a lethal bullet fired into his own temple.

As distinct from the mass media cliché, but also from major epics, the modern author resorts more and more frequently to intimate stories, which the historic event enters without bombastic shots, or weeping or cheering crowds.

One of the key events in modern Czech history was the Communist coup of February 1948. Authors dedicated to the regime described it time and again. Clips of the huge demonstration in the Old Town Square, convened by the Communists, were shown on innumerable occasions, as was the speech by the chairman of the Communist Party, Klement Gottwald.

One of the most original Czech authors, the late Bohumil Hrabal, also incorporated the Communist coup into his autobiographical novel *Městečko, kde se zastavil čas* (*The Little Town Where Time Stood Still*), but the way he did this differs totally from the method used by Škvorecký. He writes of the hero's father, the manager of a beer brewery, who is replaced by a worker-manager in those days in February. The worker-manager forbids his predecessor to enter his own office and asks him to take away his personal belongings:

> When father took away the last box with pens and calendars and small notebooks, he opened the cupboard and took two bulky lamps, the same lamps in the light of which he used to write years ago and which were ready in case the electricity was cut off, bulky lamps with green shades, and as he was taking them away the worker-manager said: "But these lamps are part of the brewery inventory...." and took them out of father's hand. "I shall pay for them," father said quietly. But the worker-manager shook his head and said in a distant voice: "You have hoarded enough, you have built yourself a house...." And when father left the office the worker-manager was waiting for this opportunity and threw the two lamps with the green shades out of the window onto a scrap heap and the

> green shades as well as the cylinders broke into small pieces and father held his head and it gave a crack as though his brain had split. "A new era is starting even here," the worker-manager said and entered the office.[9]

This very short scene about a small episode in an insignificant beer brewery magnificently captures the absurdity, inhumanity, and arrogant destructiveness of the Communist coup. Here Hrabal finds a way of capturing a dramatic moment of history without cliché, without the setting up of great events. Instead of stereotypical metaphors he chooses his own: two entirely useless, broken old lamps tell us about the character of the revolution and its protagonists.

I spoke of Kundera and his principle of using historical facts. He also mentions the fact that "in the years that followed the 1968 Russian invasion of Czechoslovakia, the reign of terror against the public was preceded by officially organized massacres of dogs. An episode totally forgotten and without importance for a historian, for a political scientist, ... By this one episode alone I suggested the historical climate of *Farewell Waltz*."[10] I must admit that I cannot remember a massacre of dogs, but basically it is not relevant whether this was a real event or the author's hyperbole. It is again a metaphor attempting to avoid the pathos of the mass media cliché.

As I've said, in modern Czech history there has been no shortage of great and dramatic events. The repercussions of these events strongly influence the life of almost every human being, often for years or even decades. In such a situation it is difficult to write a novel and entirely pass over these moments. True, the fact that literature is practically the only vehicle by which it is possible to express a view on the conditions of life in a totalitarian system has no doubt done its bit. I remember that in the seventies, when I was writing the novel *Judge on Trial*, I burdened it not only with a number of scenes which referred to historic events but even with several very brief pieces wherein I quoted documents. These documents demonstrated in a terse and effective manner the unbelievable, almost comical changeableness of Czech history, of the values and leaders whom society revered. This version was published only in German. However, that was around the time Charter 77 came out together with a number of documents concerning modern history and problems such as those mentioned in my novel. For me this was a great relief, and for the second edition I revised the novel and left out all I felt to be an excessive encumbrance burdening the composition of the novel.

In 1975, Jiří Gruša, then aged thirty-seven, an author banned at the time like most Czech authors, completed one of the most interesting works of prose written in Bohemia after the war: *Questionnaire: or, Prayer for a Town and a Friend.* Like Škvorecký's hero, the hero of this slim work is the author's contemporary, his alter ego. But in contrast to Škvorecký, Gruša covers a longer span of time, from the German occupation to the Soviet invasion, with reference to even more remote events during the previous century. The author used a character reference questionnaire as an external formal vehicle. The questionnaire allowed him, among other things, to highlight identical procedures in two totalitarian systems in which his hero lived—first in one, then in the other. As in Škvorecký's novel, the narrator's interest focuses on his personal, mainly amorous relations and experiences. Historic events are recorded only in passing, although they are of decisive importance for the heroes' lives, for, after all, they directly and indirectly threaten their livelihood—they kill, drive them out of their homes, deprive them of their freedom. Most scenes of intimacy recur with accounts of political events, realistically captured images of petit-bourgeois life with dreamlike and phantasmagoric visions. The result of this collage is a suggestive picture of the world on the brink of reality and absurdity, a life on the brink of love and death. In addition to material significance there is also a visible political significance: the folly of the totalitarian system underlines the absurdity of life and the folly of history as such.

One of the most remarkable works of contemporary Czech literature came out in 1979; in a way, it influenced and still influences a number of further literary works by other authors. I am speaking of the novel *The Czech Dreambook* by Ludvík Vaculík.

Vaculík came to literature after being a radio reporter and journalist, and his work was always marked by a reporter's pithiness, a registering of actual events intermixed with nonconformist reflections on the problems of life in a totalitarian society. Vaculík made a name for himself throughout the world with his rebellious speech at the Writers' Congress and later, at the time of the Prague Spring, with his manifesto *2000 Words*. Throughout the 1970s and 1980s, his regular monthly three-page *feuilletons* were circulated as samizdat and are, in my opinion, the best that have ever been written in this genre.

Vaculík's work became more and more documentary, and in *The Czech Dreambook* the author reaches the actual threshold of what is possible. He keeps a virtual day-to-day diary between January 1, 1979, and the beginning of February 1980: a real diary in which he puts down all major events in his life—his meetings, his interrogations, as well as most minor jobs such as work in the garden or feeding the canary and cleaning the windows, but also his thoughts about the world in which he has to move and, as the title of the novel intimates, his dreams. His work gives repeated vent to Czech common sense or, to be more exact, the common sense of the Moravian villager. As an author of *feuilletons*, Vaculík mastered to perfection the art of the punch line—brief excursions into the most varied spheres of life and the art of the most laconic and concise generalization. If I were to compare his method with the subtler construction of Kundera's works, I would say that Vaculík is Kundera's antipode. Readers were shocked that, with exceptions, the author used the real names of those closest to him. The characters enter the work as they entered the author's life: often during accidental meetings, sometimes characterized, sometimes merely mentioned by name, sometimes namelessly. The author laconically mentions some very personal facts of his life, his infidelities as well as forbidden activities, which included first and foremost the organization of the Czech samizdat *Edition Padlock*. It can be said that he sacrificed everything to the vision of authenticity. "Dear reader!" he writes in his entry on February 6, "A fat lot you know. All those deceptions that writers practice on their readers! I, however, as you can see, am not out to deceive."[11] The novel thus creates the impression—and Vaculík does his best to reinforce this all the time—that the work was not written by an author but by life: the author merely records all that life has brought along. The fact that in that year a tragic love appeared in his life is simply a coincidence.

It is true, and I myself can confirm this, that Vaculík did not invent the events he recorded, but all he recorded, all he committed, all he emphasized, all about which he brooded, all that was his own choice. In actual fact, a work which gives the impression of a chronicle of random events has been composed with utmost ingenuity and, above all, untraditionally.

Vaculík succeeded in portraying his vision of the historical reality in the late 1970s with exceptional, at times even brutal, ruthless authenticity, and he succeeded in doing this with an effectiveness achieved by no other Czech author. With his work Vaculík influenced several other Czech writers, including in part another of his world-famous contemporaries—Pavel Kohout.

Kohout published his novel of memoirs, *Where the Dog is Buried*, seven years later. His story, too, is based mainly on a record of personal experiences captured in diary form. The novel consists of two constantly intermingling dimensions. The first concentrates on an absurd game, lasting several days, which the Czech political secret police played with the author in 1978. The police sent him a letter of blackmail and then pretended that it would have to protect him against the alleged blackmailers. In this way the police forced him to agree to be followed by guards. The second dimension, covering a longer period, records all the more notable moments of the establishment of the dissident movement, as experienced by the author. It records the birth of Charter 77, of which Kohout and Vaculík were co-authors and naturally notes the hostile reaction of the regime to the charter. As a participant in these events, I can again confirm that they enter the work without major distortions. In the novel, just as in Vaculík's *Dreambook*, several characters are presented under their real names, and the condemnation of those who collaborated with the regime is much more severe. But as distinct from Vaculík, Kohout seeks to introduce a greater stylization or, rather, to produce an effect. He selects only those realities which promise to attract attention. Kohout replaces philosophizing with politicizing. Moreover, he turns a dachshund into one of his major heroes, the only one who lost his life in Kohout's struggle with the totalitarian regime. Even though Kohout was after the same authenticity as Vaculík and used similar methods, he had to sacrifice at least a little of this authenticity in his pursuit to capture the reader's attention and achieve a narrating effect.

Vaculík's novel no doubt influenced contemporary Czech literature, or, to be exact, the youngest writers. During the past few years a number of works, not only autobiographical but written in dairy or memoir form, have appeared, written strangely enough by authors under the age of thirty. I shall mention two very recent titles: *A Dairy, or the Death of a Film Director* by Igor Chaun, and *Kraft* by Martin C. Putna. The authors of other entirely autobiographical works, Zdeněk Zapletal (*Born in CSR* or *Vekslstube cimmerfraj*) and Vlastimil Třešňák (*The Key Is Under the Mat*) are only slightly older.

I have given some examples of how at least some of the most eminent Czech authors reacted to the colorful history they were made to experience, while still avoiding the danger of turning this history into a cliché. Some did this by giving history a very personal dimension in the vision of their hero; others found more effective metaphors for historic events; still others reached for a diary-form authenticity by introducing nonfictional elements into fiction.

I personally believe that the purpose of literature is to talk to man. Man is never outside of history. The fact that in the mass media and in ideological literature this history is reduced to symbols and clichés should be grasped as a challenge to the writer, inciting him to do his utmost to overcome the cliché. A literature which decides to dodge this task abandons its most innate mission, and its creators are then surprised in vain when the place they have vacated has been seized by someone else who plays a deceptive game with the lives of human beings.

Endnotes

1 Friedrich Engels to Margaret Harkness, April 1888, in *Karl Marx, Frederick Engels on Literature and Art: A Selection of Writings*, ed. Lee Baxandall and Stefan Morawksi (New York, 1974), p. 115.

2 Ibid., p. 116.

3 Milan Kundera, "Dialogue on the Art of the Novel," in *The Art of the Novel*, trans. Linda Asher (New York, 1993), p. 36.

4 Franz Kafka, *The Diaries of Franz Kafka, 1910–1923* (New York, 1988), p. 301.

5 Leo Tolstoy, *War and Peace*, trans. Constance Garnett (New York, 1904), 2:p. 244.

6 Václav Černý, *Dostoevsky and His Devils*, trans. F. W. Gajan (Ann Arbor, MI, 1975), pp. 20, 31.

7 Philip Roth, "Conversation in Prague with Ivan Klíma," in *Shop Talk: A Writer and His Colleagues and Their Work* (New York, 2001), p. 53.

8 Thornton Wilder, *Conversations with Thornton Wilder*, ed. Jackson R. Bryer (Jackson, MS, 1992), p. 66.

9 Bohumil Hrabal, *Městečko, kde se zastavil čas* [The little town where time stood still] (Prague, 1991).

10 Kundera, "Dialogue on the Art of the Novel," p. 37.

11 Ludvík Vaculík, *Český snář* [The Czech dreambook] (Toronto, ONT, 1983).

Michael Ignatieff

Berlin in Autumn: The Philosopher in Old Age

BY COMMON CONSENT Isaiah Berlin enjoyed a happy old age. The autumn of his life was a time of serenity. But serenity in old age is a philosophical puzzle. Why did he manage to avoid the shipwreck which is the more common fate of us all?

The obvious answer is that he was exceedingly fortunate. He married happily, late in life, and he enjoyed good health, good fortune, and a growing reputation. His life between 1974, when he retired from the presidency of Wolfson College, Oxford, and his death in 1997 were years both of ease and increasing public recognition. Berlin's editor, Henry Hardy, began editing and republishing his previously unpublished essays and lectures, and this transformed Berlin's reputation, giving the lie to Maurice Bowra's joke that, like our Lord and Socrates, Berlin talked much but published little.[1] He lived long enough to see his reputation, which had been in relative eclipse, blossom into what he referred to as a "posthumous fame."

Certainly, Berlin's serenity in his final years owed a great deal to good fortune. But there are temperaments which frown even when fortune shines, and even those with sunny temperaments find mortal decline a depressing experience. So Berlin's serenity is worth trying to explain, both for what it tells us about him and for what it tells us about how to face our own aging. I want to ask whether his serenity was a matter of temperament or a result of conviction, whether it was a capacity he inherited or a goal he achieved, and in particular whether his convictions—liberal, skeptical, agnostic, and moderate—helped to fortify him against the ordeals of later life.

Being philosophical about old age implies being reconciled or being resigned or some combination of the two. I want to ask whether Isaiah was resigned or reconciled and in what sense philosophy helped him to be philosophical in either of these senses.

From Socrates onwards, philosophy—especially the Stoic tradition—has made the question of how to die well one of its central preoccupations. Indeed until philosophers became academic specialists devoted to instruction of the young and maintenance of that walled garden known as professional philosophy—in other words until the second half of the nineteenth century—one of the central tests of a philosophy was whether it helped its adherents to live and die in an instructively rational and inspirational fashion. The great modern example of the philosophical death is David Hume, whose good-humored skepticism made him one of Isaiah's favorite philosophers. The story of Hume's death, told in James Boswell's *Journals* and in Adam Smith's *Memoir*, became a cause célèbre in the Enlightenment.[2] In the summer of 1776, Boswell returned repeatedly to Hume's house in the final days, awaiting some wavering which would indicate that the philosopher had recanted and embraced the Christian faith. No such wavering occurred. Hume went to his death with all the good humor of Socrates, joking with Boswell about what he might say to Charon the boatman when they met at the banks of the Styx. The jokes sent a shiver through every fiber of Boswell's errant but Christian soul. After visiting Hume for the last time, he found a whore in the streets of Edinburgh and coupled with her within sight of Hume's bedroom, as if wishing to embrace the carnal in order to drive the tormenting fear of death out of his mind. So a philosophical death was both a noble spectacle and a metaphysical puzzle.

Hume's death placed him securely in this grand philosophical tradition going back to Socrates. But his philosophical positions broke with the assumption that philosophy should teach men how to live and die well. His philosophical writings maintained—and his own experience of life deepened this into a settled conviction—that while philosophy could clarify the terms of mental and moral debate, it could not generate meaningful reasons to live or die.[3] In particular, it was not a substitute source for the consolations provided by religion. Indeed, the search for metaphysical consolations was bound to be insatiable and profoundly unsettling. If men were seeking for serenity in their final hours, they should not seek it in philosophy. Hume himself had little to say about the sources of his own serenity, but they seem to have owed more to temperament than to conviction, more to the sense of a life fully lived and enjoyed than to any received or formulated set of stoic opinions.

The same proved true of Isaiah Berlin. He was a Humean skeptic from the time he came up to Oxford in 1928, an agnostic in religion and a skeptic in philosophy. As it happened, a modern twentieth-century form of Humean skepticism was just then coming into the ascendant in Oxford analytical philosophy. While still in his twenties in Oxford, Berlin became one of the founding fathers of "logical positivism." While the immediate origins of this view were the Vienna School—Wittgenstein, Carnap, Schlick, and Waismann—Hume remains the grandfather of this view of philosophy and its most characteristic Anglo-Saxon exponent.[4] Logical positivism strengthened Berlin's Humean distrust of metaphysics and what the Germans called *Lebensphilosophie*. Philosophy, as the logical positivists conceived it, had to emancipate itself from the Socratic heritage of asking questions about the meaning of life and the manner of a good death. It would never achieve results, it would never make progress as a discipline unless it rigorously excluded unanswerable questions from its research program. This view of philosophy was in turn a view of life. It was central to this view that if you persisted in asking questions about the meaning of life, you had not understood life in any degree. Life was life and its plausibility was a matter of sentiment, not a matter of argument. Philosophical propositions were of no use at all in living or dying, and to ask philosophy to console was to mistake what it was.

Although Berlin eventually broke with the scientistic and reductive style of logical positivism, he was deeply marked by its antimetaphysical bent. Philosophy's function was to clarify common terms of argument, to elucidate the nature of moral choices, and to interpret certain puzzles in the relation between the mind and the world. It was not a substitute for religion and had nothing to say about death or how we should face it. Like most of the analytical philosophers of his generation, Berlin felt that unless philosophy kept the demarcation line with metaphysics clear, it would lose all claim to rigor, seriousness, and self-respect.

These views, developed in late adolescence, made him deeply skeptical by the time he reached his eighties about the very possibility that philosophy could assist one to be philosophical about old age. He was not scornful of those who sought comforting systems of belief, but he did not stand in need of one himself. He thought of aging and death in consistently materialist terms and believed, accordingly, that death held no terrors since, logically speaking, it was not an event in life. This formulation, adapted from Wittgenstein's *Tractatus*, implied both that death was not to be feared, since it could not be experienced, and also that death was only the end, not the defining property of life.[5]

Yet we cannot leave the matter there. Berlin the antimetaphysical philosopher may have been skeptical of the very idea that philosophical propositions can shape the encounter with death, but when it came to deciding upon his own funeral, he chose the Jewish Orthodox form of service rather than the Reform or nondenominational service his agnostic beliefs might have logically entailed. This reflected a choice of allegiance and belonging, rather than a commitment of faith. He could subscribe to the rituals of Judaism without subscribing to their content. He did so serenely, refusing to see any contradiction. The faith of his fathers had disposed of these matters of burial and mourning very well for centuries. Why should he quarrel with any of it? His skepticism about matters religious was more respectful than many of his more bone-dry skeptical friends—Alfred Ayer or Stuart Hampshire, for example. Why this is so is not easy to explain. As a refugee and exile, he perhaps needed the reassurance of religious ritual more than his English colleagues; just possibly, he thought that there was a sort of arid presumption in the modernist dismissal of ritual as superstition.

He also differed from his colleagues, ultimately, in his view of the relation between philosophical propositions and life. As a logical positivist, he was skeptical about the very attempt to justify life philosophically. But he turned away from philosophy proper in his late twenties in part because he had become fascinated precisely by the ways in which men did use ideas to justify, explain, and even modify their lives. As a historian of ideas, he was keenly aware that men do live and die by their ideas. Few philosophers had such a keen sense of the intense interaction between propositions, convictions, and temperament. If we are going to look at the impact of Berlin's thought on the manner of his own aging we shall have to look beyond the impact of logical positivism itself.

All of his thinking associated serenity with belonging, and belonging with self-knowledge. If he was serene in old age it was because he knew who he was and where he belonged. This personal sense of the necessity of roots informed all of his writing on nationalism. He always located the origins of nationalist feeling in the passion to be understood. People need to live in communities where they are understood—and not merely for what they say, but for what they mean. To have a national home was to live in a world of such tacitly shared meanings.[6]

He attached more importance to belonging than any other modern liberal philosopher. He had a clear sense of his own origins, as the son of a Baltic timber merchant born in the Jewish community of Riga in the twilight of the czarist empire. Despite going into exile he kept a strong sense of connection to these roots throughout his adult life. This organic connection was possible because his mother remained alive until he was well into his sixties. It so happened that he retired in the year of his mother's death, 1974. When he tried to speak about losing her, he used the German verb *zerreißen*, meaning "to tear in pieces." In the letters he wrote in the week after her death in 1974, he went on to say that without such living links to his past he felt accidental, contingent, directionless.[7] Life briefly lost its momentum and point. In time, he recovered it again: his organic capacities for repair and recovery were formidable. It is doubtful that he had more than several months' experience of genuine depression in his whole life, and if his mother's death occasioned one such occasion, it was brief.

His equanimity in old age had a great deal to do with the degree to which he made his own life—its needs and cravings—the tacit subject of his work, and through apparently abstract writings about nationalism explored the needs for belonging which were central to his own identity. If this produced equanimity it was because it was done tacitly, with a minimum of self-disclosure, so that his work both revealed his inner preoccupations and helped him to resolve them, without exposing him to ridicule or shame.

Among expatriates like Berlin, identities soldered together in exile often come apart in old age. In retirement and old age, people are brought up short with the realization of how far they have come from their beginnings. Often their past is now in another country and in another time. When this realization dawns, identity comes under strain. They begin to go to church or synagogue more often; they begin to dream in their languages of origin in an attempt to recover past connections; more often than not, they begin to have a sense of inner fragmentation. They are not able to pull past, present, and future together. The span of life is simply too long. There are too many twists and turns in the road.

This did not happen to Berlin. In fact, old age represented a coming together of the Russian, Jewish, and English skeins of his identity. During his years as a schoolboy and then as a young Oxford don, he assimilated thoroughly. His accent, for example, impersonated the upper-middle-class Oxford dons of his acquaintance. But with old age, the Russian and Jewish parts of his identity began to return. His voice became less English with time and more Russian in its vowel sounds. He himself was aware of this. It cannot be accidental that his most extended excursion into autobiography, the Jerusalem prize speech, was given as he turned seventy.[8] In it, he made a point of saying that his identity consisted of three elements, English, Russian, and Jewish, all braided together into one skein. The philosophical equanimity of his old age owed a great deal to this recovery of all the elements of his past, this braiding of the skein of selfhood. It made him an exceedingly economical persona: no energy was wasted in repression or denial of the origins which made him up.

There was no question of a return to Judaism in old age, because he had never left. While he did not keep a kosher table, he observed the major Jewish festivals and liked to joke that the orthodox synagogue was the synagogue he did not attend. He had no time for Reformed Judaism because he thought it was incoherent to combine religion and rationalism, to reduce an ancient faith to nothing more than an agreeable and modern ethical content. He respected the claims of the ancient Jewish tradition precisely because of their irrational and inhuman content. Igor Stravinsky came to lunch in 1963 and asked Isaiah to suggest a religious subject for a composition he had been commissioned to write for the Jerusalem Festival. Berlin went upstairs, returned with his Bible, and read Stravinsky the passage in Hebrew describing Abraham's binding of Isaac. Stravinsky took Berlin's advice and went on to compose a cantata on the theme. The Abraham and Isaac story was a parable for Berlin about the inscrutability both of God's commands and of human life itself. Unlike many of his fellow agnostics, Berlin had a healthy respect for the religious dimension in human consciousness. It also helped to sustain his ultimately metaphysical view that there were a lot of things about the shape of human life which we cannot know.[9]

Because he was a famous man, he would be asked, sometimes by complete strangers, to pronounce on the meaning of life. He found this very comic, but his replies were terse and matter of fact. When he was seventy-five, he replied to one such questioner, "As for the meaning of life, I do not believe that it has any. I do not at all ask what it is but, I suspect it has none and this is a source of great comfort to me. We make of it what we can and that is all there is about it. Those who seek for some deep cosmic...all-embracing libretto or God are, believe me, pathetically mistaken."[10]

These then were the metaphysical sources of his serenity: a deep and abiding sense of who he was and where he came from, coupled with a cool and skeptical refusal to entertain questions about the meaning of life which he thought were beyond the reach of reason.

This is about as far as doctrine and mature conviction will take us in explaining his autumnal serenity, and they do not take us very far. We need to look at his temperament, at the attitudes to self and habits of mind, which made it easy for him to greet old age with relative calm.

As his biographer I had expected that when he left Wolfson College, when he was no longer president of the British Academy, no longer Chichele Professor of Social Thought, no longer a Fellow at All Soul's, that he might have felt bereft and denuded, as professional men often do at the end of their careers. Retirement can initiate a period of lonely inner questioning. This did not happen for Berlin. This is because he was never heavily invested in these roles in the first place. He did not lack ambition; he liked to be taken seriously; he could be prickly if he felt his dignity or reputation were attacked—but he also stood outside himself and mocked his own desires for recognition. When T. S. Eliot wrote to congratulate him on his knighthood in 1956, Isaiah replied that he felt as silly as if he were wearing a paper hat at a children's party.[11] He liked recognition—the knighthood mattered deeply—but he held some part of himself back. Irony and a sense of the ridiculous, therefore, were important components of the serenity his friends admired in the autumn of his life.

Of course irony and a sense of humor about the scramble for honor and fame are easier if you've had your share of both. He always said his success had been based on a systematic overestimation of his abilities. "Long may this continue," he would say. He had very little to be bitter about, very little to regret. Yet even those who have known a success equivalent to his are often bitter and depressed in old age. He was not.

He always insisted that he was not an essentially introspective man; he was an observer, certainly, but fundamentally directed outwards rather than inwards. He never kept a diary and his most characteristic forms of self-revelation were addressed outwards in letters and conversation. He thought more about what other people made of him than he thought about himself. He found it easy to take a distance from his own life, to be ironical about himself, because he wasn't imprisoned in his own self to begin with.

He had a particular talent for imagining other lives, and that gave him a vantage point from which to see his own. He loved reading in order to lose himself in some other person, often someone radically alien to his own temperament. He had a fascination with ideas and temperaments opposite to his own: figures like Joseph de Maistre, the counterrevolutionary theorist and fanatical hater of bourgeois liberal reformism.[12] In entering into de Maistre's inner world, he could see himself as de Maistre might have seen him, and this capacity for self-distantiation freed him from excessive or burdening investment in his own roles.

Keeping himself apart from his roles followed, I think, from being a Jew and an exile. His belonging in England was both secure and conditional. Irony, self-distantiation, and self-deprecation had survival value for any Jewish exile in England. This is one of the reasons that he remained, even in secure old age, a watchful character, acutely aware that he was a sojourner and a stranger even in the Establishment which took him to its heart.

He also refused to vest his own commitments, ideas, and values with existential or historical importance. After the fall of Communism, he was constantly asked whether he felt vindicated, and his replies always challenged the premise of the question itself. Why, he asked, should any liberal feel vindicated? History, he always said, had no libretto. To claim that it vindicated him or his liberalism seemed an absurd inflation of both himself and the doctrines with which he was associated. He was also self-knowing enough to realize that he had never risked anything decisive in the struggle against Communist tyranny, as Koestler, Orwell, Miłosz, or Akhmatova had. Since that was the case, it was unbecoming to make a show of rejoicing at its fall. He did take quiet pleasure in the fact that Communism ended as his own life came to a close. He could look back across the century and feel that the intellectuals with whom he felt the closest spiritual kinship: the anti-Bolshevik writers and artists of Russia's Silver Age, 1896–1917—chiefly Pasternak and Akhmatova—would have rejoiced to have lived the hours he had been lucky enough to see. In this sense, history did shine on him in his final years.

He was distantiated from his roles, from his own ideas, and from his own posterity. He was fond of saying, *"Après moi, le déluge."* Of course, there was an element of pose in this, a very Oxford style of appearing not to care about reputation. In fact, of course, he was a careful custodian of his reputation—worrying whether he should accept such and such an honor, sit at such and such a table, with such and such a person, give his name to such and such an appeal. All of this indicates a concern to husband the coinage of his fame. But as to what came after, he always purported to be indifferent.

His attitude to my work on his biography, for example, was complex. Initially, he thought it was a ludicrous idea. "Why would I want to do such a thing?" I can remember him asking me. It was only after three years of oral interviewing—in which I would ask him a question at the beginning of the hour and get to ask him another one at the end—that he broached the issue of what would become of the tapes. The idea of a biography grew upon him as he came to trust me and grow comfortable in my company. As the years passed, he engaged with the project, checking with me about this or that detail, retelling certain stories with a new twist or nuance in order that I would appreciate its significance. But he took a fundamentally passive approach to my project, waiting for the right question before proffering the answer, and I had to wait for years for him to disclose what he took to be the essential elements of his life and thought. He seemed to have little anxiety about posterity. When I asked him how he thought he would be remembered, his replies were always of the form "how can we possibly know?" and "why should it matter?"

This attitude towards posterity was reinforced by the fact that he had no children of his own. He was quite content to be a stepfather to his wife's children, but he never evinced a very strong desire to have any of his own. The patriarchal and paternal instincts—all of which usually go with a desire to shape and mold posterity—were absent in him.

He also never had disciples. There were many former students, friends, and associates who liked to say *"Ich bin ein Berliner,"* but he never sought to create a circle of followers who would propagate his ideas and safeguard his reputation. There was no Berlin school, tendency, or faction. He disliked the idea of having to take responsibility for a Berlinian doctrine, with orthodoxy to defend and disciples to promote it.

He watched Henry Hardy, a young graduate student in philosophy, attach himself to his work; he supported Hardy's editions of his works and greatly enjoyed the revival of his reputation which Hardy's work achieved, but never took any initiative in the relationship beyond benign approval. The same genial detachment characterized his relationship to my biography. Neither Hardy nor I ever thought of ourselves as surrogate sons, disciples, or acolytes.

Isaiah simply did not want this kind of entourage around him—did not want the responsibility.

The final source of his equanimity, I believe, was in relation to aging itself. Almost all of us have a quarrel with how old we actually are, and present ourselves as younger or older than our biological age. Biological and phenomenological age are never exactly the same. Isaiah was a complex instance of this. All the people who remember him from his early youth always said that he was the oldest person in any room. When he was twenty he was already behaving as if he were a middle-aged man. Stephen Spender, one of his oldest friends, once said to me that he had trouble thinking of Isaiah as having aged at all. He was always "a baby elephant, always the same baby elephant."[13] In early pictures of him, he is wearing the same kind of three-piece suit that he wore to the end of his life. He valued continuity in the details: the same kind of polished shoes, the same look of cautious bourgeois sobriety as his father. He dressed like his father all his life, and he did so from adolescence onwards. The paradox of his extraordinary youthfulness and vitality, therefore, was that he always thought of himself as a middle-aged man. He always seemed older than he was and he always remained younger than he seemed.

Age did him many favors. He was not a prepossessing twenty- or thirty- or even forty-year-old. It wasn't until he was in his sixties that he looked fully at ease with what he had become. He thinned down, his whole face acquired a certain nobility, as if he were finally growing into the age at which he was most himself.

His vernacular of odd behavior—going to parties with crispbread in a matchbox in his pocket so that he could have his own little snacks—belonged more to the personality of an indulged child than of a sage. In a restaurant he would suddenly begin humming some little Yiddish ditty that he had heard in Hebrew school in 1915. That ability to recover his childhood and be a child again was one of the reasons that he was much loved and that he was never weighed down by life.

The other element of his aging, which he noticed himself, was that it rendered him more, not less, susceptible to pity. In a letter written late in life, he said, "The proposition that the longer one lives the more indifferent one becomes to the ills that beset one or one's dearest is totally false. I suffer much more from this than I used to and I now realize that there must have been a long period of my life when I was, comparatively speaking, too little sensitive to the misfortunes of others, however close, certainly, of my friends."[14]

In 1993, one year before his death, Steven Spender sent Isaiah the following poem, written in China in AD 835. It commemorated their sixty years of friendship:

> We are growing old together, you and I
> Let us ask ourselves "what is age like?"
> The idle head still uncombed at noon
> Propped on a staff sometimes a walk abroad
> Or all day sitting with closed doors.
>
> One dares not look in the mirror's polished face.
> One cannot read small letter books.
> Deeper and deeper one's love of old friends,
> Fewer and fewer one's dealing with young men.
> One thing only: the pleasure of idle talk
> Is great as ever, when you and I meet.[15]

That does catch perhaps the final element of what kept both of them young: the pleasure of idle talk, and the idler the better. Memory, word games and puns, the sheer pleasure of orality, which connected him to the pleasures of infancy all his life. There was nothing that meant more to him than the pleasure of talk. He died tragically of esophageal constriction, literally unable to get words out of his throat. The condition was terrible to him, and it was the only time I ever saw him depressed, because it made it difficult for him to speak to other human beings, and that was what made life worth living.

What he seemed to vindicate by his life was life itself. Life could not be philosophically justified; it could only be lived. He trusted life and certainly helped those who loved him to trust it more themselves.

Endnotes

[1] Maurice Bowra to Noel Annan, undated, 1971; see Noel Annan "A Man I Loved," in H. Lloyd-Jones, ed., *Maurice Bowra: A Celebration* (London, 1974), p. 53.

[2] I have discussed Hume's death in my *The Needs of Strangers*, chap. 3 (London, 1984). See also James Boswell, *Boswell in Extremes, 1776–1778* (New Haven, 1971), pp. 11–15; Adam Smith, *Correspondence* (Oxford, 1977), pp. 203–21.

[3] David Hume, *A Treatise of Human Nature* (Oxford, 1978), p. 264.

[4] See Ben Rogers, *A. J. Ayer: A Life* (London, 1999); my own *Isaiah Berlin: A Life* (London, 1998), pp. 80–90.

[5] Ignatieff, *Berlin: A Life*, p. 83.

[6] See Isaiah Berlin, "Nationalism: Past Neglect and Present Power" and "The Apotheosis of the Romantic Will," in *The Proper Study of Mankind*, ed. Henry Hardy and Roger Hausheer (London, 1998), pp. 553–605.

[7] Ignatieff, *Berlin: A Life*, p. 272.

[8] Isaiah Berlin, "The Three Strands in My Life," in *Personal Impressions* (London, 1998), pp. 255–61.

[9] Ignatieff, *Berlin: A Life*, pp. 237–38.

[10] Ibid., p. 279.

[11] Ibid., p. 222.

[12] Isaiah Berlin, "Joseph de Maistre and the Origins of Fascism," in *The Crooked Timber of Humanity*, ed. Henry Hardy (New York, 1991), pp. 91–175.

[13] Ignatieff, *Berlin: A Life*, p. 3.

[14] Ibid., p. 288.

[15] Ibid., pp. 287–88.

J. M. Coetzee

The Novel in Africa

AT A DINNER PARTY she meets X, whom she has not seen for years. Is he still teaching at the University of Queensland, she asks? No, he replies, he has retired and now works the cruise ships, travelling the world, screening old movies, talking about Bergman and Fellini to retired people. He has never regretted the move. "The pay is good, you get to see the world, and—do you know what?—people that age actually listen to what you have to say." He urges her to give it a try: "You are a prominent figure, a well-known writer. The cruise line I work for will jump to take you on; you will be a feather in their cap. Say but the word and I'll bring it up with my friend the director."

The proposal interests her. She was last on a ship in 1958, when she sailed from Sydney to England, to the Mother Country. Soon after that they began to retire the great ocean-going liners, one by one, and scrap them. The end of an era. She would not mind doing it again, going to sea. She would like to see Easter Island and St. Helena, where Napoleon languished. She would like to visit Antarctica—not just to see those vast horizons, that barren waste of ice, but to set foot on the seventh and last continent, know what it is to be a living creature in a land of inhuman cold.

X is as good as his word. From the headquarters of Scandia Lines in Stockholm comes a fax. In December the SS *Northern Lights* will be sailing from Christchurch on a fifteen-day cruise to the Ross Ice Shelf, and then on to Cape Town. Might she be interested in joining the education and entertainment staff? Passengers on Scandia's cruise ships are, as the letter puts it, "discriminating persons who take their leisure seriously." The emphasis of the on-board program will be on ornithology and cold-water ecology, but Scandia would be delighted if the noted writer Elizabeth Costello could find the time to offer a course on, say, the contemporary novel. In return for which, and for making herself accessible to passengers, she will be offered an A-class berth, all expenses paid, with air connections to Christchurch and from Cape Town, and a substantial honorarium to boot.

It is an offer she cannot refuse. On the morning of December 10 she joins the ship in Christchurch harbour. Her cabin, she finds, is small but otherwise quite satisfactory; the young man who coordinates the entertainment and self-development programme is respectful; the passengers at her table at lunchtime, in the main retired people, people of her own generation, are pleasant and unostentatious.

Among her new colleagues there is only one she knows: Emmanuel Egudu, a writer from Nigeria. She first met him years ago, more years than she cares to remember, at a PEN conference in Kuala Lumpur. He had been loud and fiery then; she had thought him somewhat of a *poseur*. But at least there will be someone to talk to, someone who will, in a sense, be on her side.

Egudu spends little time nowadays in his native country. He makes his living on the lecture circuit, a circuit wide enough, it would seem, to encompass the cruise ships. This will be his third trip on the *Northern Lights*. Very restful, he says; very relaxing. Who would have guessed, he says, that a country boy like me would end up this way? And he gives her his big smile.

I'm a country girl myself, she would like to say, but does not. *Nothing special in being from the country.*

Each of the entertainment staff is expected to give a short public talk. "Just to explain who you are, where you come from," explains the young coordinator in carefully idiomatic English. His name is Mikail; he is handsome in his tall, blond Swedish way, but dour, too dour for her.

Her talk is advertised as "The Future of the Novel," Egudu's as "The Novel in Africa." She is scheduled to speak on the morning of their first day out to sea; he will speak the same afternoon. In the evening comes "The Lives of Whales," with sound recordings.

Mikail himself does the introduction. "The famous Australian writer," he calls her, "author of *The House on Eccles Street* and many other novels, whom we are truly privileged to have in our midst." It irritates her to be linked once more to a book from so far in her past, but there is nothing she can do about that.

"The Future of the Novel" is a talk she has given before, in fact, many times before, expanded or contracted depending on the occasion. No doubt there are expanded and contracted versions of "The Novel in Africa" and "The Lives of Whales" too. For the present occasion she has selected the contracted version.

"The future of the novel is not a subject I am much interested in," she begins, trying to give her auditors a jolt. "In fact the future in general does not much interest me. The future is, after all, only a structure of hopes and expectations. It resides in the mind; it has no reality.

"Of course you might reply that the past is likewise a fiction. The past is history, and what is history but a story we tell ourselves, a mental construct? But there is something miraculous about the past that the future lacks. What is miraculous about the past is that whole nations, perhaps even humankind as a whole, have succeeded in making thousands and millions of individual fictions—the fictions borne by individual human beings cohere well enough to give us a shared past, a shared history.

"The future is different. We do not have a shared fiction of the future. The creation of the past seems to have exhausted our collective creative energies. Compared with our fiction of the past, our fiction of the future is a sketchy, barren, bloodless affair, as all visions of heaven tend to be. Of heaven and even of hell."

The novel, the traditional novel, she goes on to say, is an attempt to understand a human fate, to understand how it is that someone, some fellow being, having started at point A, and having gone through experiences B and C and D, ends up at point Z. The novel is thus, like history, an exercise in constructing the past. Like history too, the novel is an investigation into the power of character and the power of circumstance. By exploring the power of the past to produce the present, the novel suggests how we may explore the potential of the present to produce the future. That is what the novel does, or can do. That is why we have it.

She is not sure, reading her text, whether she any longer believes in what she is saying. These ideas must have had some grip on her when she first wrote them down years ago, but after so many rehearsals they have begun to seem tired, unconvincing. On the other hand, she no longer believes very strongly in belief. Things can be true, it seems to her, even if one does not believe in them, and conversely. Belief may be no more, after all, than a source of energy, like a battery into which one plugs the idea to make it run. Like what happens when one writes: believing whatever has to be believed in order to get the job done.

If she has trouble believing in her argument, she has even greater trouble in preventing that lack of conviction from emerging in her voice. Despite the fact that she is the noted novelist, author of, as Mikail says, *The House on Eccles Street* and other books, despite the fact that her audience is of her generation and ought therefore to share a common past with her, the applause at the end of her talk lacks enthusiasm.

For Emmanuel Egudu's talk she sits inconspicuously in the back row. They have in the meantime had a good lunch; they are sailing south on what are still placid seas; there is every chance that some of the good folk in the audience—numbering, she would guess, about fifty—are going to nod off. In fact, who knows, she might nod off herself; in which case it would be best to do so unnoticed.

"You will be wondering why I have chosen as my topic the novel in Africa," Emmanuel begins, in his effortlessly booming voice. "What is so special about the novel in Africa? What makes it different, different enough to demand our attention?

"Well, let us see. We all know, in the first place, that the alphabet, the idea of the alphabet, did not grow up in Africa. Many things grew up in Africa, more than you would think, but not the alphabet. The alphabet had to be brought there, first by the Arabs, then again by Westerners. Therefore in Africa writing, script, to say nothing of novel-writing, is a recent affair.

"Is the novel possible without novel-writing, you may ask? Did we in Africa have a novel before our friends the colonizers came? For the time being, let me merely articulate that question. Later I may return to it.

"A second remark: reading is not a typically African recreation. Music, yes; dancing, yes; eating, yes; talking, yes—lots of talking. But reading, no, and particularly not reading fat novels. Reading strikes us Africans as a solitary business, one that leaves us uneasy. When you visit great European cities like Paris and London, you see passengers climbing aboard trains and at once taking books out of their bags or pockets and retreating into their solitary worlds. Each time the book comes out it is like a sign held up. *Leave me alone,* says the sign: *I am reading. What I am reading is more interesting than you could possibly be.*

"Well, we are not like that in Africa. We do not like to cut ourselves off from other people and retreat into private worlds. And we are not used to neighbours of ours retreating into private worlds. Africa is a continent where people share. Reading a book by yourself is not sharing. It is like eating alone or talking alone. It is not our way. We find it a bit crazy."

We, we, we, she thinks. *We Africans. It is not our way.* She has never liked *we* in its exclusive form. Emmanuel may have grown older but he has not changed. Africanness: a special identity, a special fate.

She has been to Africa: to the highlands of Kenya, to Zimbabwe, to the Okavango swamps. She has seen Africans reading, ordinary Africans, at bus stops, in trains. They were not reading novels, admittedly; they were reading newspapers. But is a newspaper not as much a private world as a novel?

"In the third place," says Egudu, "in the great world-system under which we live today, Africa has become the home of poverty. Africans have no money for luxuries. In Africa, a book must give you something in return for the money you spend on it. What do I stand to learn by reading this story? an African will ask. How will it advance me? We may deplore the attitude but we cannot simply dismiss it. We must take it seriously and try to understand it.

"We do make books in Africa, but the books we make are for children, teaching-books in the simplest sense. If you want to make money publishing books in Africa, your best hope is to put out books that will be prescribed for children, that will be bought in quantity by the education system to be read and studied in the classroom. If you are a writer with serious ambitions, wanting to write novels about adults and the matters that concern adults, you will struggle to find publication. All too often you will have to look abroad for salvation.

"Of course it is not the whole picture I am giving you here today, ladies and gentlemen of the *Northern Lights*. To give you the whole picture would take all afternoon. I am giving you only a crude, hasty sketch. Of course there are publishers in Africa, one here, one there, who will support local writers even if they will never make money from them. But in the broad picture, stories and storytelling provide a livelihood neither for writers nor for publishers.

"So much for the depressing generalities. Now let us turn our attention to ourselves, to you and to me. Here I am, you know who I am, the program tells you: Emmanuel Egudu, from Nigeria, author of novels, poems, plays—winner, even, of a Commonwealth Literary Award (Africa Division). And here you are, wealthy folk, or at least comfortable, as you say (I am not wrong, am I?), from

North America and Europe and of course let us not forget our Australasian representation, and perhaps I have heard the odd word of Japanese spoken in the corridors, taking a cruise on this splendid ship, on your way to inspect one of the remoter corners of the globe, to check it out, perhaps to check it off. Here you are, after a good lunch, listening to this African fellow talk.

"What, I imagine you asking yourselves, is the African fellow doing on board? Why isn't he back at his desk in the land of his birth doing what he was born to do, if he really is a writer, namely, writing books? What is he doing here going on about the African novel, a subject that can only be of the most peripheral concern to us?

"The short answer, ladies and gentlemen, is that he is earning a living. In his own country he cannot earn a living. In his own country (I will not belabour the point, I raise it only because it holds true for so many fellow African writers) he is in fact less than welcome. In his own country he is what is called a dissident intellectual, and dissident intellectuals must tread carefully in the Nigeria of today.

"He is here, abroad, earning his living. He earns a living by writing books that are published and read and talked about and judged, for the most part, by foreigners. He earns a living, too, from the spinoffs of his writing. He reviews books by other writers in the press of Europe and America. He teaches in colleges in America, telling the youth of America about the exotic subject on which he is an expert in the same way that an elephant is an expert on elephants—the African novel. He addresses conferences; he sails on cruise ships. While so occupied, he lives in hotel rooms or rented apartments. He has temporary addresses but no fixed abode.

"How easy do you think it is, ladies and gentlemen, for this fellow to be true to his essence as writer when there are all those strangers he has to please, day after day—publishers, readers, critics, students, all of them coming to the fray armed not only with their own ideas about what writing is or should be, what the novel is or should be, what Africa is or should be, but also about what being pleased is or should be? Do you think it is possible for this fellow to remain untouched by all the pressure on him to please others, to be for them what they think he should be and to produce for them what they think he should produce?

"You may not have noticed, but I slipped in, a moment ago, a word that should have made you sit up and prick your ears. I spoke about my essence and about being true to my essence. Given half a chance I would speak at greater length about the essence of being African, about the essence of African writing; but this is not the occasion. Nevertheless, you must be asking, how do I justify the notion of essence in these anti-essential days, these days of fleeting identities that we pick up and wear and discard like clothing?

"Around essentialism there has of course been a history of turmoil in modern African thought. You may have heard of the *négritude* movement of the 1940s and 1950s. According to the founders of the movement, negritude is the essential substratum that binds Africans together and makes them unique—not only the Africans of Africa but Africans of the great African diaspora in the New World and now in Europe.

"I want to quote some words to you from the great Senegalese writer and thinker Cheikh Hamidou Kane. Cheikh Hamidou was being questioned by an interviewer. 'I have some reservations,' said the interviewer, 'about what you call African writers and African writing. In view of the fact that the African authors you refer to write in a foreign language (in this case French) and are published and, for the most part, read in a foreign country (in this case France), can they truly be considered African? Are they not simply French writers of African origin? Why should national origin take precedence over language?'

"This is Cheikh Hamidou's reply: 'They are truly African because they are born in Africa, they live in Africa, their [sensibility] is African.... [What distinguishes them lies in] vital experiences, in sensitivity, in rhythm, in style.' He goes on: 'A French or English writer has thousands of years of written tradition [behind him].... We [on the contrary] are heirs to an oral tradition.'[1]

"It is not a mystical response that Cheikh Hamidou is offering here. It is not metaphysical. It is not even anti-materialist. It is certainly not racialist. It merely gives proper weight to those intangibles of culture which, because they are not easily pinned down in words, are easily passed over. The way that people live in their bodies. The way they move their hands. The way they walk. The way they smile or frown. The lilt of their speech. The way they sing. The timbre of their voices. The way they dance. The way they touch each other; how the hand lingers; the feel of the fingers. The way they make love. The way they lie after they have made love. The way they think. The way they sleep.

"We African novelists can embody these things in our writings (and let me remind you at this point that the word *novel*, when it entered European currency, meant almost nothing, it meant the form that was formless, that had no rules, that made up its own rules as it went along, that was all it meant)—we African novelists can bring it off because we have not lost touch with the body. The African novel, the true African novel, is an oral novel. On the page it is inert, only half alive; it wakes up when the voice breathes into it, when it is spoken aloud.

"The African novel is thus, I would claim, in its very being, and before the first word is written, a critique of the Western novel, which has gone so far down the road of writing—think of Henry James, think of Proust—that the only appropriate way in which to read it is in silence and in solitude. And I will close these remarks, ladies and gentlemen—I see time is getting short—by quoting, in support of my position and Cheikh Hamidou's, not from an African, but from a man from the snowy wastes of Canada, the great scholar of orality Paul Zumthor.

"'Since the seventeenth century,' writes Zumthor, 'Europe has spread itself across the world like a cancer; stealthily at first, but now for some time [running] wild, ravaging today all sorts of [life-forms], animals, plants, [habitats], languages. With each passing day, several languages of the world disappear: repudiated, choked out.... One of the symptoms of this plague was from the beginning ... what we call literature: and literature has gained ground, prospered, and become what it is—one of the vastest dimensions of man—by denying voice. We must stop ... privileging writing.... Perhaps the great and unfortunate Africa, pauperized by our political industrial imperialism, will find herself closer to the goal than the other continents, because she is less seriously touched by writing.'"[2]

The applause after Egudu's talk is loud and spirited. He has spoken with force, perhaps even with passion; he has stood up for himself, for his calling, for his people; why should he not have his reward, even if what he says can have little relevance to the lives of his audience? Nevertheless, she does not like it, does not like the mystique of orality. Always the body that is insisted on, pushed before one, and the voice, dark essence of the body, welling up from within it. She had expected Emmanuel would grow out of it, but evidently he has not, evidently he has decided to keep it as part of his professional pitch. Well, good luck to him. There is still time for questions; she hopes they will be searching.

The first questioner is, if she is to judge from the accent, from the Midwest of the United States. The first novel she ever read by an African, the woman says, was by Amos Tutuola; she forgets the title now. ("*The Palm Wine Drinkard*," suggests Egudu. "Yes, that's it," she replies.) She was captivated by it. She thought it was a portent of great things to come. So she was disappointed, terribly disappointed, to hear that Tutuola was not respected in his own country, that educated Nigerians disparaged him and considered his reputation unmerited. Was this true? Was Tutuola the kind of oral novelist our lecturer had in mind? What has happened to Tutuola? Have more of his books been translated?

"No," responds Egudu, "Tutuola has not been translated any further, in fact he has not been translated at all, at least not into English. The reason is that he did not need to be translated, he had written in English all along, which is the root of the problem that the questioner alludes to. The language of Amos Tutuola is English, but not Standard English, not the English that Nigerians of the 1950s went to school and college to learn. It is the language of a semi-educated clerk, a man with no more than elementary schooling, barely comprehensible to an outsider, fixed up for publication by British editors. Where Tutuola's writing was frankly illiterate they corrected it; what they refrained from correcting was what seemed authentically Nigerian to them, that is to say, what sounded to their ears picturesque, exotic, folkloric.

"From what I have just been saying," Egudu continues, "you may imagine that I too disapprove of Tutuola or the Tutuola phenomenon. But in fact that is not so. Tutuola was repudiated by so-called educated Nigerians because they were embarrassed by him—embarrassed that they might be lumped with him as natives who do not know how to write proper English. No, I am on Tutuola's side. Tutuola is or was a gifted storyteller. I am glad you liked his book. Several more books penned by him were put out in England, though none, I would say, as good as *The Palm Wine Drinkard*. And, yes, he is the kind of writer I was referring to, an oral writer. I have answered you at length because the case of Tutuola is so instructive. What makes Tutuola stand out is that he did not adjust his language to the expectations—or to what he might have thought, had he been less naive, would be the expectations—of the foreigners who would read and judge him. Not knowing better, he wrote as he spoke. He therefore had to yield in a particularly helpless way to being packaged for the West, to being packaged as an African exotic.

"But, ladies and gentlemen, who among African writers is not exotic? The truth is, in the West all Africans are exotic, that is our fate. Even here, on this ship sailing toward the continent that ought to be the most exotic of all, in the sense that it has no natives except the walrus and the penguin, I can sense I am exotic."

There is a ripple of laughter; Egudu smiles his big smile, engaging, to all appearances spontaneous. But she cannot believe it is a true smile, cannot believe it comes from the heart, if that is where smiles come from. If being an exotic is a fate, then his is a terrible fate; she cannot believe Egudu does not know that, know it and rebel against it. The one black face in this sea of white.

"But let me return to your question," Egudu continues. "You have read Tutuola—now read my countryman Ben Okri. Amos Tutuola's is a very simple, very stark case. Okri's is not. Okri is an heir of Tutuola's, or they are the heirs of common ancestors, but Okri negotiates the contradictions of being himself for other people (excuse the jargon, but there are times when I must show that I too can be a literary critic) in a much more complex way. Read Okri. You will find the experience instructive."

"The Novel in Africa" was intended, like all the shipboard talks, to be a light affair. Nothing on the shipboard program is intended to be a heavy affair. Egudu, unfortunately, is threatening to be heavy. With a discreet nod the entertainment director, the tall Swedish boy in his light blue uniform signals from the wings; and gracefully, easily, Egudu obeys, bringing his talk to an end.

The crew of the *Northern Lights* is Russian, as are the stewards. In fact, everyone but the officers and the management elite is Russian. Music on board is provided by a balalaika orchestra—five men, five women. The dinnertime music is too schmaltzy for her taste; after dinner, in the ballroom, it becomes livelier.

The leader of the orchestra, and occasional singer, is a blonde in her early thirties. She has a smattering of English, enough to make the announcements. "We play piece that is called in Russian *My Little Dove. My Little Dove.*" Her *dove* rhymes with *stove* rather than *love*. With its trills and swoops, the piece sounds Hungarian, sounds gipsy, sounds Jewish, sounds everything but Russian; but who is she, Elizabeth Costello, country girl, to say?

She is seated at a table with a couple from Manchester, having a drink. They have both enrolled, they tell her, in her course, and are looking forward to it. They are not at all like her idea of Manchester.

The man is long-bodied, sleek, silvery: she thinks of him as a gannet. The woman is petite, sensual. Steve and Shirley. She suspects they are not married.

To her relief, the conversation turns not to her and her books but to ocean currents, about which Steve appears to know all there is to know, and to the tiny beings, tons of them to the square mile, whose life consists in being swept in serene fashion through these icy waters, eating and being eaten, multiplying and dying, ignored by history. Ecological tourists, that is what Steve and Shirley call themselves. Last year the Amazon, this year the southern ocean.

Egudu is standing at the entranceway to the lounge, looking around for a familiar face. She gives a wave and he comes over. "Join us," she says. "Emmanuel. Shirley. Steve."

They compliment Emmanuel on his lecture. "I was thinking, as you spoke," says Shirley, "that the printed book is probably not the right medium for you. Have you thought about composing straight on to tape? Why make the detour through print? Why even make a detour through writing? Speak your story direct."

"What a clever idea!" says Emmanuel. "It won't solve the problem for the whole of Africa, but let me give it some thought."

"Why won't it solve the problem for Africa?"

"Because I'm afraid Africans will want more than just to sit in silence listening to a tape spinning in a little machine. That would be too much like idolatry. Africans want the living presence, the living voice."

The living voice. There is silence as the three of them try to imagine what he can mean.

"Are you sure about that?" she says, imposing herself for the first time. "Africans don't object to listening to the radio. A radio isn't a living presence. What you seem to be demanding is not just a voice but a performance: a living actor before you, performing your text. If that is what you demand, then I agree, a recording can't take its place. But the novel was never intended to be the script of a performance. From the beginning the novel has made a virtue of not depending on being performed. You can't have both live performance and cheap, easy distribution. It's not possible. If that is what is demanded of the novel—to be a pocket-sized block of paper that is at the same time alive—then the novel has no future in Africa."

"No future," says Egudu reflectively. "Then what is your answer, Elizabeth?"

"My answer to what? I don't have an answer. I do have an alternative question. Why are there so many African novelists around and yet no African novel worth speaking of? That seems to me the real question. And you gave a clue to the answer yourself in your talk. Exoticism. Exoticism and its seductions."

"Exoticism and its seductions? Tell us what you mean, Elizabeth."

If it were only a matter of Emmanuel she would, at this point, walk out. She is tired of his jeering. But before strangers, before *customers*, they still have a front to maintain, she and he both.

"The English novel," she says, "is written in the first place by English people for English people. The Russian novel is written by Russians for Russians. But the African novel is not written by Africans for Africans. African novelists may write about Africa, about African experience, but they are glancing over their shoulder all the time as they write at the foreigners who will read them. Whether they like it or not, they have assumed the role of interpreter, interpreting Africa to the world. Yet how can you explore a world in all its depth if at the same time you are having to explain it to outsiders? It is like a scientist trying to give his full creative attention to an investigation while at the same time explaining what he is doing to a class of ignorant students. It is too much for one person; it can't be achieved, not at the deepest level. That, it seems to me, is the root of your problem. Having to perform your Africanness at the same time as you write."

"Very good, Elizabeth!" says Egudu. "You really understand; you put it very well!" He reaches out, pats her on the shoulder.

If we were alone, she thinks, I would slap him.

"If, as you say, I understand, then that is only because we in Australia have been through the same trial, and come out at the other end. We finally got out of the habit of writing for strangers in the 1960s, when a proper Australian readership grew to maturity. Not a writership—that already existed. We got out of it when our market, our Australian market, decided that it could afford to support a homegrown literature. That seems to be the lesson. That is what Africa could learn from us."

Emmanuel is silent, but continues to wear his ironic smile.

"I'm interested in the way you talk," says Steve. "You talk as if writing were a business, a matter of markets. I was expecting something different."

"Oh? What?"

"You know: how you get inspiration, and so forth."

Inspiration. Now that he has produced the word he seems embarrassed. There is another awkward silence.

Emmanuel speaks. "Elizabeth and I go way back. We have had lots of disagreements in our time. That doesn't alter things between us—does it, Elizabeth? We are colleagues, fellow writers. We belong to the great, worldwide writing fraternity."

He is challenging her, trying to get a rise out of her before these strangers. But she is too weary to take up the challenge. Not fellow writers, she thinks: fellow entertainers. Why else are they on board this expensive ship, *making themselves available,* as the invitation so candidly put it, to people who bore them and whom they are beginning to bore?

Emmanuel is restless, she can sense that. He has had enough of them; he wants someone new.

Their chanteuse has come to the end of her set. There is a light ripple of applause. She bows, bows a second time, takes up her balalaika. The band strikes up a Cossack dance.

What irritates her most about Emmanuel, what she has the good sense not to bring up in front of Steve and Shirley because it will lead only to unseemliness, is the way he makes every disagreement a matter of personality. As for his beloved oral novel, she finds the concept muddled. She suspects that Emmanuel and his friends in the African novel business know it is muddled too, but will go on touting it as long as it serves their own purposes. "A novel about people who live in an oral culture," she would like to say, "is not an oral novel. Just as a novel about women isn't a women's novel."

In her opinion, all of Emmanuel's talk of an oral novel, a novel that has kept touch with the human voice and hence with the human body, a novel that is not disembodied like the Western novel, but speaks the body and the body's truth, is intended to prop up the old mystique of the African as the last repository of primal human energies. Emmanuel blames his Western publishers and his Western readers for driving him to exoticize Africa; but Emmanuel has a stake in exoticizing himself. Emmanuel, she happens to know, has not written a book of any substance in ten years. When she first met him he could still honourably call himself a writer. Now his living is made on the lecture circuit. His books—if they are even in print any longer—are there as credentials, no more. A fellow entertainer he may be; a fellow writer he is not, not any longer. He is on the circuit for the money, and for other rewards too. Sex, for instance. He is dark and exotic, he is in touch with life's energies; if he is no longer young, at least he wears his years with distinction. What Swedish girl would not be a pushover?

She finishes her drink. "I'm retiring," she says. "Good night Steve, Shirley. See you tomorrow. Good night, Emmanuel."

She wakes up in utter stillness. The clock says four-thirty. The ship's engines have stopped. She glances through the porthole. There is fog outside, but through the fog she can glimpse land no more than a kilometre away. Macquarie Island it must be: she had thought they would not arrive for hours yet.

She dresses and emerges into the corridor. At the same moment the door to cabin A-230 opens and the Russian emerges, the singer. She is wearing the same outfit as last night, the port-wine blouse and wide black trousers; she carries her boots in her hand. In the unkind overhead light she looks nearer to forty than to thirty. They avert their eyes as they pass each other.

A-230 is Egudu's cabin, she knows that.

She makes her way to the upper deck. Already there are a handful of passengers, snugly dressed against the cold, leaning against the railings, peering down.

The sea beneath them is alive with what seem to be fish, large, glossy-skinned black fish that bob and tumble and leap in the swell. She has never seen anything like it.

"Penguins," says the man next to her. "King penguins. They have come to greet us. They don't know what we are."

"Oh," she says. And then: "So innocent? Are they so innocent?"

The man regards her oddly, turns back to his companion.

They will stand off Macquarie until noon, long enough for those passengers who so wish to visit the island. She has put her name down for the visiting party.

The first boat leaves after breakfast. The approach to the landing is difficult, across shelving rock and through thick beds of kelp. In the end she has to be half-helped ashore by one of the sailors, half-carried, as if she were an old woman. He has blue eyes, blond hair. Through his waterproofs she feels his youthful strength. She rides in his arms as safe as a baby. "Thank you!" she says gratefully when he sets her down; but to him it is nothing, just a service he is paid to do, no more personal than the service of a hospital nurse.

She has read about Macquarie Island. In the last century it used to be the centre of the penguin industry. Hundreds of thousands of penguins were clubbed to death here and flung into cast-iron steam boilers to be broken down into useful oil and useless residue. Or not clubbed to death, merely herded with sticks up a gangplank and over the edge into the seething cauldron.

Yet their descendants seem to have learned nothing. Still they swim out to welcome their visitors; still they call out greetings to them as they approach the rookeries ("Ho! Ho!" they call, for all the world like gruff little men). They allow visitors to approach close enough to touch them, to stroke their sleek breasts.

The boats will carry them back again at ten. Until then they are free to explore the island. There is an albatross colony on the hillside; they are welcome to photograph the birds, but are urged not to approach too closely, not to alarm them. It is breeding season.

She wanders away from the rest of the landing party, finding herself eventually on a plateau above the coastline, walking on a vast bed of matted grass.

Suddenly, unexpectedly, there is something before her. For a moment she thinks it is a rock, smooth white mottled with grey. Then she sees it is a bird, bigger than any bird she has seen before. She recognizes the long, dipping beak, the huge sternum. An albatross.

The albatross regards her steadily and, it seems to her, with amusement. Sticking out from beneath it is a smaller version of the same long beak. The fledgling is more hostile. It opens its beak, gives a long silent cry of warning.

So she and the two birds remain, inspecting each other.

Before the fall, she thinks. This is how it was before the fall. I could miss the boat, stay here. God could take care of me.

There is someone behind her. She turns. It is the Russian woman, dressed now in a dark green anorak, with the hood open and her hair tied down with a kerchief.

"An albatross," she remarks to the woman, speaking softly. "That is the English word. I don't know what they call themselves."

The woman nods. The great bird regards them calmly, no more afraid of two than of one.

"Isn't Emmanuel with you?" she says.

"No. On ship."

"You are a friend of his, I know," she presses on. "I am too, or have been. May I ask: what do you see in him?"

It is an odd question, presumptuous, even rude. But it seems to her that on this island, on a visit that will never be repeated, anything can be said.

"What I see?" says the woman.

"Yes. What do you see? What is the source of his charm? What do you like in him?"

The woman shrugs. Her hair is dyed, she can now see. Forty if a day, probably with a household to support back home, one of those Russian establishments with a crippled grandmother and a husband who drinks too much and beats her and a layabout son and a daughter with a shaven head and purple lipstick. A woman who can sing a little but will, one of these days, sooner rather than later, be over the hill. Playing the balalaika to foreigners, singing Russian kitsch, picking up tips.

"He is free. You speak Russian? No?"

She shakes her head.

"German?"

"A little."

"Er ist freigebig. Ein guter Mann."

Freigebig—generous—spoken with the heavy *g*'s of Russian. Is Emmanuel generous? She does not know. Not the first word that would occur to her. Large, perhaps. Large in his gestures.

"Aber kaum zu vertrauen," she remarks to the woman. Years since she last spoke the language. Is that what they spoke together in bed last night: German, the new imperial tongue? *Kaum zu vertrauen,* not to be trusted: she hopes she is getting it right.

The woman shrugs again. *"Die Zeit ist kurz. Man kann nicht alles haben."* There is a pause. The woman speaks again. *"Auch die Stimme. Sie macht daß man"*—she searches for the word— *"man schaudert."*

Schaudern. Shudder. The voice makes one shudder. Between the two of them passes what is perhaps the beginning of a smile. As for the bird, they have been there long enough, the bird is losing interest. Only the fledgling, peering out from beneath its mother, is still wary of them.

The voice. She remembers the year she met Emmanuel Egudu, when she was young, or nearly young, when she slept with him three nights in succession. "The oral poet," she said to him teasingly. "Show me what an oral poet can do." And he opened her out, spread her, put his lips to her ears, opened them, breathed his breath into her, showed her.

Endnotes

[1] Quoted in Phanuel A. Egejuru, *Towards African Literary Independence* (Westport, CT, 1980), pp. 87–88.

[2] Quoted in Eileen Julien, *African Novels and the Question of Orality* (Bloomington, IN, 1992), pp. 12–13.

Kenzaburō Ōe

From the Beginning to the Present, and Facing the End: The Case of One Japanese Writer

I

I WAS AT BERKELEY IN 1983. And during my stay here, I wrote a few short stories. As I reread them now, I am impressed with the accuracy of the details with which I depicted the trees on the campus. I was given an office at the Center for Japanese Studies, then in the old building, and from my window I could see a tall, beautiful tree. It had leaves like those of a camellia, brushlike flowers, and very red berries. Many trees at Berkeley are of Australian origin, and the tree outside my window was also from Australia. Its Japanese name is *Osutoraria futomomo.* Hedges of this tree are commonly seen at Berkeley, but the tree by my window was massive. The common English name for it, I believe, is brush cherry, and its botanical name is *Eugenia myrtifolia*.

I mention this because at the Center for Japanese Studies there was an able and amiable secretary whose name was Eugenie. And I wanted to tell her that her name was the same as the tree's botanical name, but I didn't, because I knew my tongue would be tied the minute she asked me: "Why are you telling me such a thing?" If any among you here are studying classical Japanese literature, I am sure you are familiar with the *choji*-dyed kimono in *The Tale of*

Genji. The dye *choji* happens to come from the *Eugenia aromatica*, a tree that belongs to the same family as the brush cherry.

The hedge around the Women's Faculty Club, where I lived, was also of brush cherry. A young lady came on weekends to clean the guest rooms. She always looked depressed, but one day she said to me, "I used to be a champion, a yo-yo champion, and I was hired to be in a Coca-Cola campaign, and I even went to Japan." I had never in my life seen a more reserved or despondent champion. And I portrayed her briefly, and the tree as well, in the short stories I wrote here at Berkeley.

In my long-standing career as a writer, I have often written and spoken about how I came in contact with literature. I clearly remember that among the first literary works I encountered was a translation of *The Adventures of Huckleberry Finn*. Reading it later, in the original, led me to the world of American short stories. And later still, while reflecting on the authors and stories I had read, I remembered something. The recollection became even clearer as I reread Hemingway in preparation for speaking at a centennial commemoration of his work. And I would like to begin my talk with this now very vivid memory.

II

We start from infancy and go on through childhood and adolescence to arrive at an understanding of the world we live in, but the real-life curriculum that teaches this to us is usually a very confused one. Nevertheless, the fundamental reason I put faith in humankind is because I know that children possess an independent sense of balance, a capacity for integration, or—to put it in yet another way—the power of imagination, with which to ride out the confusion.

Literature gives children the personal support they need to confront confusion. At times, however, it can add dangerous momentum to a child's already confused world, as was the case with me. The ponderous reality of "death" was brought home to me, in *The*

Adventures of Huckleberry Finn, by the dead man whom Huck and Jim saw in the dark of the frame house that came floating by the island where they lived. It was Jim's power of expression that caused me to discover a sense of reality even more deeply hued than reality. These were his words:

> "De man ain't asleep—he's dead. You hold still—I'll go en see."
>
> He went and bent down and looked, and says:
>
> "It's a dead man. Yes, indeedy; naked, too. He's ben shot in de back. I reck'n he's ben dead two er three days. Come in, Huck, but doan' look at his face—it's too gashly."[1]

My grandmother and father passed away the year I read this book in translation. Yet the man who just lay motionless in the dark, whose face, together with Huck, I did not see, held more reality for me than my two dead kin. And I struggled to restore order to the world that had fallen into confusion, while repeatedly sorting the two "deaths" in my family in with this man's "death."

This was part of my experience as a boy in a small archipelago on the other side of the Pacific during the Second World War. After Japan's defeat, the Occupation Forces opened American Culture Centers in various cities and towns. And at one such center, the open-shelf library, which I had never used before, became a truly memorable place. There I was to encounter another "death." For the young man who had read *The Adventures of Huckleberry Finn* in the original, guided by what I don't know, now read Hemingway's *In Our Time*. I knew nothing then of the deep linguistic relationship between the writers of English. Yet that young man sensed, in the death portrayed in one of the stories of *In Our Time*—namely the death witnessed by Nick—a distinct similarity to the death experienced by Huck. And I felt the similarity went beyond the ways the boys encountered death on their respective dark waters, Huck paddling his canoe, Nick rowing his boat. These two deaths—the one Huck did not actually see and the one Nick saw—were one and the same to me. Everyone assembled here today probably remembers the very original style used to portray what Nick saw, but please allow me to read those lines.

> [The doctor] pulled back the blanket from the Indian's head. His hand came away wet. He mounted on the edge of the lower bunk with the lamp in one hand and looked in. The Indian lay with his face toward the wall. His throat had been cut from ear to ear. The blood had flowed down into a pool where his body sagged the bunk. His head rested on his left arm. The open razor lay edge up in the blankets.[2]

Ten years later, I was a young writer myself who believed that he, in his own way, had already come to an understanding of the world, however confused it was, that he understood the world to be what it was—with all its confusions intact. Then came the news of Hemingway's death. And the deep, basic fear and loathing I had felt as a young boy toward everything in this world—all came back to me with a vengeance and permeated my whole being. I was struck down by the thought that if someone like Hemingway had taken his own life at the threshold of old age, despite his dear and deep awareness of "death" since his youth, then for me, too, there would be no way to escape.

III

As the end of the millennium draws near, newspapers and magazines all over the world are engaged in a project to ask writers to submit a short story they would like passed on to the next era, and I too received such a request. While feeling that I was not capable of carrying out so great a feat—and I even went so far as to write a letter of apology to the editor—I agreed to do my share, and for a while I entertained, and suffered through, a spell of fantasizing.

I thought of writing a narrative about a man who very intensely experiences how people live, then die, in the nuclear age. But of course I could not write this in the form of a short story. So I fantasized about a short story in which a man who knows he has to write, and knows well what he must write, before he dies, merely reminisces about the many stories he will never be able to write. The title was to be "The Snows of a Nuclear Highland." And what came to mind as I contemplated the techniques of a short story expressing the model case of a human being of this millennium were the short stories of Hemingway, which undoubtedly rank among this century's most prestigious literary works.

Rereading Hemingway in this light, I noticed anew, in *The Snows of Kilimanjaro*, a latent power that invites a fundamental reflection as we, at this century's end, contemplate the nature of the novel. The question itself is a simple one, but to answer it, a novelist has to keep working throughout his or her life. *The Snows of Kilimanjaro* puts the question in a straightforward manner.

Is a novelist someone who writes about what he or she knows? Or not? I feel that novelists of the latter half of the twentieth century, at least, have believed, or expended a lot of energy believing or trying to believe, that a novelist is someone who, aided by the power of words and structures of imagination, writes about something he or she does not personally know. However, the character Hemingway describes as lying in front of a tent set up on a highland in Africa as he watches his feet rot away reiterates that this isn't so.

Even after he falls victim to an incurable disease the man insists that, as long as he has the strength to do so, he wishes to observe the flight of the large birds that are closing in on a dying man. Even when his condition worsens, the following thoughts enter his mind:

> Now he would never write the things that he had saved to write until he knew enough to write them well. Well, he would not have to fail at trying to write them either. Maybe you could never write them, and that was why you put them off and delayed the starting. Well, he would never know, now.[3]
>
> He had never written any of that because, at first, he never

wanted to hurt any one and then it seemed as though there was enough to write without it. But he had always thought that he would write it finally. There was so much to write. He had seen the world change; not just the events; although he had seen many of them and had watched the people, but he had seen the subtler change and he could remember how the people were at different times. He had been in it and he had watched it and it was his duty to write of it; but now he never would. (p. 17)

The man goes on to say that he knows about many things so well that he could write about each of them, but that he has not written about them and he will not do so in the future. As the overtones of the man's words remind us, in Hemingway's many novels and short stories a voice has been raised of a character who has the confidence to say that he knew something well enough to write about it. So strong is the man's conviction that we have to recognize that it is impossible to write about something we do not know well, that the purpose of life is to know something to the extent that we can write about it. The writer of all these novels believed this.

Moreover, as the hero of *The Snows of Kilimanjaro* draws infinitesimally closer to death, not only does he realize that he does not know some things well enough to be to be able to write about them, but for the first time he comes to know something he knew absolutely nothing about. And dreaming of approaching this something he brings to an end a life in which he truly knew many things. As Hemingway put it:

[A]head, all he could see, as wide as all the world, great, high, and unbelievably white in the sun, was the square top of Kilimanjaro. And then he knew that there was where he was going. (p. 27)

The youth who knew very well how to write about "death," as evidenced in the short story *In Our Time*, wrote for the next ten years only about what he knew well. He lived those very years in order to learn; so that he could write about what he learned—which was the principle he lived by—and then he wrote *The Snows of Kilimanjaro*. This process reveals the complexity of the answer to the simple question I asked before: Is a novelist someone who writes about what he or she knows? Or someone who, using the power of words and structures of imagination, tries to write not only about something that the writer does not personally know but also about something that even humankind—despite the myriad things it has come to know over the past two thousand years—still does not know?

IV

This simple question must have remained with the author of *The Old Man and the Sea* fifteen years later when he had become one of the most accomplished writers of the century. Needless to say, *The Old Man and the Sea* is a work about the dangers an old Cuban fisherman faces at sea and how he overcomes them. It is a work written by a writer who knows to the gills what a fisherman experiences, and who writes only about what he knows.

Diverse and thorough studies have been conducted this century to evaluate a writer's maturity by examining how his or her works express "time." *The Old Man and the Sea*, which deserves a special place for its achievements, easily meets the criteria and does so in a very orthodox manner. It is the labor of a writer who knows precisely what "time" means as a concrete human experience, and has confidence that he knows how best to express this.

The old fisherman, about whom the writer knows everything, does exactly what the writer knows he will do. The writer even creates a scene where he makes the old man stand naked, alone, before something humankind can never quite know about.

I can quote from various places in the story to illustrate my point, but here I want to read the scene where the old man enters into his second night in his struggle with the big fish, which is still pulling him and his boat with unmitigated force. As Hemingway writes:

> It was dark now as it becomes dark quickly after the sun sets in September. He lay against the worn wood of the bow and rested all that he could. The first stars were out. He did not know the name of Rigel but he saw it and knew soon they would all be out and he would have all his distant friends.
>
> "The fish is my friend, too," he said aloud. "I have never seen or heard of such a fish. But I must kill him. I am glad we do not have to try to kill the stars."
>
> Imagine if each day a man must try to kill the moon, he thought. The moon runs away. But imagine if a man each day should have to try to kill the sun? We were born lucky, he thought.[4]

What we humans have done on our planet, from the first millennium through the second, that is, from the time our spirits were most philosophical and when our souls were most poetic, raising our eyes to the expanse of the universe—and what the old man does on his boat while drifting through the dark ocean—are hardly any different. Almost all writers today repeatedly go through the experience of lying naked at the bottom of cosmic space and gazing at the stars. Though not as happily as the fisherman...

The Old Man and the Sea may direct its readers toward something not very cheerful, but I have always found it to be a source of encouragement—from the time of my youth until now, when I am on the threshold of my twilight years. What encourages me every time I read this novel is the image of the young boy whom the old man repeatedly thinks of and addresses: "I wish the boy was here....," "I wish I had the boy....," "I wish the boy were here...."

Among the various techniques used to create this perfect novel, I feel that this repetition occasions the most danger.

I have spent more than two-thirds of my career writing about my mentally handicapped son. I have written about the things I know very well about him and about what I will never know: the unfathomable dark that lies and spreads in him like the expansive universe. And as I reflect upon it, I realize that those repeated callings-out which Hemingway penned have been echoing in my mind all along like a *basso ostinato.*

V

Will literature, specifically the novel, hold its ground for the next hundred years until writers of the future—in other words, those born this year—have their centennial commemorated? At times I think it will, with a feeling that is not altogether optimistic. And at times I think it won't, with a feeling that is not overly pessimistic. Frankly, though, while vacillating between these polar premonitions, I'm imagining only the first quarter of the next hundred years. Humankind has acquired much knowledge during this century. We can perhaps say that we have learned almost all there is to know about science, ideologies, international relations, the environment, and countless other fields. During the next hundred years, people will write about each and every one of these subjects. But will pondering such things bring joy to our hearts?

Also, during the next hundred years, human beings will write novels applying the power of words and structures of imagination to give expression to things we in fact do not know. Again, however, contemplating these things is not likely to offer us much encouragement.

Yet it would be a discourtesy to the people who will live the next century if we, who have lived this one, continue in our state of having lost courage. We must strive to revive our vitality by taking cues from a concrete person who has lived through the same period we have.

I am thinking of one of the finest models of a novelist in this century. I am thinking of a writer who wrote *In Our Time* in his youth, *The Snows of Kilimanjaro* in the prime of his life, and *The Old Man and the Sea* at the too early start of his later years. This model of a novelist remains to us a constant source of encouragement, even when we think of his death as of his own choosing—if not because of it.

For certain, the twenty-first century will continue to remember Ernest Hemingway. "Please remember, this is how I lived." These are words left by the best writer of the century in my country.

VI

The writer I just cited as Japan's best twentieth-century writer, of modern and contemporary literature, is Natsume Sōseki. I recently learned that Kobo Abe once said to a close friend that, although he believed Sōseki to be a great writer, he thought he was born a little too early. I'm very intrigued by the thought of what Abe and Sōseki would have talked about as contemporary writers had Sōseki been born later. It is particularly interesting for me because I knew Abe to be a person who rarely had anything nice to say about anybody.

I also think about Yukio Mishima, and imagine that he would have objected strongly to naming Sōseki as the greatest writer of the twentieth century. Stylewise, Mishima is about the farthest any twentieth-century Japanese writer can get from Hemingway. Not once in his life did he set foot on a battlefield, nor did he ever hunt in Africa or fish in Cuba. Nevertheless, I recall him being keenly conscious of Hemingway vis-à-vis his constant awareness of himself as a nation's representative writer of the age.

Mishima was the first among Japan's literati to want to behave "macho" in both his actual life and literature. He took to bodybuilding, and had many pictures of his pumped-up body taken and circulated. Later he committed a self-staged, self-produced suicide aimed at shaking Japanese society, creating waves that would reach to foreign shores.

Among the various reactions to Hemingway's suicide, which he committed in a secluded place and in a manner that suggested an accident, I was most impressed with what, I believe, John Updike said: "I feel that all Americans have been insulted."

I do not think that Mishima intended to insult all his compatriots, such as myself, and neither do I believe that this was the inadvertent result of his act. Mishima was not the writer of all Japanese people in the way that Hemingway was the writer of all Americans. Yet I think that Mishima carefully chose the place and method of his suicide with the desire to accomplish an act that would cause Japanese people to feel shock on a national scale. *That* he actually succeeded in doing. Staking his death on the outcome, Mishima called out to members of the Self-Defense Forces to rise up in a coup d'état, but the soldiers who heard the final speech of his life laughed and jeered at him. Mishima even scolded them and repeatedly told them to listen quietly, but to no avail. This, to me, was the most pitiful part of his death performance.

I do not believe that Mishima was seriously calling for a coup d'état. He was able to qualify for the bureaucracy, which supposedly attracts the brainiest and most superior people in Japan. And so if he had been serious, he would not have made such a hollow, ill-prepared call for a coup d'etat. So in my view, what Mishima did was stage a very theatrical suicide, in line with his aesthetic. Attaching ultranationalistic meanings to his performance is secondary.

I have a hunch that Mishima, who probably died feeling that his final performance was a success, harbored one feeling he must have kept to himself, a feeling of envy he could never overcome no matter how hard he tried. And I think I can support this conjecture. I am quite sure Mishima knew that he was not expressing an era of Japan and the Japanese people in the way that another suicide did.

Mishima had shown deep interest in the suicide note of a Self-Defense Forces member who killed himself two years before his own death. The man's name was Kokichi Tsuburaya, and he first appeared before the Japanese people at the Tokyo Olympics in 1964. It was hardly a dramatic debut when compared to that of the Ethiopian marathoner Abebe Bikila, who, in the 1960 Olympics in Rome, ran barefoot and won the race with a new world record.

Tsuburaya trailed Abebe into the very last stretch but couldn't catch up with him, and just before the finish line he was passed by a British runner and finished third. Four years later, Private Third Class Kokichi Tsuburaya, age 27, of the Ground Self-Defense Force, killed himself by slashing his right carotid artery with a razor blade in the dormitory of the Physical Education Academy of the Self-Defense Forces in Nerima.

Tsuburaya's suicide note makes mention of Japanese foods and drinks that you may not be familiar with, but I would like to read it in its entirety. Where he addresses his brothers' wives, the translation is "sister." "Kun" and "chan" are suffixes denoting endearment, "kun" for boys, "chan" for girls. This is his note:

> My dear Father, my dear Mother: I thank you for the three-day-pickled yam. It was delicious. Thank you for the dried persimmons. And the rice cakes. They were delicious, too. My dear Brother Toshio, and my dear Sister: I thank you for the sushi. It was delicious. My dear Brother Katsumi, and my dear Sister: The wine and apples were delicious. I thank you. My dear Brother Iwao, and my dear Sister: I thank you. The basil-flavored rice, and the Nanban pickles were delicious. My dear Brother Kikuzo, and my dear Sister: The grape juice and Yomeishu were delicious. I thank you. And thank you, my dear Sister, for the laundry you always did for me. My dear Brother Kozo and my dear Sister: I thank you for the rides you gave me in your car, to and fro. The mongo-cuttlefish was delicious. I thank you. My dear Brother Masao, and my dear Sister: I am very sorry for all the worries I caused you. Yukio-kun, Hideo-kun, Mikio-kun, Toshiko-chan, Hideko-chan, Ryosuke-kun, Takahisa-kun, Miyoko-chan, Yukie-chan, Mitsue-chan, Akira-kun, Yoshiyuki-kun, Keiko-chan, Koei-kun, Yu-chan, Kii-chan, Shoji-kun: May you grow up to be fine people. My dear Father and my dear Mother, Kokichi is too tired to run anymore. I beg you to forgive me. Your hearts must never have rested worrying and caring for me. My dear Father and Mother, Kokichi would have liked to live by your side.

We know from this note that Kokichi Tsuburaya was from a big family. The many names he mentions probably do not evoke any particular feeling in a non-Japanese, but to a person like myself—especially to one who belongs to an older generation of Japanese—these names reveal a naming ideology of a family in which authority centers around the paternal head-of-household. This family-ism extends to the relatives. There is probably no large family in Japan today where children are named so thoroughly in line with traditional ethical sentiments. Tsuburaya's suicide note immediately shows the changes in the "feelings" of the families of Japanese these past thirty years.

The many foods and drinks he refers to also tell of the times. Twenty years had passed since Japan's defeat, and it was not a society of food shortages. But neither was it the age of satiation and Epicurean feasting that began ten years later. The year Tsuburaya died was the year that Nikkeiren, the Japan Federation of Employers' Association, tried to counter the spring offensives—the annual demand by labor unions for wage hikes and improved working conditions—by arguing that the sharp increase in prawn imports was evidence of a sufficient rise in the standard of living. More consumers were eating imported frozen prawns. Business administrators keep an eye on such trends. And I think that honestly expresses the eating habits of Japanese people at this time.

Early in the year 1968, President Johnson sent a special envoy to Japan to request Japan's cooperation in protecting the dollar. Japanese people knew that the United States was being driven into a corner by the Vietnam War. We read in the papers about the Tet Offensive, and about Saigon coming under fierce attack by the National Liberation Front. But ordinary citizens never dreamed that the Japanese economy would soon amass enough strength to dominate the world. And probably no one imagined that later Japan's economy would fall into a deep abyss.

Domestically, 1968 saw the rage of student rebellions, among them the most noted were the struggles at Tokyo University and

Nihon University. Outside of Japan, there was the May Revolution in Paris, and the invasion of Soviet troops into Prague. In retrospect, we clearly see that the world was full of premonitions of great change.

Against this backdrop, a long-distance runner of the Self-Defense Forces—itself a typical phenomenon of the state of postwar Japan's twisted polysemous society—turned his back on the currents of such a society, prepared to die alone, and wrote this suicide note. In the note, the young man refers to specific foods and drinks, he encourages his nephews and nieces to grow up to be fine people, he is overwhelmed by the thought of his parents' loving concern for him, and he writes that he knows their hearts must never have rested in their worry and care for him. He apologizes to them because, having kept running even after the Olympics with the aim of shouldering national prestige, he became totally exhausted and could no longer run. He closed his note with the words: "My dear Father and Mother, Kokichi would have liked to live by your side."

With the passing of a quarter of a century, the style in which the note was written, its content, and the human relationships and social conditions that gave birth to it are no more. In this regard, Tsuburaya's suicide note is clearly a monumental expression of the times.

A change in international relations would not itself affect the style of the national language. However, the influx of a world subculture does change the language of young Japanese. And this in turn affects the language of the older generations. Kokichi Tsuburaya, twenty-seven years old in 1968, may be the last to write in the style of his note. For his breed has all but disappeared from the Japanese language world.

One can see, in the archives of the newspaper companies, a picture of this long-distance runner, with the competitor from Great Britain closing in on him before a standing-room-only capacity crowd at the Olympic Stadium in Tokyo. He is a handsome young man with clear-cut Japanese features. His running form, too, is beautiful, but his face shows his naked anxiety as he continues to run. Using only the elements of this photograph and Tsuburaya's suicide note, I believe that one could write a short story that would represent Japan and its people of the 1960s.

Two years after Tsuburaya took his own life, Yukio Mishima committed suicide in a truly dramatic performance at another Self-Defense Forces facility, but he was unable to make his own death an expression of a serious period of history. I imagine that had Mishima, as he died, recalled Tsuburaya's suicide, he would have envied him as an expression of an age and its people.

I have elsewhere commented on Mishima's death, but mainly in a political light. But while preparing to talk before a non-Japanese audience on how I began as a writer, how I have lived, and where I am now headed, I discovered something new about his death. Namely, the transition in the circumstances of Japanese literature since his death to the present can only be described as a decline—and his death fully prophesized this.

Mishima died as a political person in a manner suggesting a display of fireworks over the Japanese archipelago. Just prior to his death, however, he completed an epic novel, the longest he had ever written. He had also carefully prepared for the novel to be translated for an international readership. And so some people say that literature was Mishima's greatest concern until the very end of his life.

But this shows only how painfully conscious he was of the glory of his literature. "Regarding my life and literature, I would display its end in this manner," he said with his suicide. "And," he would have continued, "in Japan, at least, there is no great literature. My death announces this fact." Mishima died carrying out this pronouncement to Japan's readers of literature.

I have lived as a writer of Japanese for thirty years after Mishima's death. And I must confess that my literary career has been painful. The prophecy Mishima staked with his death has come true in terms of a resurgence and enlargement of nationalism. And I very acutely feel that he was also on the mark about the decline of literature. This is what I think, having lived these past thirty years as an intellectual in Japan and a writer of Japanese.

VII

Now I would like to talk about the novel I have just written, and what I am doing to prepare for my final days in a milieu where literature continues to decline. I was given an opportunity to give another lecture here at Berkeley, and I talked about Masao Maruyama, a scholar of the history of political thought, well known not only in Japan but also in the United States, Great Britain, and France. The lecture was also a criticism of the rising tide of neonationalism in today's Japan and the trend to deny democracy—which, in Japan, is sometimes exceptionalized by calling it "postwar democracy." It is criticized as such, albeit there is no doubt that it is the first actualization of democracy in Japan.

Certainly, momentum is gathering to embrace a neonationalism and to disclaim postwar democracy, but then what about literature and the circumstances surrounding it? Some people may say I am only venting my personal, subjective opinion when I speak of the decline of Japanese literature.

Objectively speaking, however, it is a fact that the readership of *junbungaku* or "pure literature"—which largely overlaps with what in the United States is called "serious fiction"—is dwindling. I am certain there is no publisher of a literary magazine—the conventional medium for publishing *junbungaku*—that is not operating in the red. Sales of works once published in such literary magazines, and later as a book, are at an all-time low.

But should we broaden the criteria for deciding what is and isn't *junbungaku*? That is to say, if we look at all that is produced in Japanese, there are in fact, every year, works that win readerships larger than would have been imaginable in the past. The problem is whether to view this phenomenon itself as a decline in literature.

I am a writer who cannot expect a large readership, but allow me now to talk about the novel that I have just completed. You will then understand how one Japanese writer, who feels the decline of literature, is striving, though personally, to break through that predicament.

Before coming to Berkeley, I passed to the printers a novel entitled *Chūgaeri* or *Somersault*. It is the longest novel I have ever written. And I would like to add that I consider it the most important work of my career.

The four years I portray in this novel fall in the period of the crisis-ridden recession, following the "bubble economy" that ended the high growth of Japan's economy. The story begins with the "turning" of the leader of a new religious organization, which, during this period, had many young Japanese believers. Even when the organization was at the height of the group's prosperity, its religious leader's thinking was criticized as being syncretic. His thinking is both Buddhistic and Christian, which makes it unacceptable to any orthodox Christian church, Catholic or Protestant. Moreover, it is founded on a religious tenet that would not have taken root without the influence of Christianity, which has had its place in the modernization of Japan over the past hundred years. At the same time, the religion is connected with local Japanese mystical thinking. And although it also incorporates Buddhistic and Shintoistic elements, it has no place in either of these religions.

It is also very clear that the organization's doctrine on the end of time and of the world has much in common with other fundamentalist sects. Its young members desire something that stresses the uniqueness of their faith and movement, and this desire clearly surfaces as the movement of their faith gradually becomes something more society-oriented and politically radical.

The novel is a narrative of what happens after the group's religious activities experience great conflict, from the aspect of its beliefs, and the aspect of its efforts to reach out to society. Ten years before the novel begins, the group, for a time, disbands. The disbanding was dramatically carried out amidst much television and other media hoopla. The founder and his sympathizers declared then, on television, that all of what they had created—their doctrine and all their religious activities—had been an elaborate joke—that their aim was to create a mammoth structure of comedy and to delight in its slapstick delirium.

The radical members, at this time, had deployed themselves throughout the country and had been preparing for action. Their agenda was to perpetrate terrorism on political leaders, high-ranking bureaucrats, and leading financiers and to attack nuclear power plants. At this point, the leaders of the organization are pressed with the need to demonstrate that the organization had no basis for action.

With assistance from the police and the National Public Safety Agency, the leaders succeed in aborting the acts of terrorism. The organization is disbanded and the leaders, who have "turned," disappear from the surface of society. The turning of the leaders is remembered by society as a "somersault."

The novel begins when, ten years later, the leaders who had gone into hiding begin new activities. Their goal is to establish an entirely new church. Obviously, things do not proceed as planned, since the believers they abandoned through their "somersault" have already formed various groups on their own, and have continued to practice their faith. The radicals have embraced stronger political beliefs, while a group of female believers have strengthened their faith in the mystical. The leaders need to respond to their demands. But how, having once entirely abandoned their doctrine and group, will the leaders establish a new church with their former believers? This is the problem that forms the framework of the novel.

The idea of a messiah-like leader of a religious group suddenly making a complete turnabout came to me as I read, over many years, Gershom Scholem's *Sabbatai Sevi: The Mystical Messiah*. Isn't it strange that a false messiah, who converted from Judaism to Islam in seventeenth-century Turkey, captured the fancy of a Japanese novelist?

I happened to find a copy of Scholem's voluminous book at Berkeley's student bookstore. Since then a translation of the original work has appeared in the Bollingen series, and ten years have passed. And I have been reading it over and over ever since. At first, Nathan of Gaza, Sabbatai Sevi's sympathizer, fascinated me. Later my attention turned to Rabbi Sasportas, his unrelenting disapprover.

However, what I found most intriguing were the believers in Sevi after his apostasy—namely, those who remained at various places in Europe, Asia Minor, and Africa with faith in their turnabout leader. If a messiah figure were to appear in Japan today, and one day he abandoned his faith, what would be the fate of his believers? A novel formed in my mind as I contemplated this question, in connection with the Aum Shinrikyo incident.

VIII

Time keeps me from talking further about the novel. However, I want to add that, toward the end, the leader, who has rebuilt his church after once abandoning his faith—although he has lost, to the terrorism of former radicals, a man who for him plays the role of the prophet Nathan of Gaza—upon coming across the words "new man" in the New Testament, in Letters to the Ephesians, adopts this concept and makes it the center of his activities.

I belong to the "children's generation" of the intellectuals who, after defeat in the Pacific War, hoped and struggled to create a new culture of Japanese people and thereby resuscitate Japan. I have hoped to carry on their legacy, in terms of both the system of postwar democracy that they conceived, and the postwar literature with which they reformed the style and themes of Japanese literature.

And now I have reached the age of the old fisherman who fought a big fish on the dark sea of Cuba. I have told you of how the old man's calling out to the little boy has attracted me. The expectations I have of the "new man" I wrote about in my novel, which may be my last, stem from the same wish as that of the old man. It is my personal feeling that, for Japanese society and literature—with its 130 years of experience after the Meiji Restoration, and 50 years of postwar experience—to resist the resurrection of its negative inheritance and preserve its positive legacies, however few, we have but to place our hopes on the new generation. What I am now thinking is not just due to a personal feeling. Rather it comes from a more general awareness of crisis.

Endnotes

1 Mark Twain, *The Adventures of Huckleberry Finn* (San Francisco, 2009), p. 60.

2 Ernest Hemingway, "Indian Camp," in *In Our Time: Stories by Ernest Hemingway* (New York, 1925), p. 20.

3 Ernest Hemingway, "The Snows of Kilimanjaro," in *The Snows of Kilimanjaro and Other Stories* (New York, 1995), p. 5.

4 Ernest Hemingway, *The Old Man and the Sea* (New York, 1996), p. 59.

Anthony Grafton

Traditions of Conversion: Descartes and His Demon

Conversion and Vocation

LOOKING BACK IN SATISFACTION from the end of a long and productive life, Athanasius Kircher could identify many points at which providence had reached down to shape the path he followed. In his adventurous boyhood, God had saved him from drowning as he swam too near a millrace; later on, a divine hand protected him from racing horses, armed brigands, and Protestant soldiers bent on lynching him. In his more studious youth, God had given him the reputation of a great mathematician. One night in 1631, Kircher lay peacefully snoring in his order's college at Würzburg. He slept the sleep of the just, not only because he had found his special aptitude, but even more because the Holy Roman Empire had reached an uneasy state of truce. The emperor had conquered his Protestant enemies; no one, the Jesuit later recalled, could even imagine that heresy would revive. Suddenly a bright light filled the room. Waking, he leapt out of bed and ran to the window. He saw the open square before the college full of armed men and horses. Running from room to room, he found that everyone else was still deeply asleep and decided that he must have been dreaming. So he hurried to the window again. There he saw the same terrifying vision. But when he finally woke someone to serve as a witness, it had vanished. In the next few days, Kircher became prey to fear and depression. He ran about, as he later recalled, "like a fanatic," predicting disaster. The others made fun of him—until the Swedes invaded. Suddenly, the prophet was treated with honor in his own country.[1]

Kircher usually appears as a figure in more placid cultural landscapes. He was one of the most erudite men in Europe's great age of polymaths. His skills at mathematics and natural philosophy won him a European reputation—as well as at least one accusation of practicing magic. His all-embracing historical and philological interests expressed themselves in works of textual exegesis as unbelievably long and learned as they were varied in subject matter, works which shed light on everything from the route followed by Noah's ark during and after the Flood to the achievements of the Nestorian church in ancient China. Kircher discovered the historical relation between the ancient Egyptian language and Coptic, collected giants' bones, deciphered hieroglyphs, explored volcanoes, and experimented with magnets. As a scholar he adopted one of the characteristic styles of his erudite and cosmopolitan age: that of the polymathic dinosaurs who made the world into their own Pedantic Park. They wrote more than any of us now has time to read, and read more than we can now imagine. The hot pursuit of learning was their passion, one that sometimes induced them to lower the political and confessional boundaries that normally separated them from their enemies—as Kircher did when he invited Protestant scholars like John Evelyn to inspect the ancient inscriptions and shin-bones of giants stored in his celebrated museum in the Collegio Romano. To the modern onlooker, Kircher's career seems a splendid case in point of that thirst for knowledge in all its forms which led some of the literati of his day to take such a passionate interest in schemes for creating universal languages, combinatoric systems, and universal libraries.[2]

In Kircher's view, however, the diversity of his pursuits was only apparent: in fact, his life had been propelled by God along a clear trajectory toward a single goal. Not only had divine providence reached down and inspired him with prophetic knowledge; it had also given him a scholarly vocation. In 1628, during his scholasticate at Mainz, Kircher was sent to the library of the Jesuit house to look for a book. He later recalled:

> While I went through the books one by one, chance or providence led me to hit upon a book, in which all the Roman obelisks that Pope Sixtus V had set up in the city were elegantly represented with their hieroglyphical figures. Immediately fascinated, I tried to work out what sort of figures those were, for I thought that the sculptor had put them there arbitrarily. But the text informed me that those figures were monuments of ancient Egyptian wisdom, inscribed since time immemorial on these surviving obelisks at Rome, and that no one had given an explanation of them, since the knowledge of them had been lost. I was possessed by longing, as a hidden instinct drove me to see if I could apply myself to knowledge of this sort. And from that time to this, I have never abandoned my intention of arriving at them. For I thought in the following way: the characters survive, the genuine Egyptian ones. Therefore their meanings must also be hidden somewhere even now, scattered in the innumeral works of the ancient authors. If they are not to be found in the Latin and Greek writers, perhaps they are in the exotic books of the Oriental writers. From that time to this, I began to examine all the texts of those authors, in the hope that I could restore the whole body of the Egyptian religion, by collecting the fragments of their learning that were scattered everywhere.[3]

Like Gershom Scholem in the years around 1920, so Kircher in the years around 1620 found himself committed, to his own surprise, to a scholarly work of redemption: he would spend his life collecting and repairing the broken fragments of a lost tradition.[4] Like Scholem, Kircher succeeded marvelously at this task. In his later years in Rome, he became the reigning expert on hieroglyphs anywhere in the world, not only the author of a series of weighty books on the subject but also the scholarly adviser on those most dizzyingly scenographic of seventeenth-century urban projects, Bernini's sculptural ensembles for the Piazza Navona and Santa Maria sopra Minerva. Kircher composed Latin inscriptions for these great architectural and sculptural sites. In them he made clear that the Egyptians had cultivated an essentially monotheistic theology and a profound natural philosophy, from both of which Christians could still learn much.[5]

When Kircher made this case, he implicitly called central beliefs and ritual practices of his own church into question. Though obelisks and hieroglyphs had always formed a prominent feature of Rome's cyclopean landscape, the popes who first began to move and re-erect these Egyptian monuments saw them as frightening remnants of a deeply pagan order. Sixtus V, who had the Vatican Obelisk transported to the position it now occupies in front of the Basilica of Saint Peter's, also had it ceremonially exorcised by a priest. He aspersed it with holy water and drove out the evil spirits that inhabited it with a variant of the usual formal: *"Exorcizo te, creatura lapidis."* Sixtus set a cross on its summit to indicate that Christ had vanquished the Egyptian demons that had once inhabited its shaft.[6]

Sixtus did the same to the four other obelisks that he raised in strategic places like the Lateran, where they served as focal points, visible from a long distance, for the processional life of the holy city. Before these products of Egyptian natural magic could become the dramatic punctuation marks that transformed the experience of reading Roman and Christian public space, they had to be formally converted, like recalcitrant living creatures, to their new religion.[7] Kircher, by contrast, treated the obelisks and their inscriptions as remnants of a pagan wisdom that had much in common with Christianity. He held, and showed, that they did not need to be transformed in order to serve as central parts of the Roman architectural and ceremonial order in a Christian city.

Kircher, in other words, argued that the obelisks and the inscriptions they bore, which explicated the secrets of God and nature, did not represent the alien, impure forms of wisdom which biblical metaphors about the Egyptians called to mind. Rather, they belonged to the same tradition of divinely revealed wisdom as the Hebrew and Christian scriptures: indeed, they formed its oldest, and perhaps its most profound, part. Kircher's enterprise adumbrates Gershom Scholem's effort to reconfigure the Jewish tradition, by emphasizing the central place of magical beliefs and practices which previous scholars had rejected as evil and irrational.

Yet the early modern German Jesuit naturally differed in fundamental ways from the modern German Jew. In retrospect, as Kircher retraced his story, he saw his dedication to the obelisks as the result of a providential intervention in his life, one as direct and clear as the one that inspired his prophecy of invasion. What seemed at the time perhaps a chance occurrence—his discovery of a book about obelisks—his later experiences showed to be the result of a divine plan. When Kircher examined Roman obelisks that were lying down, with one face concealed, he could guess exactly what figures would be found on the side not visible to him. When he studied the broken obelisk later set up in the Piazza Navona, he found himself able to fill in its gaps, supplying by conjecture figures carved on fragments of it that had passed into the hands of private collectors, when those greedy antiquaries would not show him their treasures. Again and again "the light of divine grace"—as well as Kircher's "skill, acquired over a space of many years"—saved him from the machinations of his enemies.[8] Kircher, in other words, literally divined both the form and sense of these inscriptions before he saw them. And he could do so because God guided him. Like Augustine, he knew that any particular encounter with a text could be meaningless. But his own encounter with Herwart von Hohenburg's *Thesaurus hieroglyphicorum*, like Augustine's reading of the life of Antony in the garden, had been charged with meaning. For Scholem, the task of restoring unity to the broken fragments of a tradition fell not to a divinely anointed prophet, but to someone without traditional faith—a modern scholar, living in the modern world, who could no longer cherish the beliefs that had once animated those whose texts he studied. Kircher, by contrast, did not represent himself as simply adopting a scholarly vocation, but as being converted to it, by direct divine intervention. The choice of an intellectual career thus became endowed with the same high drama, moral weight, and potential risks as Augustine's conversion to the true religion. As Augustine had his Donatist critics, who questioned what they saw as his easy acceptance of the coexistence of good and bad Christians in the church, so Kircher had his philological ones, who questioned his easy assimilation of all fragments of ancient tradition to one great, more or less Christian whole. And like Augustine, Kircher defended himself volubly and ably.

Kircher's account, like other spiritual autobiographies, imposed a retrospective order on events that he had experienced very differently at the time of their occurrence. It also included a number of exaggerations and a few whopping lies. Kircher, who represented himself as a kind of super-archaeologist, able to imagine in detail the stones that he could not see, in fact rarely bothered to inspect the obelisks in his own city of Rome, but drew his illustrations of them from a book published in Germany, errors and all. What is clear, however, is that Augustine's narrative of conversion—a narrative of a radical shift in allegiance and understanding of the world—gave Kircher the template for his account of his own archaeologist's process. Conversion formed one of his most vital intellectual and stylistic resources. It inspired him, moreover, to develop and propagate, in books and sculptures, theories at variance with the orthodoxy he, as a Jesuit, was pledged to defend and make others believe in, as well as to record his experiences in order to edify the young. A Jesuit's autobiography, his tale of conversion, surprisingly became the story of a voyage out—to something like the foundation of a new religion.

Autobiography and Its Discontents: Genre Trouble

> *1 January 1404.* I know that in this wretched life our sins expose us to many tribulations of soul and passions of the body, that without God's grace and mercy which strengthens our weakness, enlightens our mind and supports our will, we would perish daily. I also see that since my birth forty years ago, I have given little heed to God's commandments. Distrusting my own power to reform, but hoping to advance by degrees along the path of virtue, I resolve from this day forward to refrain from going to the shop or conducting business on solemn Church holidays, or from permitting others to work for me or seek temporal gain on such days. Whenever I make exceptions in cases of extreme necessity, I promise, on the following day, to distribute alms of one gold florin to God's poor. I have written this down so I may remember my promise and be ashamed if I should chance to break it.
>
> Also, in memory of the passion of Our Lord Jesus Christ who freed and saved us by His merits, that He may, by His grace and mercy, preserve us from guilty passions, I resolve from this very day and in perpetuity to keep Friday as a day of total chastity—with Friday I include the following night—when I must abstain from the enjoyment of all carnal pleasures. God give me grace to keep my promise, yet if I should break it through forgetfulness, I engage to give twenty *soldi* to the poor for each time, and to say twenty Paternosters and Avemarias.[9]

This irresistible confession by the Florentine merchant and historian Goro Dati raises most of the right questions about this complex, even baffling subject. What, it makes us ask, was a conversion in early modern Europe? What was an autobiography? What relation, if any, did the spiritual experience which the term "conversion" seems to denote have to the texts that claimed to describe it?

These questions, unfortunately, are much easier to raise than to answer. Conversion, in the first place, ranks with the slipperiest of human experiences, the most difficult to identify or to describe—and certainly to evaluate. The meaning of the term itself has changed radically over time: Augustine, as Karl Morrison has recently pointed out, normally applied it not to the process of searching and suffering that a soul had to undergo before it found rest in God—the story, that is, told in his own *Confessions*—but to God's conversion, his turning outwards, toward the individual's soul.[10]

Even in its normal sense, moreover, conversion can take many forms, as A. D. Nock showed in his classic study of the subject, itself inspired by William James. It could refer to a straightforward, nonviolent process of "adhesion," enlistment in a new religion, as happened in ancient cities that received new gods. Or it could be applied to a more complex, difficult, and protracted process, a breaking of old ties, a cutting loose from one web of social and political and kinship connections, usually in order to attach oneself to another. It could describe a mass phenomenon: the decision, voluntary or compelled, by which a group adopts a new liturgy, a new calendar, a new discipline, and a new god. Or it could evoke the trajectory traced by a single person, jaggedly propelled back and forth by good and evil impulses like the ball in a cosmic pinball machine.[11]

In the Christian tradition, conversion has taken any number of forms. Some convert outwards, following a course normally described as a movement from darkness into light, as Paul did when he went from Judaism to Christianity. Others convert inwards, experiencing a change normally represented as a rise in spiritual temperature, one that involves passing from a lukewarm to a burning commitment to one's own faith, as many Florentines of a generation after Dati's did when they torched their vanities at Savonarola's urging. One can describe conversion as instantaneous or protracted, easy or difficult, painless or torturous. One can praise it as self-discovery of the highest order or dismiss it as self-hatred. And one must never forget that conversion, in most cases, is not a clearly defined hundred-yard run from a well-marked starting block to a clear goal, but an uncertain motion toward a state that is changed by the one who adopts it.

Yet even once we have set out all these possible classifications for it, Dati's experience flutters away from the lepidopterist's net and killing bottle. Evidently he moved—or hoped to move—back, not out, to a deeper commitment to the Christian faith and discipline into which he was born. But what moved him to do so, the extent of the distance he traversed, and the inward content, if any, of his reregulation of his outward content remain unclear. This problem, moreover, is typical. A few early modern Europeans found graphic ways to describe the actual feel and texture of conversion. Luther effectively deployed the vocabulary of "scruples" to describe his own condition of stark terror before his discovery of grace. But Thomas Platter, later the publisher of Calvin's *Institutes*, found it harder to identify the springs of his radical break with the old church. While working as a janitor in the Zürich cathedral during his school days, he had run out of wood for the stove. Seeing a statue of St. John, he seized it and hurled it into the fire—a story clearly suggesting that he had arrived at a radical, but painless, rejection of the old forms of devotion. Yet Platter admitted that he still prayed regularly to the saints until he heard a sermon by Ulrich Zwingli, which gave him the feeling of being pulled out of his seat, brain first. When did Platter—or Augustine—actually convert? Opinions differ, legitimately.

If conversion is never easy to describe with precision, past conversion— the form historians normally try to deal with—is even harder to seize. It survives only as recorded, after all, in biographical or autobiographical texts. And these pose enormous analytical problems in their own right. Though we often speak freely of early modern autobiographies, the term was not widely used until the early nineteenth century. The now traditional outline history of the genre moves lightly and easily across the centuries from Marcus Aurelius to Augustine to Abelard and beyond, until the genre reaches perfection and full self-awareness with Goethe.

But the texts corralled by such sweeping analyses lack the internal unity, the intertextual coherence, of those that belong to clearly defined genres like epic or pastoral. The autobiographical tradition is really an artifact of the late nineteenth and early twentieth centuries, when Wilhelm Dilthey and his disciple Georg Misch, hoping to trace the history of human consciousness, decided that autobiography could play a central role in it.[12]

Those historians who have concerned themselves most systematically with such documents in recent times have emphasized the diversity of the forms that "life-writing" could take from the fifteenth to the eighteenth century.[13] Autobiography, in the words of James Amelang, "was a practice before it was a program."[14] Men and women who wrote their own lives did so in radically diverse forms: diaries aimed at their family circles and meant to be held under lock and key; letters directed to their children; remarks dictated to their pupils; pleas directed to their confessors; notes composed for their own use; and formal Latin treatises, drafted and polished for formal publication. They drew on a rich heritage of examples from the past, which they not only imitated but also resisted. Intertextual relationships ran the gamut from incestuous to patricidal. When Girolamo Cardano, for example, set about writing his last and most formal autobiography, he seized upon the work of Marcus Aurelius, recently translated into Latin, as a model of how not to write one's life. Marcus, as he saw, had written in order to make himself a better man, eliminating any details that did not help attain that end. Cardano, by contrast, wrote to describe all of his faults, from his silly walk to his obsessive pursuit of fame.[15]

In Dati's case, the wording of his text suggests that the passage of time inspired him to change his religious state: reaching the age of forty, seen as old in his time, and arriving at the first day of the Christian, if not the Florentine civil year, apparently led him to repent. Dati, like so many of his contemporaries, took a serious interest in the calendar, which he saw as more than an abstract classificatory system. In his history of Florence, he wrote with passionate enthusiasm about the 24th of June, the Feast of St. John's, and the joy that it evoked in all Florentines. It is entirely possible, then, that the other end of the ceremonial year inspired him with very different feelings. But his work as a whole took the normal Florentine form of a collection of dated notes on everything from business to the births of children (and the deaths of wives) to trouble with the servants. The calendrical inspiration might merely reflect the literary form he chose to use.

If autobiographies are not free expressions of personality, but varied applications of stiff, preexisting templates drawn from high and low, literary and practical traditions, there is some case for arguing that no conversion experienced in premodern times can ever be accessible to us except as a representation. We can identify the existing resources mobilized in a given case. But we cannot hope to penetrate behind it to some putatively deeper reality of vision and emotion—especially as any given autobiographical text will also pose problems of comprehension and evaluation.

Even if we can only hope to identify the tools used to trace a spiritual experience in a given text, however, the effort seems worth making—if not with the aim of uncovering "how he really changed his life," at least in the hope of identifying the intellectual resources that early modern individuals mobilized to portray and defend their spiritual decisions. After all, students of fields as diverse as literary history, philosophy, and administration have argued in recent years, following and updating Burckhardt, that early modern Europe played a crucial role in the development of a modern self, a self with clear boundaries, a consciousness of its independence from others, and a sense of its own interiority. Sensitive recent scholarship has taught us much about the ways that individual Catholics used the language of Christian conversion to particular ends, not always those desired by the authorities who tried to guide them.[16] Kircher's example has already suggested that one characteristic form of modern intellectual life, scholarship as vocation, was formed in the capacious, flexible crucible of conversion. It may prove, paradoxically, that the tools forged to create Catholic converts could support more than one form of conversion, even one of those most characteristic of the modern world: conversion to a new intellectual position.

The Philosopher in the Stove

Let us attend, then, to one of the most famous scenes of conversion in the history of early modern Europe: the one that took place in Germany, somewhere near the Rhine, on the night of the 10th to 11th of November, 1619, and found its most famous record in a manifesto of the New Philosophy. René Descartes, finding himself shut up in winter quarters with Imperial soldiers whose conversation did not interest him, "spent the whole day shut up alone in a stove-heated room," plunged into a systematic consideration, as he put it in his *Discourse on Method*, "of his own thoughts." In one sense, Descartes admitted, his life up to that point had already involved a conversion: the shift from one set of beliefs to another. He had been brought up "in one of the most celebrated schools in Europe," the Jesuit college of La Flèche, founded by Henri IV and designed to produce good Catholic lawyers and officers. He had "learned everything that the others were learning there": in other words, the basic encyclopedia that included the humanistic studies of grammar, rhetoric, and moral philosophy and the more technical disciplines of mathematics and natural philosophy. And he had come to esteem "the strength and beauty" of eloquence, the "entrancing delicacy and sweetness" of poetry, and the subtlety of mathematics. But he had also come to feel that these studies had only limited value. Learning the ancient languages and reading the works of the ancients, for example, had made him cosmopolitan, showing him that "everything contrary to our ways" was not "absurd and irrational." But he had also realized that he had no way of telling which of the ancient histories were true. As important, he had decided that he could learn the same lessons that history taught from traveling, from "reading the book of the world," and that he could do so without becoming an antiquary, as ignorant of the customs of his own time as he was steeped in those of the past. He had come to see that the philosophies of the ancients, though they exalted the virtues, failed to define them; theology rested on an exaggerated faith in human reason, which was incapable of reaching heaven; and mathematics, though rigorous, seemed oddly sterile, since no system had been built on its foundations.

Accordingly, as soon as Descartes reached the age when he could "pass from under the control of [his] instructors," he abandoned formal study and turned to travel and introspection. He served at courts and in armies and mingled with varied individuals and groups, in order to see what results they had arrived at by applying their common sense to practical problems—a process in which he had more faith than he did in the abstract reasoning of a scholar in his study. In the end, he decided not to accept any belief that he had not arrived at by his own independent reasoning. After thinking matters through in the intense concentration made possible by the "stove-heated room," he knew his vocation: to reject everything he did not know evidently, to divide up every problem into as many parts as necessary, and to build a new philosophy from the foundations, using "the long chains of perfectly simple and easy reasonings by means of which geometers are accustomed to carry out their most difficult demonstrations." Descartes found that he was thinking—and knew that he existed. And he went on to become the first Cartesian and to assert the existence of the *moy*, the hard, individual, irreducible self.[17]

Modern readers of the first chapters of the *Discourse* have traditionally seen Descartes's account of his development as an autobiography of a particular kind. They have argued that Descartes used the language of secular essayists and moralists like Michel de Montaigne and Pierre Charron to describe the intellectual labyrinth in which he found himself before he arrived at his new method. Descartes derived from them both much of the language he deployed and the dramatic description he offered of the condition of human thought in the years around 1600. Long before Descartes, Montaigne had subjected the reigning philosophies of his time—above all the morality of the Stoics—to what he called "trials," the form that became the new genre of the essay. Like Descartes, Montaigne had insisted that existing philosophies had reached an impasse to which only a form of skepticism could do justice. He could know only his own self directly, and had devoted large sectors of his work—for example, his great last essay "On Experience"—to describing the flow of his own existence, day by day and kidney stone by kidney stone. Unlike Descartes, to be sure, Montaigne had not been able to construct a positive philosophy, a new system to replace the old ones that his critical intellect demolished. But he evidently provided the positive source for Descartes's self-portrait as the embodiment of disembodied critical intellect, the mind not troubled by or caught up in the illusions normal in his epoch, willing to subject itself, at least provisionally, to the norms of society.

In the seventeenth century, however, others read the published record of Descartes's life very differently. In particular, many traditional intellectuals—men who felt more sympathy for Kircher's style of polyglot erudition than for Descartes's austere definition of the rigorous knowledge that alone was worth having—saw the Cartesians as the members of something like a sect, blind followers of a leader who had engaged in something more like self-torment than reasoning.[18] The erudite Anglican clergyman Méric Casaubon was no enthusiast for all traditional forms of learning: in 1659 he published the diaries of John Dee's dealings with spirits, which did much to sink the natural magic of the Renaissance into terminal discredit.[19] But he firmly believed that anyone who hoped to pursue knowledge should do so through civil conversation and reading, in great libraries and centers of learning like the collection of the Cotton family. He lampooned Descartes's autobiography as the story of a vainglorious man who had locked himself in an isolation ward in order to dramatize an enterprise that was really nothing but "vanitie, futilitie, nugacitie":

> What a mysterie doth he make of his *Ego sum: ego Cogito . . .*, to attaine to the excellencie whereof, a man must first strip himselfe of all that he hath ever knowne, or beleeved. He must renounce to his naturall reason, & to his senses: nothing but caves and solitudes will serve the turne, for such deepe meditation, such profound matter: rare inventions to raise the expectation of the credulous, & in the end to send them away pure Quacks, or arrand Quakers.[20]

Casaubon compared the author of the *Discourse* not to Montaigne and Charron, but to the religious enthusiasts he loathed: "The man seemes to me to take the same course with his disciples, as many Jesuited Puritans doe with theirs." Such Puritans deliberately cast their followers down "to the lowest pitt of despaire," before raising them up again by teaching them a new theology and rationale for Christian life. This left them cheered up but also in "a great dependencie." Similarly, Descartes, "after he hath obliged his disciples, to forgett & forgoe all former præcognitions & progresses of eyther senses or sciences; then he thinks he hath them sure; they must adheare to him tooth & nayle, or acknowledge themselfes to have been fooled."[21]

In his work *Of Credulity and Incredulity*, Casaubon traced these methods to their source. Descartes resembled the Puritans, who taught that "there is no true Conversion, but through the horrors of a sad kind of desperation, as antecedent to it, or always concomitant," and developed a method of systematic prayer and exhortation to reduce their disciples into a receptive state.[22] But the Jesuits—or some of them—were also "said to use some such thing, to get themselves some confidents."[23] In fact, Casaubon found these tactics typical of Counter-Reformation Christianity. Reading a Catholic tract which accused the Church of England of lacking "seriousness," he countered this charge by insisting that the Catholic Church was too serious—so much so that it committed emotional violence on those it proselytized. Augustine, he noted, marked the "fourth degree" of conversion "to consist in a kind of mourning, proceeding from the first degree, a godly fear."

> But their way is a shorter way: first desperation, or somewhat very near to it: then an absolute confidence, grounded upon it. Neither will I deny, that it may happen so, to some, sometimes, who become true converts. But, that to be the only way, is an invention of their own, that I think hath more of policy in it, in the first inventors, at least, and chief abettors, than of ignorance; not to be reconciled, I am sure, with the example of the thief upon the cross.[24]

Casaubon suggested that the Puritans might have learned their tactics from the Jesuits, and that Descartes had something in common with the Puritans. What he did not point out was that Descartes had actually gone to school with the Jesuits. In fact, it seems likely that Descartes's conversion to his new method, like Kircher's conversion to the religion of hieroglyphs, was in part made possible by methods for managing and transforming the self that he had learned, with the humanities, at La Flèche.

The Documents in the Case: Descartes the Dreamer

In the *Discourse on Method,* Descartes emphasized the purely intellectual nature of his conversion, insisting that he "was not troubled by any cares or passions" and that both his experience in the "stove-heated room" and the consequences he drew from it were purely intellectual. But in one of several sheets of notes that Descartes kept, headed *"Olympica,"* he gave a very different account. In this intimate journal written in Latin—a standard development of the humanistic notebook, that magnificent tool for ordering all the texts in the world and making the world into a text—he made clear that as he prepared his first public appearance on the theater of the world, he knew that he might have to conceal and mislead: "Just as comedians are counseled not to let shame appear on their foreheads, and so put on a mask: so likewise, now that I am to mount the stage of the world, where I have so far been a spectator, I come forward in a mask." He recorded that the "foundations of [his] wonderful discovery" lay not in a calm day's reasoning, but in a dream that he had had in November 1619, about a poem by the late Roman writer Ausonius, which discussed the question "What road in life shall I follow?" And he insisted that he had been perfectly justified in drawing inspiration from a verse that had come to him in a dream: "It might seem strange that opinions of weight are found in the works of poets rather than philosophers. The reason is that poets write through enthusiasm and imagination; there are in us seeds of knowledge, as [of fire] in a flint; philosophers extract them by way of reason, but poets strike them out by imagination, and then they shine more bright." The whole series of his later discoveries unfolded from this dream.[25]

In the remainder of this text, which Descartes never finished, he told in detail what had happened to him in the stove-heated room. His state was not, he wrote in his Latin account, one of calm but of violent agitation. Exhausted, he fell into "a sort of enthusiasm," dreaming three dreams in one night. In the first, frightened by some phantoms, he walked toward the left, since he felt weak on his right side. Ashamed at his awkwardness and pushed bodily by a sort of whirlwind, he tried to reach a nearby college. There he encountered, among others, someone who called his name and told him that if he would go and find Monsieur N, he would be given something. Descartes imagined that the gift would be a melon from a foreign country. Though the wind made it impossible for him to make progress, he saw others standing without difficulty. Terrified by this incongruity, Descartes woke in great pain, which made him fear that an evil demon was persecuting him. Turning on his right side—since he had slept and dreamed on the left—he prayed for protection, slept again, and dreamed of a terrifying thunderclap, only to wake and find the room full of sparks. Deciding that this was not an evil portent, but a form of illumination, he fell back to sleep. In a third dream, he was delighted when he found a dictionary and then an anthology of Latin poets—one which contained, among other poems by Ausonius, the one on choosing a way of life, and which he discussed in some detail with a man who questioned him before disappearing.

While still asleep, Descartes decided that this series of experiences was a "songe" or "vision"—that is, in the Latin of traditional oneiromancy, a form of prophetically inspired dream. He began to interpret it, and continued even after he awoke. He took the dictionary as representing the whole corpus of the sciences, the *Corpus poetarum* first as the union of philosophy and wisdom and then as offering to open the truths of all the sciences. He took the third dream as marking his future path, the two former ones as describing his past—when he had not sought the proper form of solitude, represented by the melon, and had been tormented by an evil genius, represented by the wind. He understood his pain as representing his own conscience, repenting of his past life, while the thunderclap stood for the spirit of truth descending. The whole series of dreams, he decided, had been a supernatural revelation. In gratitude, Descartes promised to go on pilgrimage if he could to the house of the Virgin in Loreto.[26]

Through much of the twentieth century, historians of philosophy did their best to explain these dreams away by taking them, for example, as consciously composed allegories.[27] But more recent scholarship has scraped the hagiographical whitewash away and revealed the foreign texture and form of Descartes's experiences. Alice Browne, John Cole, and Sophie Jama have subjected Descartes's dreams to magnificently wide-ranging examination, and in his intellectual biography of Descartes Stephen Gaukroger has given them a substantial place, though not a central role.[28] These scholars have shown that as Descartes dreamed he referred to, and was affected by, a vast range of identifiable beliefs and practices. Some of these he would have known as a child: for example, that St. Martin's Eve, the harvest festival on which he had his dreams, was normally a time for getting drunk and celebrating fertility. Others, like the interpretative techniques he applied to his dreams, were practices that he had formally studied. Browne, an expert student of ancient and Renaissance theories of dream interpretation, has shown how traditional Descartes's terminology and tactics were.

Jama, for her part, has traced the connection between Descartes's dreams (and his reading of them) and his experience as a pupil in the Jesuit college of La Flèche. There, like the other collégiens, he went on retreat with a Jesuit spiritual director. Under the Jesuit's guidance, he carried out the *Spiritual Exercises* laid down by Ignatius Loyola, the founder of the Jesuit order, on the basis of his own experience. That is to say, Descartes underwent a long series of experiences, divided into weeks, and many of them based on the precise, meticulously detailed imagination of scenes, from Christ's crucifixion to Hell itself. He took in all the details and considered their meaning, ridding himself of his besetting sins and cultivating his virtues. Finally, after long preparation, he had—as the *Exercises'* terminology put it—"elected" the way of life that God had in mind for him. In the course of his retreats, evidently, Descartes mastered and internalized the Jesuits' technology of self-scrutiny, a craft created by Ignatius, who drew on a wide range of later medieval and Renaissance precedents and techniques as he converted his first associates in Paris. When Descartes locked himself up, stripped all superfluous concerns from his consciousness, and scrutinized both his own life to date and the meaning of his dreams, detail by detail, trying to pull out and capture every atom of meaning, he clearly adapted the techniques he had learned while on retreat, and applied them to their normal end of finding a vocation.[29]

Yet Descartes's experience—and his own understanding of it—also clearly deviated from the normal practices of the Jesuits. He allowed himself to be guided by dreams rather than by meditations carried out while awake. He served as his own spiritual director—a task normally carried out only by Jesuits. And he made the course of his life turn not on a systematic, staged inquiry into God's plan for him, but on the aleatory method of dream interpretation. Only the divinely guaranteed truth of his experience—not the tried protocols of the order—ensured that the path he took was the right one, not a detour staged by his evil genius or demon.

In presenting his situation in this way, Descartes enacted a conversion. It was not the stately, austere, considered decision that a pupil of the Jesuits was supposed to make, but a wild, passionate gamble. His experiences resemble those prescribed in the *Spiritual Exercises* less closely than those recorded in Ignatius's own autobiography, which the founder of the Jesuits dictated to young followers near the end of his life. Ignatius, like Descartes, made his life-determining decisions aleatory. He let the hand of God steer him. Hearing a Muslim deride the Christian doctrine of the Immaculate Conception, the former soldier was not certain whether to follow the infidel and beat him or go on his way to a spiritual victory. He allowed his horse to choose which path to follow—and thus involved the divine hand in his decision making. And he experienced, as Descartes did, numerous visions, some of which he interpreted as diabolic, others, like his experience of the divine presence as a bright, round object, as divine. Like Ignatius's account, Descartes's represents a divinely inspired but highly individual experience of conversion to a vocation.[30]

The fact that Descartes laid so much weight on revelatory dreams reveals much, both about his debt to the Jesuits for teaching him particular technologies of self-scrutiny and about the formidable independence with which he used them. The *Spiritual Exercises*, as we have seen, recommended meditation, not dreaming. Ignatius's own account of his dreams was not published until long after Descartes's death, for fear of inspiring unsanctioned efforts at emulation. But Jesuits talked and wrote a great deal about dreams in Descartes's time. For the late sixteenth and early seventeenth centuries saw a number of dreaming prophets—mostly, but not entirely, women—proffer their revelations to kings, ministers and prelates.[31] And Jesuits were regularly called upon to advise on how to handle these people, who saw their sleeping states as direct conduits of divine counsel. For dreams could come—as Descartes knew—from the devil as well as from God. And Jesuits knew the devil's ways better than anyone. Their deftness at exorcising devils in public, in fact, provided one of their most effective forms of propaganda in the France of Descartes's youth.[32]

José de Acosta, the author of a brilliantly iconoclastic *Natural and Moral History of the Indies*, served as assessor in 1578 at the trial of Francisco de la Cruz. This "learned Divine and Professor (or Doctor) of Divinity" attached himself to Maria Pizarro, a woman who received divine revelations in "trances and raptures, which carried her quite besides her self." He claimed that he would do miracles, that he had spoken with God himself, that he was holier than any of the angels. And despite five years of imprisonment during which even his breviary was confiscated, he cited scriptural passages in support of his views, "so many and so long, that his very memory caused great admiration"—though his explications of the passages inspired only ridicule and pity. Led out to be executed, he looked up to the heavens, expecting fire from above to consume the court and the spectators: "But in very deed," Acosta noted with satisfaction, "no such fire came from above; but a flame came from below, which seized upon this pretended King, and Pope, and Redeemer, and new Law-giver, and quickly did reduce him into ashes."[33] So much for those who set too much store by false or diabolic visions.

Martín Del Rio, the Spanish Jesuit who wrote a standard handbook of demonology, retold this story and told a number of others about bad dreams and dreamers. He recalled, with some nostalgia, how in his happy days in Belgium he and the great philologist Justus Lipsius had discussed the case of an old woman who claimed that a divine spirit appeared to her in her dreams, in the form of a vague, bright sphere, the precise outlines of which she could not see. This spirit both foretold future events—like the death of the viceroy, Requesens—and forced her to reveal them in public. Del Rio admitted that opinions about this visionary had varied.[34] But he also pointed out that diabolic visions were especially likely to come to women of low social position, like this prophetess. More generally, he argued that excess interest in dreams usually had dire consequences. Some dreams, of course, were purely natural, caused by environmental influences on the sleeper's body: they were neither meaningful nor worrying. Some were genuinely prophetic. Del Rio conceded that the recipients of truly divine dreams were normally also instilled with absolute confidence in the truth of their revelations—very likely one of Descartes's criteria for accepting the validity of his own dreams. But he also insisted that only experts, priests experienced in the difficult craft of "discretion of spirits," as laid down by older authorities like Jean Gerson, could really decide if a dream was divine or diabolic. And he suggested that in cases of doubt, "it will be safest if you distance yourself from it, and despise it, as something diabolic."[35]

It seems clear that Descartes learned in the Jesuit world he inhabited while young to take dreams seriously. He acted like a good Jesuit when he examined the "causes and circumstances" of his dreams, tested the feelings that they inspired in him, and decided which supernatural being had sent them to him. But he rejected the cautious, sober protocols that were meant to govern the Jesuits' practice of dream interpretation even as he accepted and applied their normal methods.

Descartes did not insert any account of his dreams—or even the mood in which he dreamt them—into his *Discourse*, and generations of his philosophical readers have taken his effort to create a baseline of interiority, an irreducible thinking self that could construct a world, as purely philosophical. This view, which inspired young mathematicians and philosophers for centuries to choose Descartes's vocation as their own, still surfaces in Charles Taylor's brilliantly teleological reconstruction in the *Sources of the Self*. Descartes's dreams are told, and retold, as a philosopher's primal scene—like Wittgenstein's encounter with Piero Sraffa on a train, or Nelson Goodman's famous double positive. But it is rare for historians of philosophy to see the *Olympica* as part of Descartes's comprehensive effort at autobiography, or his dream experience as central to the philosophy he founded. What did Descartes intend by separating his account into two parts?

The Name of the Rose: What Is an Autobiography?

A fuller understanding of the range of autobiographical practice in early modern Europe may clarify what Descartes was about when he composed these very different accounts, one nearly contemporary and one retrospective, of his life, and preserved them both. Modern writers characteristically see autobiography as a single, coherent effort—the writing of a single, fixed text. But in the sixteenth and seventeenth centuries, those who converted most radically—as Ignatius and Descartes did—often wrote multiple accounts of their experiences, ranging from formal, relatively austere documents destined for publication to multiple, less formal, more vivid records, meant to be preserved by friends and used by biographers. The spiritual directors of Spanish saints, recently studied by Jodi Bilinkoff, regularly collected and used similar documents, always editing and adapting them, often in radical ways, and sometimes rewriting them entirely.[36]

Personal records of experiences of the divine were meant to be preserved and used; the Bollandists, the Jesuit specialists in hagiography who compiled the *Acta Sanctorum*, became masters at collecting and evaluating them.[37] Adrien Baillet, who included Descartes's account of his dreams—literally translated into French, in his biography of the philosopher—also published a four-volume set of lives of the saints, in Latin, into which he intercalated numerous similar documents. Even before publication these might circulate widely among the friends and acquaintances of the person in question. Descartes both crafted an economical, sharply pointed account of his life as a preface to several of his works and recorded the same decisive moment, in a very different, more emotional, pious, and traditional way, in pages destined for his own eyes and for the eyes of his friends. He wrote his autobiography in two complementary modes and at two different times. In doing so he made clear not how trivial his dreams seemed, but how seriously he took them and how much he wished them to figure in future accounts of his life—just as Blaise Pascal, in most respects a radically different figure, did when he preserved his personal record of his *"nuit de feu."*[38]

Descartes the Convert

Descartes the dreamer found little comprehension from his first readers. Committed though he was, after all, to the significance of his dreams, he certainly recognized that they did not fit the rest of his philosophy very well. This may explain what he meant when he said that he would have to wear a mask in order to come forward onto the public stage. Later in life he would make clear that he saw men in their early twenties as still immature and liable to attacks of enthusiasm—a remark that makes his distance from his early self quite clear. Cartesians, as well as the many non-Cartesian admirers of his mathematical proficiency who engaged in debate with him, were often embarrassed by the existence of the *Olympica*. Even Baillet was too critical a hagiographer to take Descartes's dreams very seriously. A disciple of the Bollandists, he assured the reader of his *Lives of the Saints* that "I report dreams and visions when nothing in them is contrary to the gravity of history."[39] He had no trouble dismissing the account of the "simple" priest de Bosco, who dreamed in 1511 that the Old Testament heroine Susanna and Daniel, her rescuer, appeared to him. They told him that her bones were buried in the church of St. Servin in Toulouse—where they appeared in due course, accompanied by a nicely aged written attestation of their identity, and were, again in due course, reinterred with splendid rituals, reenacted every year.[40] Accordingly, he admitted that Descartes's visions revealed him to be an "enthusiast." The historian, he slyly suggested, might be tempted to suspect the philosopher of having had a bit too much to drink on St. Martin's Eve—though he also admitted that Descartes insisted on his own sobriety, and that it was a "*Génie,*" not wine, that had set his brain on fire.[41] Yet Baillet showed more sympathy than Constantijn Huygens, who remarked that even pious Catholics would find Descartes's description of his dreams "a great weakness," or Leibniz, who agreed.[42]

Perhaps Méric Casaubon, that diligent collector of traditions and sharply observant critic of intellectual fashions, was more insightful than the philosophers. He insisted on the continuity between the Jesuits' technologies of self-mastery and Descartes's philosophical conversion. Evidence that Casaubon could not have had access to confirms this ingenious conjecture. Descartes was clearly inspired by his reading of his dreams not only to embark on a particular kind of career, and to defy all opposition, but also, many years later, to portray his own life as a model—a secular saint's life pivoting on a philosopher's conversion—in the teeth of his own insistence that no one should emulate historical examples, since the sources that described them exaggerated and overpraised their subjects. As Casaubon suggested, the new philosophical sect that Descartes created probably owed much of its ideological force and unity to the technologies of conversion that he ingeniously secularized and applied to systems of ideas. In the world of learned practice, conversion—and the now unfamiliar forms of autobiography that recorded it—played a vital role, offering a new way of representing the path to method and knowledge. Though its origins were soon forgotten, this model survived until relatively recent times, when metaphors of the market replaced metaphors of conversion, in the intellectual as in other spheres. It remains to be seen if the new language can yield accounts of conversion as attractive and durable as the old one did.

Endnotes

Warm thanks to Michael Heyd for his critique of an earlier draft of this essay.

1 Athanasius Kircher, "Vita ... a semetipso conscripta," Vienna, Österreichische Nationalbibliothek, MS 13752, pp. 18–19. On this text and its roots in Jesuit practice see esp. H. Louthan, "Popular Piety and the Autobiography of Athanasius Kircher, SJ," in *Catholicism and Austrian Culture*, ed. R. Robertson and J. Beniston (Edinburgh, 1999), pp. 3–15.

2 See, e.g., Thomas Leinkauf, *Mundus combinatus* (Berlin, 1993); P. Findlen, *Possessing Nature* (Berkeley, 1994).

3 Kircher, "Vita," pp. 17–18.

4 Cf. Gershom Gerhard Scholem, *Von Berlin nach Jerusalem* (Frankfurt am main, 1977).

5 See esp. Erik Iversen, *Obelisks in Exile*, vol. 1, *The Obelisks of Rome* (Copenhagen, 1968).

6 See esp. *Ordo dedicationis obelisci quem S.D.N. Sixtus V Pont. Max. in Foro Vaticano ad limina apostolorum erexit, et benedictionis item crucis* (Rome, 1586).

7 Torgil Magnuson, *Rome in the Age of Bernini* (Stockholm, 1982), 1:pp. 16–25.

8 Kircher, "Vita," pp. 28–35.

9 *Two Memoirs of Renaissance Florence: The Diaries of Buonaccorso Pitti and Gregorio Dati*, trans. Julia Martines, ed. Gene A. Brucker (New York, 1967), p. 124.

10 Karl Frederick Morrison, *Conversion and Text* (Charlottesville, 1992).

11 Arthur Darby Nock, *Conversion* (Oxford, 1933); for a more recent survey see *Oxford Classical Dictionary*, 3rd ed., s.v. "conversion" by Philip Rousseau.

12 For fine studies in this vein see Karl Joachim Weintraub, *The Value of the Individual* (Chicago, 1978); John Sturrock, *The Language of Autobiography* (Cambridge, 1993).

13 See the studies collected in *Ego-Dokumente*, ed. Winfried Schulze (Berlin, 1996); Hans Rudolf Velten, *Das selbst geschriebene Leben* (Heidelberg, 1995).

14 James S. Amelang, *The Flight of Icarus* (Stanford, 1998).

15 Anthony Grafton, *Cardano's Cosmos* (Cambridge, MA, 1999).

16 See, e.g., Alison Weber, *Teresa of Avila and the Rhetoric of Femininity* (Princeton, 1990).

[17] René Descartes, *Discours de la Méthode; Oeuvres philosophiques*, ed. Ferdinand Alquié (Paris, 1988), 1:pp. 570–91.

[18] See the learned and sensitive account of Michael Heyd, *"Be Sober and Reasonable": The Critique of Enthusiasm in the Seventeenth and Early Eighteenth Centuries* (Leiden, 1995), esp. chaps. 3–4.

[19] See the splendid account in Méric Casaubon, *Generall Learning*, ed. Richard Serjeantson (Cambridge, 1999), to which I am much indebted.

[20] Ibid., p. 153.

[21] Ibid., pp. 153–54.

[22] Cf. Norman Pettit, *The Heart Prepared* (New Haven, 1966).

[23] Méric Casaubon, *Of Credulity and Incredulity* (London, 1670), p. 151, quoted by Serjeantson, in Casaubon, *Generall Learning*, pp. 153–54n169.

[24] Casaubon, *Of Credulity*, p. 153.

[25] René Descartes, *Oeuvres*, ed. Charles Adam and Paul Tannery (Paris, 1967), 10:pp. 217–19.

[26] Descartes's Latin text does not survive; I follow the French paraphrase in Adrien Baillet, *La vie de Monsieur Des-Cartes* (1691; reprint, New York, 1987), bk. 2, chap. 1; 1:pp. 81–86.

[27] E.g., Henri Gouhier, *Les première pensées de Descartes* (Paris, 1958).

[28] Alice Browne, "Descartes' Dreams," *Journal of the Warburg and Courtauld Institutes* 40 (1977): pp. 256–73; John Cole, *The Olympian Dreams and Youthful Rebellion of René Descartes* (Urbana, 1992); Sophie Jama, *La nuit de songes de René Descartes* (Paris, 1998); Stephen Gaukroger, *Descartes: An Intellectual Biography* (Oxford, 1995), pp. 104–11. Gaukroger shows in detail that Descartes would have a number of intellectual experiences and personal encounters before formulating what became his definitive "method," and reads the dreams as the account of a breakdown, and Descartes's account of his recovery as the way he "rationalized his recovery in terms of a great discovery" (p. 111).

[29] See the excellent recent treatment of the *Spiritual Exercises* in John O'Malley, *The First Jesuits* (Cambridge, MA, 1993). Another body of literature that fascinated Descartes at this point—and that contained some elaborate accounts of dreams and conversions—was the body of Rosicrucian texts that appeared at exactly this time. But as Gaukroger points out, there is no proof that Descartes read the text that offers the closest parallels, Rudophilus Staurophorus's *Raptus philosophicus* of 1619 (p. 108); by contrast, it is certain that Descartes knew the Jesuits' techniques of meditation and dream interpretation.

[30] See *The Autobiography of Ignatius Loyola*, trans. Joseph F. O'Callaghan, ed.

John C. Olin (New York, 1974); original in *Fontes narrativi de S. Ignatio de Loyola*, 4 vols. (Rome, 1943–65), 1:pp. 354–507.

[31] See, e.g., Richard L. Kagan, *Lucrecia's Dreams* (Berkeley, 1990).

[32] Daniel Pickering Walker, *Unclean Spirits* (Philadelphia, 1981).

[33] José de Acosta, *De temporibus novissimis libri quatuor* (Rome, 1590), pp. 54–56, quoted by Martin Antoine Del Rio, *Disquisitionum magicarum libri sex* (Cologne, 1679), pp. 534–36; trans. Méric Casaubon, *A Treatise concerning Enthusiasme* (1656; reprint, Gainesville, 1970), pp. 102–6.

[34] Del Rio, *Disquisitionum magicarum libri sex*, pp. 636–37.

[35] Ibid., p. 635.

[36] Jodi Bilinkoff, "Confessors, Penitents, and the Construction of Identities in Early Modern Avila," *Culture and Identity in Early Modern Europe (1500–1800): Essays in Honor of Natalie Zemon Davis*, ed. Barbara D. Diefendorf and Carla Alison Hesse (Ann Arbor, 1993), pp. 83–100.

[37] Karl Hausberger, "Das kritische hagiographische Werk der Bollandisten," in *Historische Kritik in der Theologie*, ed. Georg Schwaiger (Göttingen, 1980), pp. 210–44.

[38] On this point see the excellent treatment by Browne in "Descartes' Dreams."

[39] Adrien Baillet, *Les vies des Saints*, 4 vols. (Paris, 1701–3), 1:pp. iv–v.

[40] Ibid. 5:pt. 2, p. 30.

[41] Baillet, *Vie de Des-Cartes*, 1:p. 85.

[42] Quoted by Jama, *La nuits de songes*, pp. 9–10.

Michael Pollan

Cannabis, Forgetting, and the Botany of Desire

I WANT TO GET a couple things about myself out of the way before I start. The first one is that, as you know, I write about plants. Whenever I take questions from an audience, there's always someone who says, "Is that your real name?" I mean, it does seem awfully convenient, I realize that. But I've also learned from people asking these questions that it is a certain genre of name called the "career natural," or an even better term is the "aptonym." So I guess I have a good aptonym. I've been collecting others. The last time I was in the Bay Area I was told about a podiatrist named Dr. Toesy, which I kind of like. There are always doctors with these great names. I collected Drs. Slaughter, Smother, and Kaufman. There are lots of great urologists. There's a Dr. Klap in Buffalo, and Dr. Peckler somewhere else. And, of course, the head of the Audubon Society is John Flicker. Over Friends of Animals, Priscilla Ferrell presides. But one of my favorites is a woman named Angela Overy, who wrote a wonderful gardening book called *Sex in Your Garden*.

So we're going to talk a little bit about sex in your garden, and drugs, and rock and roll. I want to start by briefly explaining what I mean by the botany of desire, about my approach to plants and their relationship to people, and then get on to marijuana. Those who have the book, *Botany of Desire*, will recognize some of what I'm saying, at least at the start. But I then want to go a little bit deeper into what we've learned and what we're learning about cannabis and the cannabinoid network and memory since the book has come out. We're learning things actually almost every day about this very exciting area of brain science. But fitting this Avenali Lecture, and the setting, actually, I come to this scientific topic from very much a humanities point of view. I'm told now I'm a science journalist, which came as something of a surprise to me. I didn't know I was writing science. I felt a little like the character in Molière who didn't know he was speaking prose, but apparently that is what I write.

We have a bad habit in the humanities of assuming that scientists have the last word. But when I was doing the research for my chapter on cannabis in the book, I remember asking a pharmacologist in New York, who had studied drugs for years and years, "Well, what does it mean scientifically to be high?" He said something very interesting: "Well, you know, we don't understand consciousness yet scientifically, so how can we hope to understand changes in consciousness scientifically?" He and others basically told me that, for now, you're better off with the poets on this one. This is one area where the philosophers and the poets may yet have much to teach the scientists.

I also chose this topic for tonight, though, because here in California we're in one of the most important theaters in the battle over marijuana—medical marijuana—which is the battle to relegitimize this powerful plant. But I want to get past the drug war and the political perspective tonight. I'm not going to talk that much about it, although we could address it in the question period if you like. Rather, if we can, I want to look at the plant and other plant drugs as Darwinians, rather than as drug warriors.

The last reason I chose this topic is that I think I'm in a room full of people who are very well equipped—better than I, I think—to pursue at length some of the paths I'm hoping to point toward with regard to our understanding of consciousness and drugs.

But let me start with the plants. They possess an astounding and really overlooked power to nourish us and poison us, to delight our senses of sight and smell and taste, to calm our nerves or wake us up, even to change the contents of our minds and experience of consciousness. This to me is just an amazing fact, and it's an everyday fact that we don't really deal with. That's really what I undertook to deal with in the book. The first question is: why should plants have these powers? Those of you who have read the book know that the beginning of my answer—or my attempt to find an answer—as in so much of my writing, began in my garden. I really began as a gardener/writer, in many ways. One of the things I love about gardening is that it is a very desultory kind of work; it doesn't occupy all of your brain, by any means, at least the way I do it, and so there's plenty of room for speculation and for posing to oneself silly questions while one labors. It's not the same with carpentry, about which I've also written (I wrote a book on architecture and building). If you let your mind wander while you do carpentry, you end up wounded. But in the garden this isn't likely to happen. One day, during the first week of May, I was planting potatoes, and right next to me was a flowering apple tree. It was that week in May, in Connecticut where I live, where the apples were just in spectacular blossom, and the bees were going crazy, and this tree was just vibrating with the attention of the bumblebees. So I asked myself this sort of silly, but ultimately to me quite profound question: what did I have in common with those bumblebees as workers in this garden? Now, I wasn't thinking about Marx, and many people on this campus have reminded me that Marx has a whole riff on bumblebees. This wasn't on my mind, so don't read that into what I'm saying.

I realized that the bumblebee and I had a lot in common. We were both going about getting what we wanted from nature, but at the same time we were unwittingly disseminating the gene of one species and not another. The bee, like me, to the extent he thinks about this at all, thinks he's calling the shots. (Actually, it's she.

In the case of bumblebees, apparently it's female bees that do the work.) The bee has chosen to go to that particular flower, breaks in, grabs the nectar, runs off, gets away with the goods. But we know that this sense of control the bee feels, assuming she feels it, is simply a failure of bee imagination. What is really happening is that the plant has cleverly manipulated that bee into paying it a visit. And in the case of the bee, the plant does this by evolving precisely the right combination and kinds of molecules—the right color, the right shape, the right attitude toward the sun—to gratify the bee's desires. We know this from elementary or college botany. This is co-evolution, two species coming together to advance their own self-interest. They wind up trading favors, often without knowing it.

So how are matters any different between me and the potatoes I was planting, or me and the marijuana plant I wasn't planting in my garden? The plants, too, in those cases, have evolved to gratify our desires. That potato has developed precisely the flavors, the shapes, the colors, to earn a spot in our garden. In this case, I was seduced by the pages of a seed catalog, and I ordered these potatoes from a firm in Oregon, and the genes were flown across the country, or shipped across the country, and that potato seized a little bit of habitat, a couple of rows in my garden.

Plants, too, evolve to gratify our desires—a certain select group of angiosperms, the domesticated plants—which we happen to reproduce. We give them more habitat, and we carry their genes all around the world. This is what I mean by the botany of desire. Our desire, and the desire we're going to talk about tonight—specifically the desire for intoxication, for changes in consciousness—possesses a powerful force in natural history, in evolution, in much the same way that the hummingbird's desire and love of red is a case of co-evolution.

Now for the first of two disclaimers: this process is not intentional. When I talk about these plants cleverly manipulating us, I'm obviously using figurative language. We don't have a very good vocabulary for talking about how other species act on us, about their agency. We see the world as if we're the thinking subject, and then you've got that subject's object. And so, you know, I pull the weeds, I plant the potatoes, I harvest the crops. But this is just a limitation of our language. Even real evolutionary biologists talk about things like evolutionary strategy. And the word "strategy" has intent in it, but, of course, we know that's not how evolution works. The first red apple was not the result of a bunch of green apples sitting around a table saying, "Let's try red today. We'll do a red apple, we'll see if we get noticed, and we'll see if we get..." It was a mutation, strictly an accident. So even though I'm going to use this language of intention, I don't think plants are conscious. I'm not the Oliver Stone of the plant world. There's no conspiracy here.

Now, why do plants need to go to all this trouble? The THC molecule, one of the active ingredients in marijuana, is a very complicated molecule, and it takes some expense, metabolic expense, for the plant to produce it. These colors, these scents, all these are expensive propositions. Well, the main reason plants need to do all this, to gratify our desires, is that they can't move. The single great existential fact of plant life is..., well, they can't locomote. They can move with the wind and water, but they can't pick themselves up and go. So what they've worked on, what they have, are chemicals instead of legs. Cannabis works on our minds in order to borrow our feet, basically. And plants have developed this incredible variety of molecules—and, again, we're only going to concentrate on one or two today—either to attract or repel other species. They have to rely on chemistry for their defense and for their propagation: for their movement. And they've gotten really, really good at this.

You know, they're so unlike us. We really fail to appreciate their genius. And although I won't speak in terms of plant consciousness, I will speak in terms of genius. I think you can make a case that they are as advanced as we are. You look a little skeptical. But when you think about it, what does that mean, to be an advanced creature, an advanced being? It all depends on what advances you value, and who is drawing up the yardstick. You know, we value consciousness, and toolmaking, and the ability to write books, and give lectures. But by the yardstick of organic chemistry, they are so far beyond us. They've been evolving even longer than we have, just in another direction, working on other ways to confront the same challenges of life on earth, especially the challenges of reproduction and defense.

Now, you still look skeptical. Another measure we could look at—I'm trying to be objective about this—has just recently come out, and that is the size of the human genome. I don't know if you followed this, but I think the most interesting thing to come out of the much-ballyhooed mapping of the genome was the number of genes we apparently have. The first estimate is—and this came as something of a surprise—only about 35,000. This is actually kind of scandalous, if you consider that the roundworm, a creature that can't do all sorts of things, has something like 20,000 genes. How is it that we ended up with so many fewer genes than were predicted? They predicted over 100,000, I believe. Another species we've mapped at the same time is rice. You know how many genes rice has, first count? 50,000—15,000 more genes than we have. Why should this be? I don't know that that's a fair standard for being more advanced, but it is one snapshot on complexity. The reason for its complexity probably has to do with the fact that everything rice does depends on producing interesting molecules—proteins—and you need genes to do that. So perhaps that's why.

So I have enormous respect for the sophistication of these plants. We shouldn't sell them short. While we were nailing down consciousness and locomotion, they were perfecting organic chemistry, and they've achieved, you know, the arts of molecular seduction and defense; they are nature's alchemists, indeed.

There are lots of examples. I'll just give you one: Photosynthesis is, of course, one of the great examples. This is an astonishing trick, to be able to take sunlight and water—very common elements—and create sugars, food, energy. We can do nothing like this. But the other example I've come across recently is the lima bean. I like this one, as a gardener. Do you know what a lima bean does when it's attacked by spider mites? It releases a volatile chemical from its leaves. The chemical goes off in the air and summons another insect that dines exclusively on spider mites. So the lima bean sends out this chemical SOS, insects come to its rescue, they eat all the spider mites, and everybody's happy. You know, our idea of a pesticide, by comparison, is just so crude it's not even funny. So when people ask me things like, "Do you think your plants are conscious?" I say, "Isn't it enough that they can eat sunlight and do these things?" I'm a believer in plant genius.

Let's get to the case of drug plants. One of the most important relationships we have with plants involves, as I've said, changing consciousness. Now, when I talk about changing consciousness, I'm not just talking about illicit drugs. I'm also talking about things like coffee and nicotine and tea, anything that changes the texture of consciousness. We're not talking about hallucinogens, although we'll talk a little bit about them.

Apparently, all cultures except the Inuit have used plants to change consciousness, and the Inuit are truly the exception that proves the rule. The reason the Inuit never did it is that nothing very psychoactive grows where they live. As soon as plants with these powers were introduced, they took to them pretty quickly.

Andrew Weil calls this desire for changing consciousness the fourth human drive, after food, water, and sex. I think he is right. It certainly is a very widespread activity—a lot more widespread than we realize—and it doesn't always involve drugs. In his first book, *The Natural Mind*, which is still well worth reading, Weil points out that kids love to change consciousness, and they do it by swinging and by getting dizzy. We do it with exercise and meditation and fasting and thrill seeking. We're creatures, apparently, who just happen to like to fiddle with our brain chemistry.

Most cultures, curiously, promote one plant for this purpose, or two, and condemn others. They fetishize one and they have taboos on others. And if you look at things historically or geographically, cross-culturally, you will see that it's very relative and subject to change. In my garden, I have apple trees that were planted in the teens. Back in the '20s, during prohibition, those apple trees were regarded the way marijuana plants are today. They were the root of all evil, producing alcohol. And they were chopped down in many places by Carry Nation. That's what her hatchet symbolized: something to chop down apple trees because they were used for cider. At the same time, you could go into any pharmacy in America and buy preparations containing cannabis, tinctures of cannabis, as well as tinctures of opium. And, of course, between the Muslim world and the West, you have a flip between opiates and alcohol. This plant is a panacea and this one is a panapathogen, a root of all evil. It's a constant in human societies.

Now, what's the use of these drug plants in evolutionary terms? Well, one of the more interesting theories proposed by Steven Pinker, the brain scientist, is that our attraction to plant drugs is the coming together of two distinct adaptive traits. We have a system of brain rewards, such that any time we do something very heroic or useful, our brain is flooded with chemicals that make us feel good, and that's very adaptive. We also have this big brain designed for solving problems. So you bring the second trait to bear on the first, and you figure out a way to trick the brain into triggering its reward system. It's a pretty good theory.

We're not the only species who do this, though. You know, animals also get high, like to be intoxicated. Everyone is familiar with the example of catnip and locoweed. And, in fact, it appears that animals were our Virgils in the garden of psychoactive plants. We learned about a lot of these plants from watching animals get high. Coffee was discovered, apparently, by Abyssinian goat herders watching their goats. What their goats would do is eat the red berries off this one particular bush and get really frisky. And the herders thought, "Well, we're going to try this too." And somewhere along the line they learned to roast the beans, and we had coffee.

Now, it would seem to be maladaptive, though, to use these plant drugs. It does make creatures more mistake-prone. Animals that get high blow childcare, make lots of mistakes, have accidents, ruin their health. There's an herbivore that will eat a psychoactive lichen off of rocks until it has completely destroyed its teeth and can no longer eat and thus dies. Yet plant drugs do have utility. On our evolutionary journey, something that gives us pain relief, or lends us mental acuity in the case of things like coffee, something that helps smooth the waters of social relationships, helps us to work and to hunt—these things are useful. Many cultures use drugs in a very specific way, right before the hunt to give them powers of endurance and things like that. So they can also be powerful mental tools on life's journey.

Drugs also can relieve existential pain and boredom. There's this very depressing quote from Huxley: "Most men and women lead lives that are . . . so painful, at the best, so monotonous, poor and limited that the urge to escape, the longing to transcend themselves if only for a few moments, is and has always been one of the principal appetites of the soul."[1]

Are plant drugs or psychoactive drugs good or evil? I think, like a lot of things in life, that the answer to the question is "both." They're both a blessing and scourge. The Greeks pretty much had it right. They had one word, *pharmakon*, that meant both medicine and poison.

Now to pot, to marijuana, to this particular co-evolutionary relationship. Why did this plant make THC in the first place, THC being the main psychoactive ingredient? It certainly wasn't so people could get high. Marijuana did not produce THC so we could change our consciousness. It probably produces chemicals for its own purposes, and these are still unknown. There are theories. One is that THC helps protect the plant against insects. Another theory is that it helps protect against ultraviolet radiation. You find more THC as you go up higher in elevation and you have more UV rays. Another is that it's an aid to help the plant defend itself against predators. And if that's true, it's kind of a brilliant defense. You know, when you're playing around with the arms race between plants and their predators, outright poison is sometimes not the best way to go. When you put out a powerful poison, you select the resistance, and very soon you've developed it, and the poison becomes ineffective, as we find with pesticides all the time. But think how much more clever it would be to have a defense against predators that makes them forget where they saw you last time?

Now, I have some firsthand experience with this.... Well, second-hand, actually, not exactly firsthand. My cat has it firsthand. I grow catnip for my cat; he definitely has a problem with it. And during the garden season, every evening when I'm harvesting something for dinner, he comes down to the vegetable garden, and he waits to be let in. I open the gate and he comes in, and he wants to find his catnip. And every night, I have to show him where it is again. Catnip is very different from THC, but you can see the usefulness of a chemical that would cause the predator to forget where you are. That's my own theory. I hasten to add I don't think there's any science behind it.

Marijuana was discovered, it appears, in Central Asia, perhaps thanks to birds. Pigeons love the seeds of marijuana, and get a little tipsy on them. And this may be what tipped people off to what it was. It was probably purely accidental that this plant, this chemical, happened to be active in the human brain. But that's no different from any other of the accidents on which evolution and co-evolution are built. The plant seized on this accident.

Marijuana became one of the earliest plants to be domesticated. Its first use, by the Chinese, was as fiber, hemp. It's been so changed by its fifteen thousand years of co-evolution with us that apparently marijuana in its wild form doesn't exist anymore. We don't really know what the plant in the wild was like, how psychoactive it was, how good a fiber it was. The plant comes down on two lines of co-evolutionary descent, which is very interesting. You start with the same plant, but over time you develop one plant for the fiber—marijuana has the longest, strongest fiber. We're not going to talk about hemp very much, but that's how the Chinese started with it. It was, in fact, the most important fiber for both paper and cloth, up until the invention of the cotton gin in the nineteenth century. On that path of descent marijuana moved west from China, to northern Europe, and on to America.

The other path of descent was as a medicine, and people selected that strain for stronger and stronger medicine. It was used for pain relief, help with childbirth; as an anti-inflammatory, antispasmodic, anti-anxiety drug; and as a treatment for insomnia. On its second path, it moved from central Asia, down into India, and to Africa. And from Africa, it appears to have come to the "new world," to South America, first with the slave trade, and then it came up from Egypt to Europe with Napoleon's army returning to France. So it came kind of late to Europe.

Along the way, we changed the plant, selecting for either a better fiber or a stronger drug, and the plant changed us—individually, by giving us this tool, helping us with pain and that sort of thing—but also collectively. And, of course, that's something else that plant drugs do: besides being mental tools, plant drugs work on us at this higher level, at a cultural level.

Now I'm entering a very speculative area, and this is where I hope I can inspire someone to take this further. You could write—and a few people have tried—a natural history of religion, in which you would find, or speculate, on the role of plant drugs in a great many religions. In many traditions, cannabis has been used—the shamanic tradition in South America, Indian religion. Also cannabis in witchcraft: cannabis was used as an anti-sacrament in medieval witchcraft. There's also wine, which was mixed with other things in ancient Greece.

Drug plants have been a bridge between our world and other worlds. To what extent? We don't really know. But the '60s literature about this can be kind of dubious. A historian of religion writing in the early '60s asks: "Which was more likely to happen first ... the spontaneously generated idea of an afterlife in which the disembodied soul, liberated from the restrictions of time and space, experiences eternal bliss, or the accidental discovery of hallucinogenic plants that give a sense of euphoria, dislocate the center of consciousness, and distort time and space, making them balloon outward in greatly expanded vistas?"[2] If you put it that way, you know, it's hard to imagine this idea of an alternate universe, or a heaven, or a hell without drugs. But who knows?

I also think you could write—and it would be a very interesting book—a natural history of the imagination, looking at the role that plants, drugs, and fungi have played in certain movements in our cultural history. We know that many of the great thinkers of ancient Greece participated in an annual religious rite at which a hallucinogenic potion was consumed; for example, the mysteries of Eleusis, a harvest festival for Demeter. Everybody was sworn to secrecy about what was going on, but the theory is that ergot, a fungus that grows on grain—which ties into the Demeter thing—was consumed. At a molecular level, ergot is very closely related to LSD. We don't know what impact, if any, this had on Greek thought. It seems almost impious to suggest it had any, but what would we think if we discovered, say, a secret manuscript telling us that Plato's metaphysics were the result of his drug trips? For sure, one of the effects often reported by people who have used drugs could be called the Platonic effect. I'm quoting one writer, who talked about how under the influence of drugs "a cup 'looks like' the Platonic Ideal of a cup, a landscape looks like a landscape painting, a hamburger stands for all the trillions of hamburgers ever served, and so forth."[3] Drugs can make people feel as though they've been admitted to this realm of archetypal forms. A highly provisional idea.

Less provisional, though, is the role of drugs in romanticism. Coleridge spoke of it, and attributed to opium his notion of suspension of disbelief. There is also the idea of the secondary imagination, which starts with the world of fixed and dead objects and then "dissolves, diffuses, dissipates, in order to recreate."[4] This is an entirely new mode of imagination, and moving toward something much more like modern art. And this idea is owed to experiments with opium.

David Lenson, an interesting literary critic and musician, has written a great book called *On Drugs*. I recommend it, though it got very little attention when it came out a couple years ago. In an essay developed from *On Drugs* Lenson writes: "Our operative idea of imagination, dating back to the tail end of the eighteenth century, is inextricably linked to our history of intoxication. However criticism has tried to sanitize this process, we have to face the fact that some of our poets and theorists when apparently talking about imagination are really talking about getting high."[5]

Another area to look at, which Lenson looks at too, is improvisation. It's an amazing invention: folk, jazz, and rock improvisation. Without THC, specifically, I think improvisation is a very hard thing to imagine ever happening. I'm thinking in terms of the breaking of the linear flow, and the spatialization of time that goes on. And if you look at the history of rock and roll, you find that even a lot of the musicians whom we think of as acid- or LSD-influenced restricted themselves to cannabis when they were performing, and that acid was a whole other part of their lives. But THC was the drug for improvising. Lenson, talking about this now more as a musician, says about the solo,

> What is shared, the melody, is now his or hers to diffuse, dissolve, dissipate and recreate. The song's spatial aspect is redrawn, the improvisational expanse must be filled. Pot makes improvisational space virtual, opening dimensions and possibilities, so that the apparent infinity is interesting, rather than terrifying. Marijuana, the most user-constructed of all drugs, is the great yea-sayer, supporting and encouraging whatever is going on anywhere, and introducing very little of its own, or nothing of its own. It helps you understand that there is no predetermined right or wrong thing to do with the enormous space at your disposal, there is only what you do.[6]

With this very sketchy idea of a naturalistic imagination, I come to my second disclaimer. I don't want to sound like I'm offering a brief for drug use. I see drugs acting on human culture as mutations, in the same way that we understand that ultraviolet radiation creates mutation in genetic copying. Mutations are mistakes, and 99 percent of them are disastrous for the creature. Yet mistakes are a very important part of cultural evolution. Think of Harold Bloom's idea of the creativity of productive misreading. If nothing else, drugs lead to plenty of misreadings, most of them stupid. But every now and then, one comes along that changes everything. And that's really what I'm talking about, that drugs can do this for us.

Let me go a bit more into the harder science. One of the hardest clichés of the 1960s was that drugs like cannabis and others would unlock secrets of consciousness. Well, it turns out that Timothy Leary, Allen Ginsberg, and others were sort of right. THC, in particular, has thrown open a door onto the workings of the mind that they never would have imagined. We have learned things about neuroscience by studying cannabis. So the answer to understanding consciousness through drugs is from studying it, not from smoking it.

Trying to figure out how this plant works, Raphael Mechoulam isolates THC, delta-9-tetrahydrocannabinol—an important moment for neuroscience. And then a couple of years later, in 1988, a researcher at St. Louis University, named Allyn Howlett, discovers receptors in the brain and elsewhere, some very interesting places, that THC activates. One of those places is the uterus, which in view of the history of the drug helping with childbirth, makes a certain amount of sense. Mechoulam hypothesized that humans did not have these receptors in order to respond to THC in particular, so therefore the brain must produce another chemical—an endogenous cannabinoid—that these receptors were designed to interlock with. Four years later, in 1992, he discovers what this endogenous cannabinoid is, and he names it anandamide, which is the Sanskrit word for inner bliss. This is a man working in Israel and not in the US, under a grant from the National Institute of Drug Abuse. I don't think that name would have washed here. Later, another cannabinoid called (less poetically) 2AG was also discovered.

The question arises, what do we have this endogenous cannabinoid receptor system for? This is where it gets really interesting. Anandamide works very much like THC, but as a neurotransmitter it needs to be shorter-acting. You don't want your neurotransmitters hanging around in the brain for too long, or you'll just get clogged up with stuff. So they break down very quickly. You have re-uptake of your serotonin and things like that. But it does everything THC seems to do. It affects your short-term memory, pain, emotion, and appetite. One way you can prolong the effect of anandamide once it has been released in your brain, interestingly enough, is with chocolate. People often talk about the effects of chocolate on mood. Not so much that it's a drug itself, but it seems to prolong the effect of other drugs in the brain, anandamides specifically. And that may be why it makes us feel good.

I want to focus on memory, but this exploration of anandamide and 2AG has opened up some other interesting things, and one, of course, is appetite. The neuroscience of the munchies has basically been discovered. This just happened recently. Scientists were able to breed knockout mice, mice that don't have these receptors, and they found something very interesting. These knockout mice do not nurse. They do not have the desire to suck at their mother's breast, and they eventually die. But if you then administer THC to them, their appetite is restored and they thrive. So it appears that anandamide acts in a kind of seesaw relation with another chemical called leptin, the brain's signal for satiety. This opens up enormous possibilities for control of appetite, a very significant finding.

There's also been a lot of work done on another constituent of marijuana, cannabinoid, which is not psychoactive by itself. A lot of research has shown that it's a great anti-inflammatory, it's a neuroprotectant, and it may be what gives medical marijuana patients relief from things like epilepsy and anxiety. Now that cannabinoid can be separated from THC, you can actually produce a nonpsychoactive kind of drug, but there are a lot of patent issues. Well, actually, no one wants to develop a plant drug because you can't patent it, so nothing is happening with the discovery. There is a company, though, in England, GW Pharmaceuticals, that's in stage-three trials with a cannabinoid aerosol that you put under your tongue, which they're hoping to sell as a help for MS patients.

But back to this neuronetwork and anandamide. I asked both Howlett and Mechoulam why we have this cannabinoid system in the first place. Remember, it works just like THC. It's involved with pain relief, loss of short-term memory, sedation, mild cognitive impairment. Howlett said, "All those things that you've just said are exactly what Adam and Eve would want after being thrown out of Eden. You couldn't design a more perfect drug"—this is her quote to me—"for getting Eve through the pain of childbirth and helping Adam endure a life of physical toil." She's basically saying that this is a brain-zone drug for coping with the human condition.

Mechoulam had an even more interesting take on it. He thinks anandamide would be found to be crucially involved in emotion. For example, if the experience of seeing his grandson entering the room brings happiness, the brain's cannabinoid could be the missing link that "translates" the objective reality of the grandson rushing toward him into a subjective change in his emotions.

But then I asked Mechoulam, "Why would we evolve a chemical that would make us forget, that would affect our short-term memory?" That seems maladaptive. His answer was one of the great "aha!" moments I had when I was working on this book. He said, "Well, do you really want to remember all the faces you saw in the subway this morning, all the faces in the supermarket?" And I realized at that moment, well, of course, forgetting is not a defect of a mental operation, although it can certainly be that; forgetting is a mental operation. It's almost as important as remembering. He believes that there is another seesaw there. There is a chemical that helps us lock in memory, and anandamide works on the other side to make us get rid of memory.

This also relates to memory loss with regard to trauma. We need cannabinoids to forget horrible things that have happened. Scientists have worked with mice that got an electric shock every time they heard a certain tone. This conditioned them to be fearful when they heard the tone. When you play the tone for normal mice, the first time they react fearfully, but over time if you play the tone enough they forget and they just go about their business. And this is what happened. But these preconditioned shock-treatment mice that cannot use the anandamide their brains are producing never forget the fear—it is never extinguished. So I think it's very interesting that if we didn't have anandamide we might not ever be able to get over things like posttraumatic stress phobias and neuroses of various kinds, even chronic pain. It's often been observed that pain is the hardest of all experiences to summon with memory. You know something felt really bad, but it's very hard to recreate that emotion the way you can recreate other emotions, and it may be that we have the cannabinoids to thank for that.

Now, as I looked for literature on forgetting, I found that there's very little of it. There's a lot more on memory, which makes sense, I guess, given that memory is crucial to identity, to culture. But I would argue that forgetting is really crucial, too, for our psychological health, for certain spiritual experiences, and even for learning. Memory is important for learning, but so is forgetting. One great thinker who has written a little bit on forgetting is William James. Daniel Boorstin, in *The Discoverers*, quotes James: "In the practical use of our intellect, forgetting is as important a function as remembering.... If we remembered everything, we should on most occasions be as ill off as if we remembered nothing. It would take as long for us to recall a space of time as it took the original time to elapse." That's a kind of spacey idea. And James goes on, "We should never get ahead with our thinking. All recollected times undergo...foreshortening; and this foreshortening is due to the omission of an enormous number of facts which filled them. 'We thus reach the paradoxical result'"—he is such a blind writer, isn't he?—"'that one condition of remembering is that we should forget. Without totally forgetting a prodigious number of states of consciousness and momentarily forgetting a large number, we could not remember at all.'"[7] A very sweet idea.

We actually do have one great case study of a man who remembered everything. I don't know if any of you are familiar with a book by the great Russian psychologist, A. R. Luria, *The Mind of the Mnemonist*. Luria is a very interesting writer; he's the model, I think, for Oliver Sacks's work. Luria wrote a book about a Russian Jew he treated in the '30s whom he calls "S." Any sequence of words or numbers or abstract symbols Luria presented to this man, "S" could remember and recall. The limit of his memory was never reached in any test he took. He could bring it all back indefinitely. He saw the figures as images, everything presented itself as sheets of paper, and he could see all the numbers you gave him. He could recite them forwards or backwards or any way you wanted. He visualized it all, sort of like a memory palace. And he became a mnemonist, a professional memory performer, and he did three shows a day, where people would put forth these outrageously long list of words and things, and he would remember them all.

But as time went on, "S" became tormented by his inability to forget, either long- or short-term. Luria says that "traces left by one stimulus did not inhibit those of another. They showed no signs of becoming extinguished with time, nor did they become any less selective with the years." Images of these numbers and words he was memorizing in these performances would just come unbidden to his mind, and they began to drive him crazy. And he devised mental exercises—he did visualize everything—where he would actually crumple up these pages in his mind and burn them, throw them in the fire. And then he would look in the fire, see the crumpled paper, and still make out the words and images and numbers. It was a torment. And when you read him a story, every word summoned another image, so that if you said, "The man leaned on a tree," "S" would get this image of a forest, and then if the next line was, "and he looked into a shop window..."—you get the idea. "S" is quoted as saying, "No, this is too much. Each word calls up images, they collide with one another, and the result is chaos; I can't make anything out of this."

Just imagine if you couldn't lose images that came into your mind. "S" couldn't get the gist of a story or an argument, because he couldn't forget what wasn't important. All that suggests that abstracting, or distilling, depends on forgetting, depends on mental editing. "S" had to learn tricks for forgetting, the way we have to learn tricks for memory. He would close a white curtain, the image would disappear, and that seemed to work. Perhaps "S" was like those preconditioned shock-treatment mice.

Friedrich Nietzsche is the other writer who has written about forgetting. An essay written in 1876 called "On the Uses and Disadvantages of History for Life" is just a paean to the virtues of forgetting. It starts like this, "Consider the cattle, grazing as they pass you by: they do not know what is meant by yesterday or today. They leap about, eat, rest, digest, leap about again, and so from morn till night and from day to day, fettered to the moment and its pleasure or displeasure, and thus neither melancholy nor bored." No mnemonist here. "A human being may well ask an animal, 'Why do you not speak to me of your happiness but only stand and gaze and me?' The animal would like to answer and say, 'The reason is I always forget what I was going to say'—but then he forgot this answer too, and stayed silent."[8] It's a great essay, and he's talking about how cheerfulness, the good conscience, the joyful deed of doing anything really depends on forgetting. He's very much like Emerson and Thoreau in this. He believes you can't have a great passion without conviction, or without forgetting. He says those who can act are those who, "forget[] most things so as to do one thing."[9] To do, or I would add, to think or to feel, and certainly to write. I know writing for me involves prodigious amounts of forgetting. And all this I'm very attracted to, because I have a terrible memory. This is always a consolation to me. But Emerson and Thoreau, too, have this idea of laboring under the weight of convention in the past, and nature became their technology to help them forget and to push things out of the way.

To paraphrase Nietzsche, the ability to forget most things in order to attend to one is the key to what I hope is going on, still, in this room right now. Your ability to attend to my words, think about it, depends on forgetting 99 percent of the sense information coming in right now. Think about all you're not thinking about right now, just for a second—the discomfort of your chair for sitting this long, the roar of the ventilation systems, the lights, the architectural detailings, the screen, your dinner plans, your homework, the taste in your mouth, the smells, how all of this talk of intoxication, maybe, makes you want to have a drink or maybe something stronger. I mean, forgetting is not just about the past, it's an important thing to remember. To be here now depends on forgetting a great deal of sensory information in the near present, and even forgetting the future, too—worries, anticipations, intentions, all these things can be forgotten also.

So what I'm suggesting is that anandamide is crucial to this operation, to editing out all of the near-term memories, so that you can attend to what is before you.

Andrew Weil, as I mentioned earlier, talks about a lot of this in *The Natural Mind*. "Disturbance of immediate memory," he says, "seems to be a common feature of all altered states of consciousness in which attention is focused on the present."[10] So I think this goes beyond the altered states of consciousness. We've been talking about cannabis, but sport gives it to us also, and thrill seeking, any of the different technologies we have for immersing ourselves in the present. You cannot toe that line, Thoreau said, without ridding yourself of the past and the future.

This notion of the present is the goal of meditation, and it's the goal of experiencing what we call transcendence. The seeker, the spiritual seeker, if you think about it, works to put aside past and future, the better to toe the line of the present moment. There are many examples in both Eastern and Western thought where this experience of the present becomes our door onto eternity. In the West, Boethius said, the spiritual goal is "to hold and possess the whole fullness of life in one moment, here and now, past and present and to come."[11] And there's the Zen master who said, "Awakening to this present instant we realize the infinite is the finite of each instant."[12] What I'm suggesting is we can't get from here to there without first forgetting, and we will find that it is the cannabinoids that mediate this process.

But isn't there something a little artificial about this? How does this make us feel? Is a chemically conditioned spiritual experience any less real? Does it make a difference that the chemical involved is endogenous or artificial, and why? Huxley wrote about this a little bit. He said that all our experiences are chemically conditioned, of course, and if we imagine that some of them are purely spiritual, purely intellectual, or purely aesthetic, it is merely because we have never troubled to investigate the internal chemical environment at the moment of their occurrence. So humans have found many ways to fiddle with their brain chemistry. And that's exactly what's going on—meditation, fasting, risk. Even with the placebo effect, we're not just fooling ourselves into thinking we're happier when we take a placebo antidepressant, we're actually producing more serotonin.

So why does using a plant like cannabis still strike us, for spiritual purposes, as false and cheap? Is it the work ethic—no pain, no gain? I think the problem is really the provenance of those chemicals in this case, that they come from outside us, and even worse, that they come from nature, from plants. We have a name for someone who believes spiritual knowledge might come from such a corridor, and it's "pagan." And we have the story about that, and it's called Genesis. So what was the knowledge God wanted to keep from Adam and Eve in the garden? I would argue that the content was not nearly as important as the form, that there was spiritual knowledge to be had from nature, from a plant. The tree in the garden was a seriously psychoactive plant, and the new monotheistic faith had sought to break the human bond with magic nature, to disenchant the world of plants and animals by directing our gaze to a single God in the sky. But this new God can't just pretend the tree of knowledge doesn't exist, not when generations of plant-worshiping and -consuming pagans know better. So the tree of knowledge is allowed to grow in the Garden of Eden, but ringed around it now is the powerful taboo—taste it and you will be punished. And interestingly, the punishment involves remembering, involves falling into history and shame. This, I suggest, is the drug war's first victory.

But I want to end on a much more positive and, well, intoxicating note. This is a passage from my book:

> Plants with the power to revise our thoughts and perceptions, to provoke metaphor and wonder, challenge the cherished Judeo-Christian belief that our conscious, thinking selves somehow stand apart from nature, have achieved that kind of transcendence.
>
> Just what happens to this flattering self-portrait if we discover that transcendence itself owes to molecules that flow through our brains and at the same time through the plants in the garden? If some of the brightest fruits of human culture are in fact rooted deeply in this black earth, with the plants and fungi? Is matter, then, still as mute as we've come to think? Does it mean that spirit too is part of nature?
>
> There may be no older idea in the world. Friedrich Nietzsche once described Dionysian intoxication as "nature overpowering mind,"—nature having her way with us. The Greeks understood that this was not something to be undertaken lightly or too often. Intoxication was a carefully circumscribed ritual for them, never a way to live, because they understood that Dionysus can make angels of us or animals, it all depends. Even so, letting nature have her way with us now and again still seems like a useful thing to do, if only as a check on our

abstracted upward gaze back down to Earth for a time. What a reenchantment of the world that would be, to look around us and see that the plants and the trees of knowledge grow in the garden still.[13]

Endnotes

1 Aldous Huxley, *The Doors of Perception and Heaven and Hell* (New York, 1963), p. 62.

2 Huston Smith (quoting Mary Barnard), "Do Drugs Have Religious Import?" (1964), in *Cleansing the Doors of Perception: The Religious Significance of Entheogenic Plants and Chemicals* (New York, 2001), p. 19.

3 David Lenson, *On Drugs* (Minneapolis, 1995), p. 104.

4 S. T. Coleridge, "On the Imagination, or Esemplastic Power," in *Biographia Literaria* (Oxford, 1907), p. 202.

5 David Lenson, "The High Imagination," Hess Family Lecture, University of Virginia, April 29, 1999, p. 8.

6 Ibid., pp. 14–15.

7 Daniel J. Boorstin, *The Discoverers: A History of Man's Search to Know His World and Himself* (New York, 1985), p. 488.

8 Friedrich Nietzsche, "On the Uses and Disadvantages of History for Life," in *Untimely Meditations*, trans. R. J. Hollingdale (Cambridge, 1997), pp. 60–61.

9 Ibid., p. 64.

10 Andrew Weil, *The Natural Mind: An Investigation of Drugs and the Higher Consciousness* (Boston, 1986), p. 90.

11 Boethius quoted in ibid., p. 91.

12 Quoted in Lama Surya Das, *Awakening the Buddha Within* (New York, 1997), p. 305.

13 Michael Pollan, *The Botany of Desire* (New York, 2001), pp. 178–79.

Part II: Dialogues

Maya Lin

with Thomas Laqueur, Andrew Barshay, Stephen Greenblatt, and Stanley Saitowitz

Grounds for Remembering

Thomas Laqueur

MY PARTICULAR INTEREST is the question of how a name relates to place and memory, a problem that goes back almost to the beginning of Western thinking on the subject of commemoration. Quintilian, as well as Cicero, cites as the inventor of mnemonics Simonides the poet, who could identify the mangled and apparently unidentifiable bodies of those who had been crushed in a collapsed palace by remembering where they had stood when they were alive.

In general, the idea of connecting a name and the place of a body in war had almost no resonance until, very dramatically, in late 1914, in the early stages of a war of unimaginable destruction, there began an unprecedented and massive bureaucratic effort to mark the graves of each and every dead soldier. It then left on the battlefronts of Western Europe over four million names in relatively close proximity to where the body that had been associated with that name fell. To be even more specific, we have in the archives of the

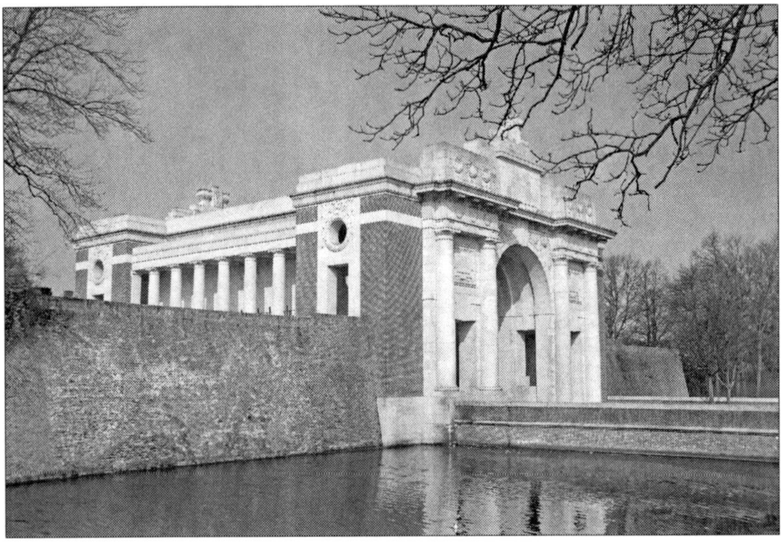

Menin Gate, Ypres, Belgium

organization that finally took over the task of counting the dead, ordnance survey maps which give within ten meters the location of over 350,000 bodies that were disinterred so as to be identified and reburied nearby under a name-bearing marker or one announcing that the name was unknown but to God. World War I, in short, witnessed the most dramatic explosion of names on a landscape in world history.

Let us take the British experience as an example. There were 1,075,293 British dead in World War I. Of these, 557,520 bodies were identified and buried in individual marked graves. A further 180,861 dead were found, but even after tremendous effort of the sort suggested by Simonides—asking survivors where they had last seen someone, consulting official diaries that recount daily military action—they could not be identified, and were buried under markers bearing the legend "Known but to God." Their names joined the names of 336,912 other bodies that had simply disappeared, bodies that were never found—fragmented, beaten into the mud as the war moved back and forth over them—on a series of memorials which follow the battlefronts of World War I, and which were meant to place the name near the place where the person had fallen.

Let us consider some of the monuments starting at the northern part of the Western Front in Ypres. In the city of Ypres, on a long, tunnel-like structure modeled on a seventeenth-century fort in Nancy, the distinguished architect Sir Reginald Blomfield managed to arrange panels bearing about 55,000 names. The original idea had been to place all the unidentified dead from the three major battles of Ypres on this one monument, but it turned out there were simply too many. Then the problem became how to make each set of lists mean something that was not too self-evidently arbitrary. This particular assemblage of names, for example, came to be defined as all those who had died unknown in the Salient before August 1917. One walks into this structure through a classical arch. A niche in one pillar offers a book listing, with numbing specificity, the names engraved on every inch of the walls, stairwells, and passageways.

From the time the memorial was built in the late 1920s, visitors have left poppies and wreaths near the names of those they came to commemorate. Often the ashes of poppies were put on individual names by veterans' organizations. I think this activity underscores the extent to which, as would become the case in the Vietnam memorial, the names *themselves* almost immediately became places of pilgrimage.

Other monuments to the fallen whose names had become unmoored from their bodies trace the contours of the front. The Tyne Cot Memorial, in the midst of turnip fields that had witnessed the horrible fighting of November 1917 through early 1918 at the Battle of Passchendaele, encloses 33,488 names on the four sides of the courtyard, in which there are another 11,980 gravestones. The disembodied names of 11,447 men dead from the battles of Armentières, Aubers Ridge, Hazebrouck, and more line the colonnades of the Ploegsteert Memorial. At Vimy Ridge in the valley

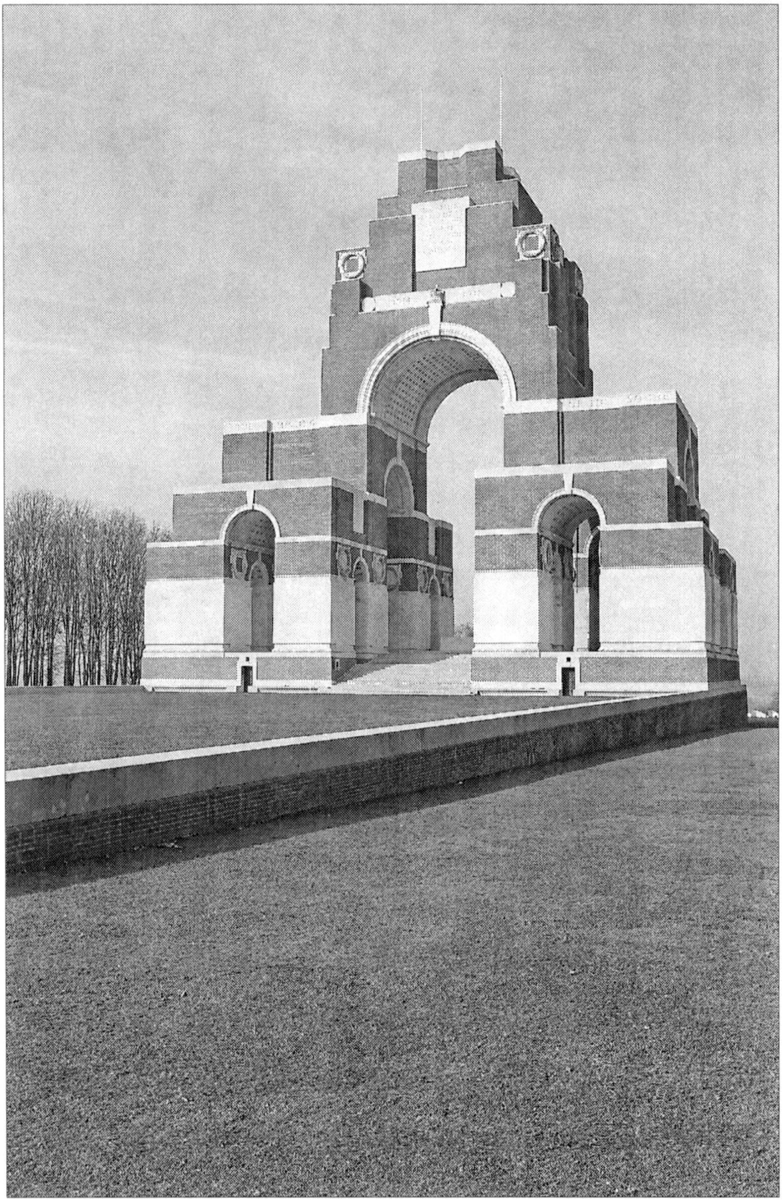

Thiepval Memorial, France

of the Somme, a memorial by Walter Allward overlooks the hill up which Canadian forces fought their way: two burning figures frame the names of 11,500 men with no known resting place. And so on.

The vocabulary of the Thiepval Memorial, however, is very different from these other monuments. The architecture alludes to the cathedral in Albert, a small city near Thiepval, which was famous because the Madonna on its steeple was almost knocked off her perch during a period of heavy shelling but miraculously held on. The Thiepval Memorial was meant to speak to this local event, but it was also, and perhaps incongruously, meant to be a modernist grid for 73,412 names.

Thiepval is a massive brick structure with sixteen huge columns that bear, on three of four sides, the seemingly endless panels of names. Here, as elsewhere, each name is intended to refer to one specific body and only to that body. When there are two R. Clarks, for example, they are distinguished by their serial numbers. When someone is "known as" someone else—i.e., by another name—that fact, too, is specifically noted.

The British had no mass graves; the Germans had a goodly number. That said, however, the names were also a central feature of memorialization in these mass graves. The names of several thousand German students who died in the Battle of Langemarck in Belgium, one of the earlier battles of the war, are recorded on the walls of a small Greek chapel on the side of the entry gate to an enormous memorial space that shelters the bodies of tens of thousands of the fallen from later battles near the site. Immediately beyond this chapel, one comes to a mass grave of unidentified bodies whose specificity as the locus of memory is thematized in the inscription: "In the cemetery rest the remains of 44,061 German soldiers of the war, 1914 to 1918," followed by an inscription that refers to Jacob's being renamed Israel after his struggle with the angel: "I called you by your *name*, and you are mine."

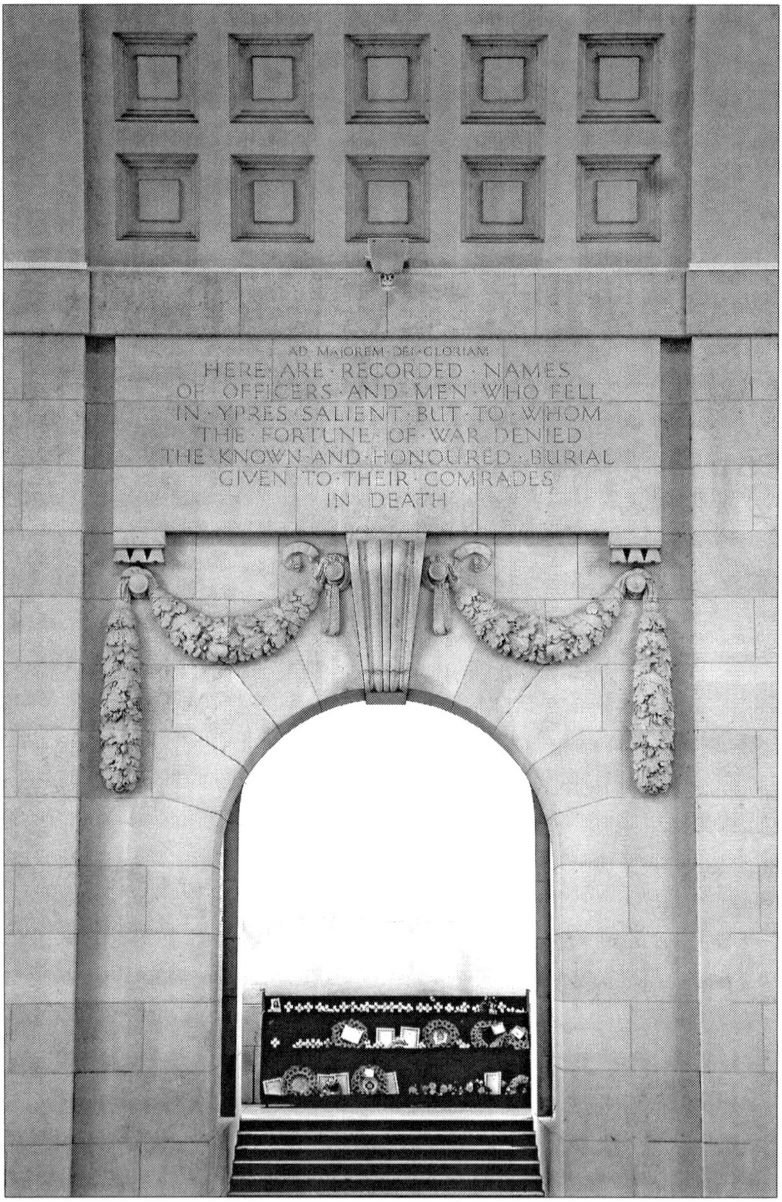

Interior, Menin Gate. Inscription: HERE ARE RECORDED NAMES OF OFFICERS AND MEN WHO FELL IN YPRES SALIENT BUT TO WHOM THE FORTUNE OF WAR DENIED THE KNOWN AND HONOURED BURIAL GIVEN TO THEIR COMRADES IN DEATH

Pictures make clear that naming is in some sense about the arithmetic sublime, the notation and representation of a gigantic number—in this case, of bodies. A tablet listing all the German names in the cemetery has them in run-on form; you read it without breaking. The views of the cemeteries at the Battle of Verdun show rows of Christian graves (marked by crosses), Muslim graves (marked by stones), and Jewish graves (by a portion of the Star of David). At the other end of that scale are the bodies that were gathered up into thousands of very small cemeteries.

Quite frequently, comrades would draw maps locating the battlefield graves of fallen soldiers and send the maps to the deceased's relatives. There are tens of thousands of these maps extant. In addition, the Imperial War Graves Commission in 1915 began paying photographers to provide pictures of temporary graves using these maps to locate them. (The case I'll cite at the end will show that in some instances the place where the person was buried had been obliterated by the war and the map was useless for locating the grave.) A great deal was made at the time of the fact that people were actually interested in the location of a particular person's remains, or of a name.

Names, as Proust puts it at the beginning of *Le côté des Guermantes,* offer us "an image of the unknowable which we have poured into their mold. They are transformed to suit the life of our imagination."

The point that I want to emphasize is that the number of things that one can and did do with these names—how the imagination transformed them—is legion. Hidden from what you have seen in the slides and monuments are the sheer technical difficulties of gathering so many names into any sort of meaningful assemblage. We can imagine the man in charge of building a memorial writing his boss and asking, "Is there any reasonable interpretation of the data that would give us so low a figure as 50,000 missing, and if so, what is that interpretation?" What does it mean to have those 50,000 names rather than some other 50,000 names organized in some other fashion?

There are also tremendous design problems in how to list names in an era when nobody had actually built memorials listing numbers of such magnitude. Harvard Memorial Chapel, with about 200 names, for example, is on an entirely different scale. In response to this situation, the artistic advisor to the War Graves Commission had proposed a solution which Maya Lin later adopted in the Vietnam Veterans Memorial: listing them as if in a great, long sentence to be read. This was opposed by the Labor and Socialist members on the commission, who argued that a crucial objective in these monuments would be making it easy for relatives to find the names of the deceased. It would not do to tell the bereaved that the appearance of the monument would gain if the names were grouped together in continuous lines. He thought, and the commission agreed with him, that each name should stand for itself, one to a line, and hence the sort of listing that we have seen here. That, it turns out from the veterans' response to Maya Lin's monument, was a misreading of the psychology of survivors.

This leads again to the issue of representing the sublime. People at this time had to answer the question, "How do we actually imagine a million dead people?" The answer was reached, in a kind of hypernominalist way, by showing them as specifically as possible. "Do you want to know what a million people looks like? That's what a million looks like." It's extremely specific and, in their account, *anti*representational.

There are also issues of nationalism and imperialism—the politics of mass democracies, of how to explain armies that became conscript armies, though much of this began before conscription in the British case—but I would prefer to conclude with an instance that is about something much more intimate than these issues. As Stephen Greenblatt told me earlier, my account of the development of naming as a central feature of commemoration seemed to say that it is all because of Trollope. In some sense, he's right.

There was an exchange of letters between Will Martin, who was an infantry private and one-time groom in the British army, and his fiancée, Emily Chitticks, who was a servant on the next farm. There are seventy-five manuscript letters from him to her until he was killed in March 1917, and there are twenty-three letters from her to him extant. Five of those letters he never saw. They were returned to her unopened in a little package appropriately stamped "Killed in Action." In 1921 she collected these letters into a bundle called "Will's Letters" along with a chronology of their relationship, a pencil verse about how she wouldn't see him on earth again, and a couplet in ink saying,

> Sleep, darling, sleep on foreign shore
> I loved and loved you dearly, but Jesus loves you more.

And there is also a note saying that she wanted this packet buried with her just as her heart was already buried in Flanders Field. Her life, she said, had ended with his.

Emily Chitticks actually died in a council flat about four years ago and was buried at the expense of the state. Some time subsequently, someone cleared out her effects, found these letters, and gave them to the Imperial War Museum, where I opened them.

It's a remarkable letter exchange in its novelistic quality. What I mean is that these people attempt to read feelings into each other; that they write with the sensibility of domestic fiction. They talk about their dreams. "It was strange to dream of you in civilian clothes," she writes to him, "because I never saw you in civilian clothes." He writes to her, "I didn't want to act this way because I knew it would make you anxious." She tells him about the two little, dear puppies born at Suffolk House in her last letter to him, "Two sheepdogs they are, and such pretty and playful ones." He tells her about death on the front. "I've seen some graves today, dear, of officers and men who were killed in action. They had wooden crosses and wood railings around the graves. They were really done up very nicely. Well, dear Emily, I hope you've received all my letters."

Her last letters to him come back and she hears nothing. Finally she gets a letter from his friend saying where the body is—in a temporary grave. She writes back, "How can I thank you for the information you sent me regarding my sweetheart Will Martin? It's a terrible blow. No one knows but myself what it means." Then she writes to the War Graves Commission as to where Will's grave is. She gets a little card saying that he is buried at a point just southwest of Écoust-Saint Mein, which is southeast of Arras. That site however, she learned later, was shelled, so the grave had disappeared and no trace could be found of Will Martin.

After several more inquiries, the War Graves Commission assured Emily that Will's name would be preserved.

> You may rest assured that the dead who have no known resting place will be honored equally with the others and that each case will be dealt with upon full consideration of its merits as regarding the site and place of the memorial.

In fact, and I saw it there, Will Martin's name along with 10,000 others is on the Memorial to the Missing at the Faubourg d'Amiens for soldiers who were lost in the Arras sector in the Battle of the Somme.

Maya Lin

I will continue discussing these World War I memorials, but I'll be taking them in a different direction. I too am going to mention Lutyens's Thiepval Memorial because for me it is the prime inspiration for the Vietnam Veterans Memorial.

There are two points I should mention before I begin. I've never seen the Thiepval Memorial. My accounts of it came through an art history professor and his experience and description of it in a class I took. I would also like to draw attention to the notion of the individual name and the importance of the name. In reflecting on the work I've done in designing, specifically in designing the

Vietnam memorial, a certain name comes to mind in addition to Thiepval, and that's Woolsey Hall at Yale University.

Any undergraduate who was at Yale when I started there in 1977–78 saw one or two men in Woolsey Hall always etching the names of the alumni from Yale or of the Yale students who had been killed in Vietnam. As you walked through the hall to and from classes, you'd register that there were these two men etching the names. And you'd unconsciously register the time it was taking to etch in each name, and the time somebody had lost. It was always *there*. It was ever present. The actual work stopped some time in my sophomore or junior year, but I think, like every other student passing through there, you could not help but be quiet as you walked through that hall. Also, you couldn't *not* touch the names. This, I think, is very important and always will be in my work. The opportunity to touch the names is a little different from the experience of a lot of the World War I memorials, where in many cases you cannot approach the names, even though you are reading them, because they're much higher off the ground. I would draw attention to the symbolic nature of listing the names and the impossibility of reaching some of them.

I designed the Vietnam memorial in a class on funereal architecture. In all, it took me a few weeks to design it. It also took me nearly the whole semester to learn how to describe it. In the class we had focused on architecture's involvement in how we grieve, how we mourn, how we deal with the notion of death through the built form. A previous assignment had been to design a memorial to World War III. I had come up with a design that proved to be a futile, somewhat terrifying journey. My professor at the time was horrified. In fact he came up to me afterwards and said "Maya, if I had a brother who had died in this war, I'd be so offended that I would never want to come to this memorial." I looked at him and said, "Andy, it's World War III. We're not going to be around afterwards."

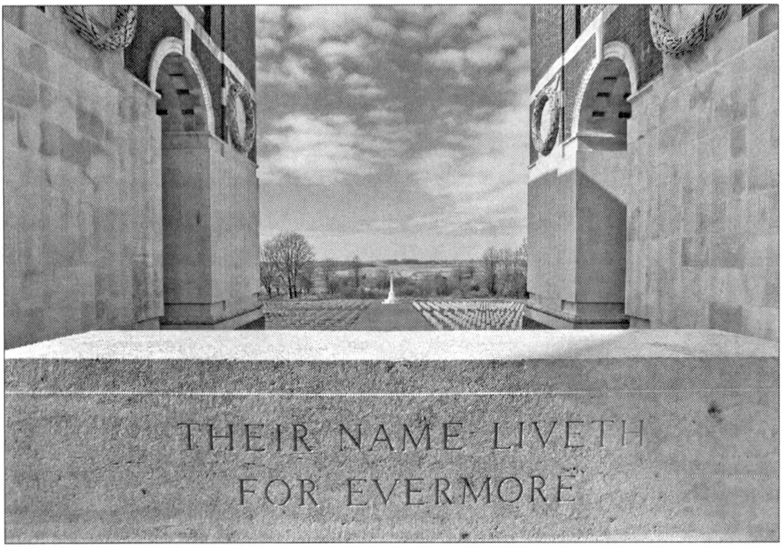

Thiepval Memorial. Inscription: THEIR NAME LIVETH FOR EVERMORE

That incident underscores the question that preoccupied me while designing the Vietnam memorial, "What is the purpose of a memorial?" I made some conscious decisions before ever designing it, verbally articulating what I wanted to accomplish. One thing that was very important to me was to be extremely honest about the facts of not so much the *politics* of war but the *results* of war. I also thought it important to register loss on a fundamental, individual level. The memorial focuses on the *individual* loss, because I thought the experience of visiting the memorial should be a private awakening, a private awareness of that loss.

Although I studied memorials from the earliest funeral steles to contemporary commemorative works, I was most moved by the World War I memorials, particularly those photgraphed by the British War Graves Commission. What I found most influential was the expression of great loss and tragedy surrounding these works; they focused on the people who gave their lives rather than on a

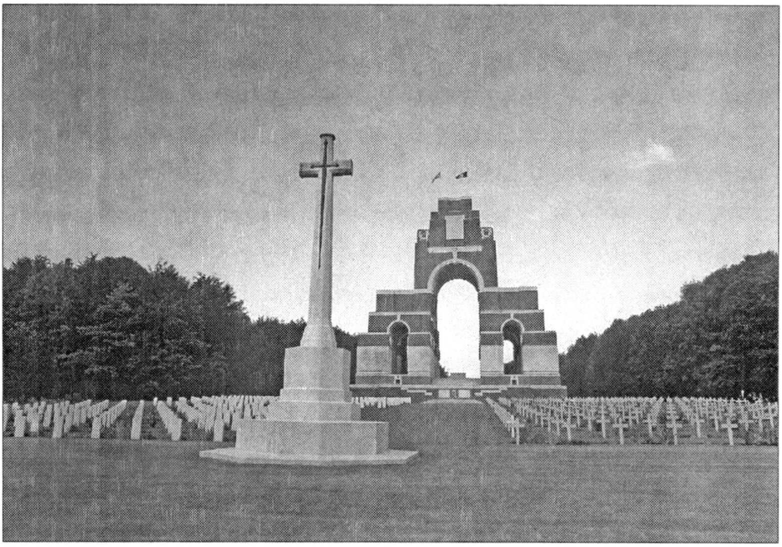

Lawn and cemetery at Thiepval Memorial

country's or leader's politicized statements of victory. You begin to see emerging the acknowledgment of the individual.

I designed the project that everyone now sees, but at the time I hadn't decided to enter it into the competition. I made that decision the following semester, and, although the design was essentially complete, it took me weeks to write a description of the design, which I felt would be as essential to understanding it, since the design seemed to be so simple in the drawings.

About that time, Professor Scully started talking about the Thiepval Memorial in class. He described it as an abstraction of a scream that you walk through. The design of the Thiepval Memorial is based on the church Tom Laqueur mentioned earlier, the church at Albert that had been shelled and whose Madonna remained just barely attached during the shelling. The shelling of the church reiterated itself into the abstraction of the memorial and also, as Professor Scully had mentioned, the expression of pain and anguish—the open, gaping mouth you walk through as you enter the structure.

As you drive up to the memorial you see it surrounded by a lawn. You have to break through and walk across this encircling lawn in order to approach the structure. As you enter and finally stand at the center of the memorial you are flanked by views of cemeteries; crosses on the left, stones on the right. Professor Scully describes this experience as a passage to an awareness, where you stop at the center and are fully aware of the immensity of the loss. You've walked through names of fallen soldiers, and you are left overlooking these very simple gravestone markers. As he described it, the journey takes us to a certain point of awareness that we cannot go beyond, even though we can continue walking.

I started writing the final part of the design, the accompanying written description, while he was lecturing. He couldn't figure out what I was doing. I had pretty much finished writing by the end of his lecture. I made several careful revisions afterwards because I realized that a lot of what I was doing wouldn't be immediately understood just by looking at the design. I ended up drafting this text directly onto the boards because I could never get it "right." It took me longer to write this than it took me to design the piece itself. I thought I'd read it today because it's something I've never really discussed publicly.

> Walking through this park, the memorial appears as a rift in the earth, a long, polished black stone wall emerging from and receding into the earth. Approaching the memorial, the ground slopes gently downward, and the low walls, emerging on either side, growing out of the earth, extend and converge at a point below and ahead. Walking into the grassy site contained by the walls of the memorial, we can barely make out the carved names upon the memorial walls. These names, seemingly infinite in number, convey the sense of overwhelming numbers while unifying those individuals into a whole. For this memorial is meant not as a monument to the individ-

ual, but rather as a memorial to the men and women who died during this war as a whole.

The memorial is composed not as an unchanging monument, but as a moving composition to be understood as we move into and out of it. The passage itself is gradual; the descent to the origin, slow; but it is at the origin that the meaning of this memorial is to be fully understood. At the intersection of these walls, on the right side, at the wall's top, is carved the date of the first death. It is followed by the names of those who have died in the war in chronological order. These names continue on this wall, appearing to recede into the earth at the wall's end. The names resume on the left wall as the wall emerges from the earth back to the origin where the date of the last death is carved at the bottom of this wall. Thus, the war's beginning and end meet. The war is complete, coming full circle, yet broken by the earth that bounds the angle's open side and contained within the earth itself. As we turn to leave, we see these walls stretching into the distance, directing us to the Washington Monument to the left, and the Lincoln Memorial to the right, thus bringing the Vietnam memorial into historical context. We the living are brought to a concrete realization of these deaths. Brought to a sharp awareness of such a loss, it is up to each individual to resolve or come to terms with this loss. For death is, in the end, a personal and private matter and the area contained within this memorial is a quiet place meant for personal reflection and private reckoning.

The thick granite walls, each two hundred feet long and ten feet below the ground at their lowest point, gradually ascending toward ground level, effectively act as a sound barrier, yet are of such a height and length so as not to appear threatening or enclosing. The actual area is wide and shallow, allowing for a sense of privacy, and the sunlight from the memorial's southern exposure along with the grassy park surrounding and within its walls contribute to the serenity of the area. This memorial is for those who have died, and for us to remember them.

The memorial's origin is located approximately at the center

> of this site, its legs each extending two hundred feet toward the Washington Monument and the Lincoln Memorial. The walls contained on one side by the earth are ten feet below the ground at their point of origin, gradually lessening in height until they finally recede totally into the earth at their ends. The walls are to be made of hard, polished black granite with the names to be carved in a simple Trajan letter three quarters of an inch high, allowing nine inches in length for each name.
>
> The memorial's construction involves recontouring the area within the walls' boundaries so as to provide for an easily accessible descent, but as much of the site as possible should be left untouched, including trees. The area should remain a park for all to enjoy.

The only significant change that had to be made on the original design was the size of the names. I'd made a horrible error in mathematics, and each wall would have ended up being too long. In order to accommodate the names at the original size, the walls of the memorial would have touched the Washington Monument and cut through the Lincoln Memorial because, as Tom mentioned, the immense number of the names made the sizing of the names the biggest technical problem. I think that this memorial couldn't have been done in the past, because at the time the World War I memorials were being built, for example, each name had to be hand cut. At the size we needed to carve the letters, the work couldn't have been done manually. Each letter ends up being about half an inch tall, which was considered impossible. But because of computers and new mechanical etching techniques, the engravers were able to do it.

I'm going to end my talk with a few points about memorials in general and my work in particular.

I consider the work I do memorials, not monuments; in fact I've often thought of them as antimonuments. I think I don't make objects; I make places. I think that is very important—the places set a stage for experience and for understanding experience. I don't

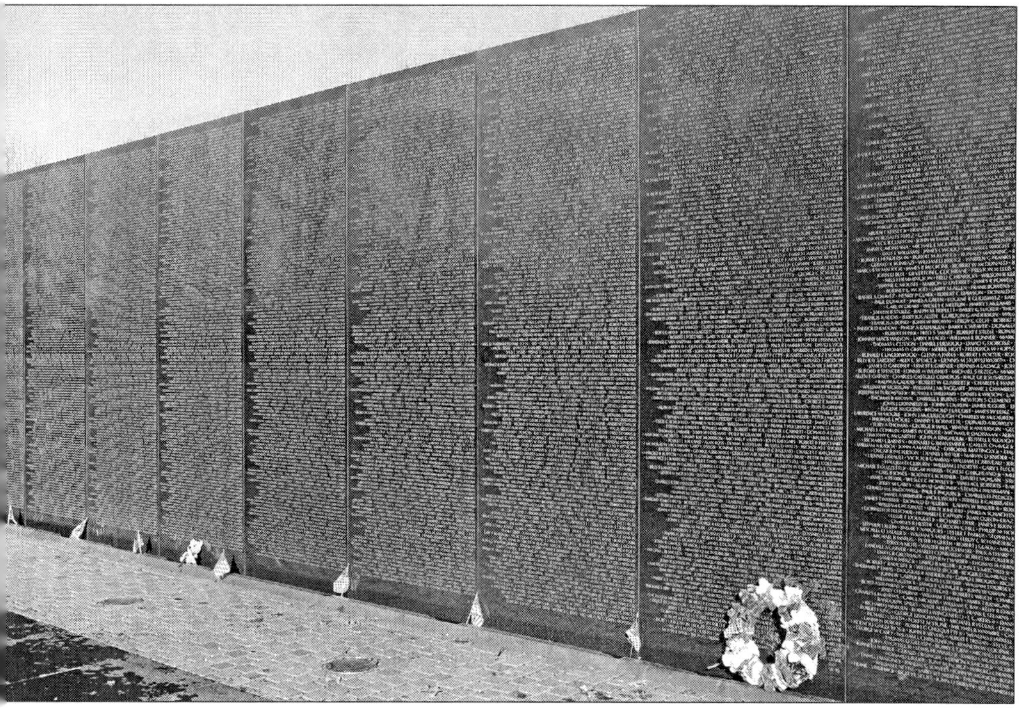

Vietnam Veterans Memorial, Washington, DC

want to say these places are stages where you act out, but rather places where something happens within the viewer.

I think there's a very big difference between reading a book in a public place and reading a billboard in a public place. My works try to bring out the notion of the intimacy of reading that which is a book—literally. Even in the Vietnam memorial you'll notice that the panels open like a book. The panels are numbered like the pages in a book. At the apex you can see that on the right-hand panels the words rag right, and on the left they rag left. One change we made to the original design was to add a prologue and an epilogue. This is an interesting point of convergence between the notions of text and art and content.

I faced two design problems aside from the political controversies concerning the building of this piece. The first one was the chronology, which was absolutely critical. One of the things about

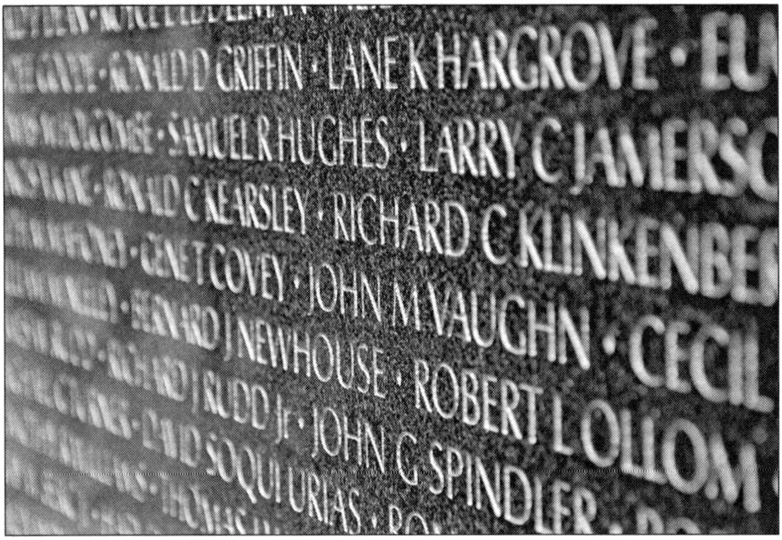

Lettering detail, Vietnam Veterans Memorial

remembering the past is that you really have to make it relevant to the present. You have to bring it to life. My task seemed to be to convince people that the memorial is a thread of life that we can put ourselves into. Keeping the order of names chronological allows a returning veteran literally to find his time. Within a couple of panels he will also find the names of other people who served with him. He is brought into an immediate experience of the past. MIA advocates wanted to list MIAs separately and alphabetically. I was able to convince these groups that separating out the MIAs would have been a disaster and would have broken the entire context of the piece. We finally convinced them to agree to a notation so that if an MIA later came back or was officially declared dead, the notation could be changed.

The second problem was the size of the text, the technical problem of placing such an enormous text on the form of the monument. We debated the issue of how small the letters could be and still be read. I came up against incredible opposition, because any stonecutter will tell you that you absolutely cannot read a letter less than an inch tall. They were thinking in terms of a very public monument and these were conventional measurements. In order to fit the text and have the lettering be of a size that wouldn't overpower the site, we went down to about five eighths of an inch. In so doing, I really came to see the text as a book that happens to be there for everyone to read, but not to be read the way public monuments are normally read, which would have required a much larger text. The size of the letters also allows people to see the lettering as a part of the form itself, like a beautiful fabric, so that the text begins to symbolize something other than just the names carved there.

Andrew Barshay

I want to shift the scene from Europe and America to Asia. The grotesque harvest of bodies and souls that we know about from Europe in the First World War and the Second World War has, in the case of the Second World War, its counterpart in Asia. I want to talk about some aspects of issues relevant to war memories and memorialization in Asia.

The last time I lived in Tokyo I took a bus every day past a nondescript little park that was on a hill overlooking one of the main train lines that runs through the city and also overlooking the Kōrakuen Stadium where the Tokyo Giants play. This park had many of the typical features of parks in larger Japanese cities: sandy ground, benches, low fences or hedges surrounding planted trees. Very modest, very unglamorous, but it was a place for local kids to play. There was a small stone monument recessed in the very back of the park close to where one could look out over the hill to the train tracks and the stadium and amusement park below. I didn't actually spend time in it, but in passing by every day I did notice what the park was—it turned out to be Tokyo's memorial park for its own war dead (*senbotsusha*).

At the end of this week [March 6, 1995] fifty years ago, Tokyo was firebombed, and approximately 100,000 people died overnight from March 9 to March 10. This park to memorialize the war dead is essentially a park for the victims of that firebombing. The striking thing about the park is that there is no aura of sacredness, no aura of death surrounding it. It's a normal place where people play. Its simplicity made me wonder, "Where are the dead in a city like Tokyo?" They're not there in the park.

One answer is that they are in a place not far from there, at Chidorigafuchi along the Imperial Palace moat. In 1959 the city of Tokyo erected a tomb to the war dead, people whose identities are not known. It's called Mumei Senshisha Byō —a very un-Japanese-sounding name—The Tomb of the Unknown War Dead. It doesn't sound Japanese at all. Particularly when seen in Chinese characters, it almost reads like a translation. Nevertheless, this is the place where the ashes of the people whose identities were not known are interred; ashes because that is what they had become, and because since the seventh century cremation has been the accepted means of handling the remains of the dead in Japan.

Again, I stress that this place sounds and feels somewhat foreign. Unlike Arlington, its closest analogue, it's not a place in which people feel connected to each other or to their shared past. There is, so to speak, no "there" there, no greater self, even an anonymous one, in which they share. Ultimately, real life and death in Japan must be mediated by *family*. The prewar state in Japan referred to itself as a literal, not metaphorical, "family state." Without consanguinity, or better, the "sentiment of consanguinity," the collective experience of war would become unbearably senseless.

These considerations lead me to my main focus today—the *site* of my concerns. I confess to feeling rather strange about not making Hiroshima or Nagasaki my subject; but I want instead to speak about the only other place in Japan that can "compete"—forgive me this term—with them. In fact, from the point of view of memories, memorialization, and the political economy of war death in Asia, this place may be of greater significance.

I'm talking about the Yasukuni Shrine, which is located atop Kudan Hill in Tokyo. "Yasu-Kuni" means something like "to soothe" or "to pacify the country." The Yasukuni Shrine is the main shrine to the war dead in Japan, specifically, to those people who have died in service to the emperor of Japan, roughly (via its antecedents) since the 1850s, which is when Commodore Perry arrived, but formally speaking since 1869. It is important to understand that the Yasukuni Shrine is a Shinto shrine and that all the soldiers enshrined there must have been killed in action. These soldiers become *kami*, deities who are worshipped there not only by their own families, as members who brought honor to the family, but also by the emperor. The fact that many, indeed millions of heroes are acknowledged there distinguishes the Yasukuni Shrine from the many shrines to individual imperial heroes and soldiers. In this function, it is a shrine dedicated not to one person, but to everybody who had died in combat for Japan. The emperor's visits there, varying in frequency depending on political and historical conditions, may be understood as the sole occasion on which he performs acts of worship to his people.

When Japan fought its first modern wars in 1894–95 and again in 1904–5 against China and Russia respectively, the emperors made visits to the shrine not only to preside over the enshrinement of the dead but also to announce the beginning or the end of the war. Those wars ended in victory, of course, but the number of visits that the emperor made to the shrine at that time was not great—fewer than five or seven. During World War II, which we think of as beginning in 1941 even though there had been significant military activity since 1937, the emperor made approximately twenty visits to Yasukuni Shrine on one occasion or another.

As a shrine, Yasukuni has festivals in the fall and in the spring. Like most such festivals, it was traditionally a somewhat gaudy and tacky affair. The number of imperial visits increased as the

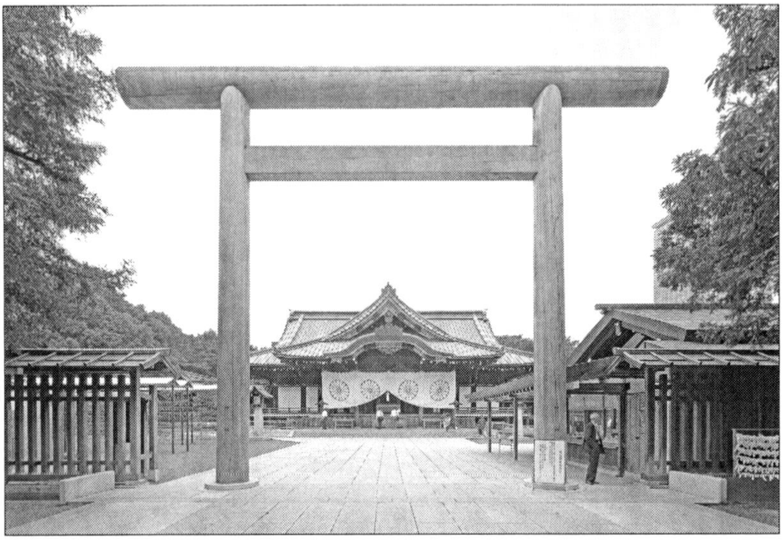

Yasukuni Shrine, Tokyo

number of casualties increased dramatically. If we compare the early decades of the twentieth century to the middle decades, we see a sharp increase in the number of war dead. At present, there are 2,453,199 dead enshrined at Yasukuni. In the Japanese context, one way of handling the issue of millions and millions of dead is to honor them by making them *kami*. As such, they are represented collectively by a single mirror kept in the shrine sanctuary. As *kami*, they live in connection with their families and link generations of those families. Yet once enshrined, in a real sense those *kami* no longer belong strictly to their families; they belong to the state.

The deification of those fallen in combat is an aspect of today's discussion that deserves particular attention. One striking feature of the slides we have seen is that all the structures are monumental yet retain the possibility of connection between the living and the dead at an intimate level: we see how shatteringly true this is at the Vietnam memorial. But there are "only" 59,000 names to be touched, not 2,500,000, or, by some estimates, 20,000,000, as in China. The Yasukuni Shrine, by contrast, cuts off the families from their dead in the very act of enshrining them. I want to illustrate this point with a court case that will lead us from the question of memorialization to the related questions of the politics of death and memorialization in Japan.

Before I do that, let me just mention that the Yasukuni Shrine is in fact a hierarchical organization; along with the main Tokyo shrine are local branches throughout the nation. It was originally intended only for people who had died *in combat,* and sometimes people weren't qualified, even though they had died of war wounds or had been taken prisoner and died in captivity. Those people were originally excluded. It was considered a tremendous privilege and honor to be enshrined in Yasukuni. The regulations were loosened later on, but were still reserved for military deaths. When the future of the shrine was being debated by American occupation forces after 1945, one eminent scholar, D. C. Holtom, suggested that the enshrinement be opened to meritorious civilians; but that didn't happen.

There was a court case some years ago which involved a member of the Japanese Self-Defense Forces (SDF), Nakaya Takafumi, who died in a traffic accident near Tokyo in 1973 and was properly cremated. The local branch of the Yasukuni Shrine wanted to apotheosize (*gēshi*) him, make him into a *kami,* as would be proper for someone who had died in service to the country. The SDF made an official request to this effect with the support of the local veterans' organization. But his widow, Yasuko, refused to allow the apotheosis to occur. She was a Christian and didn't want her husband to be enshrined. In defense of her claim over her husband's remains, she argued that it violated her constitutional and human rights to have her religious wishes overridden by the state.

She sued the shrine and won ... twice. In the first suit, the apotheosis was not permitted, so there was a countersuit. She won the countersuit, and the shrine was ordered to pay her compensation of about one million yen. Finally, the case went to the Japanese Supreme Court, where in 1988 she finally lost. The court decided that once the woman's husband had died and the desire to apotheosize him had been made known, it was neither a question for his wife to decide nor, in particular, a question of her individual religious preference. The state ruled that once the dead were dead, those religious rights didn't matter. There were two reasons for this decision. The court decision stated that it was not the wife's decision but the man's family's decision, since what mattered most was the continuity of the house line. To recall one of those crude proverbs that tell so much, women have wombs and "wombs are borrowed things" (*hara wakarimono*); the parents of the deceased, not the widow, have first claim to the son's spirit. The court also ruled that in assisting the apotheosis, the SDF was not patronizing Shinto, nor was the widow compelled to participate, both of which would have been unconstitutional. In the end, Nakaya Yasuko lost her case and the apotheosis was carried out.

This story speaks to the meaning of Yasukuni in the context of war memory, memorialization, and, of course, the meaning of "postwar" in Japan, insofar as Japan has a democratic constitution that enshrines, so to speak, political and human rights that did not receive much attention in the prewar constitution. For the state to win a case like this is important, because it suggests that in some ways, despite the enormous political differences in the relations between the emperor, the state, and the people from the pre- to postwar periods, and despite the much greater degree of political openness, there are areas where the state can, in fact, reach into the most intimate concerns of people, including the disposition of their dead.

Yet the significance of Yasukuni and its differences from the World War I and Vietnam memorials become clear only when seen in an Asian context. The Yasukuni Shrine brings out and dramatizes fears of the revival of militarism, because along with the millions of departed heroes, it also enshrines Japan's official war memories. It remains the site of Japan's only public military museum, displaying weaponry and equipment: everything from swords to tanks. As you enter the shrine's precincts, there are two massive stone lanterns with metal plaques on them depicting the exploits of Japanese forces at different points in their history. Much of what is memorialized there has to do with the war in China, which began in earnest in 1937, and eulogizes the sacrifices made by imperial troops. On October 17, 1978, General Tōjō Hideki was enshrined there as one of the "Martyrs of the Shōwa Era." (Tōjō, you might recall, was executed as a Class A war criminal in 1948, having been convicted of "the grossest crimes against humanity.") I don't want to get into the issue of "victor's justice" here, but I think it fair to say that Tōjō had set a good many of the "departed heroes" on their path to "martyrdom," along with their millions of victims.

Particularly after the enshrinement of Tōjō, the practice of Japanese cabinet members, especially the prime minister, making regular appearances at the shrine has outraged the sentiments of the Chinese, as well as those of other nations for shared, if somewhat different reasons. I don't want to minimize the degree to which expressions of outrage are politically motivated, but there is a core of unassuaged bitterness that must not be denied. For the Koreans, Yasukuni is a very complex issue. Korea was a colony of Japan at that time. There were also many Koreans who served in the Japanese military during World War II, but who were excluded from Yasukuni even though they died for the emperor. I will also note in passing that at Hiroshima, as well, Korean victims are not memorialized within the official confines of the Peace Park.

Thus, the Yasukuni Shrine may be said to form one side of a triangle in the political economy of war memory in Japan. The other two sides of the triangle are formed by Hiroshima and Nagasaki, and by the city of Nanjing in China. Nanjing was the capital of the Nationalist government that fell to the Japanese in the winter of 1937–38. When Japanese troops entered the city, they carried out atrocities that took approximately 300,000 civilian lives after the city's military defeat. For the Chinese, Nanjing is just one of those sites on which Japanese forces vented their fury for being resisted by people whom they (the Japanese) considered inferior to themselves.

The practice of official observances at Yasukuni crystallizes the issue of war memory in Asia in a way we in this country are not really aware of, except perhaps by analogy. When the Japanese cabinet, for example, under Prime Minister Nakasone, that great friend of Ronald of Bitburg, insisted that his full cabinet make a formal appearance at Yasukuni Shrine, there was tremendous controversy. The spectacle of the prime minister with his cabinet signing his name in the registry as prime minister of Japan, appearing in mourning clothes, going in official cars paid for by state funds raised constitutional issues about the separation of "shrine" and state in Japan and provoked all kinds of problems in Japan's relations with China.

Yasukuni regularly surfaces as an issue. It is not settled, and I don't see it being settled in the foreseeable future. This may in fact be an optimistic conclusion. On the one hand, over the course of the 1960s and 1970s, there were five instances when the Liberal Democratic government pushed bills in the Diet to allow for official worship by the cabinet at Yasukuni. Five times they were defeated. On the other hand, Nakasone did go, decked out in tails. And there is the Nakaya ruling of 1988 to consider. The issue is the place of Yasukuni in relation to postwar political institutions and to Japan's presence—historical and contemporary—in Asia. But ultimately, the meaning of Yasukuni will depend on the extent to which the continuity of family, of house, is linked to national identity and the collective experience of being Japanese. Which identity, which experience will it be—an official version that overrides private concerns and convictions, or a reimagined one that respects the real diversity of sentiment and experience that will never disappear from Japanese life—remains to be decided.

Stephen Greenblatt

This is an occasion, first of all, in which I can express my gratitude for Maya Lin's presence during these past weeks as the Avenali Professor at Berkeley and, beyond this, my gratitude for her extraordinary gifts. These gifts are not by any means restricted to the arts of memory, but today's focus on remembrance makes it inevitable that we reflect on that aspect of her achievement for which she is most famous. In what I have to say today I will try to blur the lines between memorials, architecture, and works of art, understanding, of course, that these are all separate genres but that they all frequently refer to each other.

Since powerful works of art tend very quickly to acquire an air of inevitability, and since academics are usually in the business of reinforcing this air of inevitability by amassing sources, precedents, and historical causes, it may be worth reflecting on how wildly improbable the Vietnam Veterans Memorial is. For the United States, at the height of its military and economic world domination, to lose a war against an insurgent peasant army was virtually unthinkable. For a country dispirited and bitterly divided by this war and its disastrous conclusion to undertake to erect, at private expense, a major national monument to its fallen soldiers was unlikely, and still more unlikely to elect to locate this monument on the central triumphal axis of its national institutions and collective memory. For the commission to design the monument to be awarded to a very young, unknown architecture student, a woman, and, what is more, an Asian American woman, was unprecedented. For this design to be realized over the vehement, vociferous, and, on some regrettable occasions, vicious opposition of some of the most influential politicians in the land, was astonishing. And then for the completed work of art—a work predicted to be divisive, unpatriotic, coldly abstract—to become one of the most influential and beloved monuments in the United States, the center of a virtual cult of remembrance—that is the wildest improbability of all.

Even if it manages to reconstruct a perfect causal chain, a historicist criticism whose underlying meaning is "this must be so" or "things had to be this way" necessarily misrepresents the way works of art are actually made. It is far better to understand that the Vietnam Veterans Memorial could not have been built, could not work, and could not possibly exist. We know that it could not exist not only because of the historical factors I have just sketched but also because of a long-term, persistent resistance to monuments in our culture, a culture shaped from its seventeenth-century origins by a deeply iconophobic Puritanism.

It is no accident that Milton's fallen angels excel at architecture—it is practically the first thing they do when they pull themselves off the burning lake—and that *Paradise Lost* reserves a special contempt for the monument builders of antiquity:

> Let none admire
> That riches grow in Hell; that soil may best
> Deserve the precious bane. And here let those
> Who boast in mortal things, and wondering tell
> Of Babel, and the works of Memphian kings,
> Learn how their greatest monuments of fame
> And strength, and art, are easily outdone
> By spirits reprobate, and in an hour
> What in an age they, with incessant toil
> And hands innumerable, scarce perform.

The implication here is not that monumental architecture is itself inherently satanic: the principal designer of the capital of Hell, Mulciber, had already been famous for his architectural projects up above. "His hand was known," Milton writes, "In Heaven by many a towered structure high, / Where sceptered angels held their residence." But there is something troubling, something wrong with trying to preserve memory, and particularly the memory of name and fame, in material structures. Again, the desire to preserve memory is not in itself evil. In Eden, too, Milton imagines the impulse to commemorate by digging in the earth and assembling polished stones (collected from the brook, let us note, rather than polished by human labor) and making offerings. One of the things, indeed, that most afflicts Adam at the prospect of leaving Paradise is the lost opportunity to build monuments for ensuing generations:

> Here I could frequent
> With worship place by place where he vouchsafed
> Presence Divine; and to my sons relate,
> 'On this mount he appeared; under this tree
> 'Stood visible; among these pines his voice
> 'I heard; here with him at this fountain talked':
> So many grateful altars I would rear
> Of grassy turf, and pile up every stone
> Of lustre from the brook, in memory,
> Or monument to ages; and thereon
> Offer sweet-smelling gums, and fruits, and flowers.

But if the impulse to build monuments is a pious one for Adamic man, after the fall it becomes deeply suspect: it is not strictly forbidden, but it easily becomes unacceptable, improper, vain, an offense to the very values it pretends to honor.

There is a famous passage in Isaiah in which the Lord rails against "a people that provoketh me to anger continually to my face; that sacrificeth in gardens, and burneth incense upon altars of brick; Which remain among the graves, and lodge in the monuments... Which say, Stand by thyself, come not near to me; for I am holier then thou. These are a smoke in my nose, a fire that burneth all the day" (65:3–5). "Which remain among the graves, and lodge in the monuments": the passage points us toward a set of deeply rooted cultural beliefs that make the building of any successful monument difficult. Monuments, like high places, altars of grassy turf, and offerings, were very early identified with stiff-necked self-righteousness, with hypocrisy, with settled landedness rather than nomadic searching, with the stony performance of a piety that does not in fact exist. Holiness and authentic remembrance are in the heart, not in outward signs, in rituals, in monumental observances that always tend, as the prophet goes on to make clear, toward idolatry.

Idolatry has two faces, both of them unacceptable, both of them lurking in monuments: the first is inert matter, the second is demonic. The demonic is the lurid threat, and the one most explicit in a writer like Milton, but it has, over the centuries, proved to be less enduring—though it has had sudden and surprising resurgences in recent years in the spectacle of public statues pulled down, defaced, and dismembered in carnivalesque rituals of rage and liberation. I think one of the most extraordinary trends the world has witnessed in the last five years is the attacking of public monuments as something actually satanic, not simply as inert matter. But the sense of inert matter, of monuments as dead substitutes for living memory, has, if anything, steadily increased, so that we have as a culture grown exceedingly uncomfortable with cenotaphs and obelisks and statues of heroic warriors. For our attempts at memorialization, we prefer narratives and movies and interactive museums.

The point is not that we have stopped building monuments—our cities are littered with them. For if we are heirs to an ancient fear of idolatry, we are equally heirs to a shame and honor system in which monuments have always played a crucial role. Milton's contemporary Thomas Hobbes draws upon a very old tradition of distinguishing between idol worship and what he calls "civil honoring." Making images of God or angels or even dead men violates the second commandment, he writes in *Leviathan,*

> unless as monuments of friends, or of men worthy of remembrance: for such use of an image is not worship of the image, but a civil honouring of the person; not that is, but that was: but when it is done to the image which we make of a saint, for no other reason but that we think he heareth our prayers, and

> is pleased with the honour we do him, when dead and without sense, we attribute to him more than human power, and therefore it is idolatry.

The notion of "civil honouring" dominates the building of monuments in American cities, but almost all of them arouse a vague uneasiness. We can use as a literary emblem of this uneasiness the monument that old Montague and Capulet vow to erect in memory of the children they have managed to destroy: "For I will raise her Statue in pure gold," says Montague about Capulet's daughter Juliet,

> That whiles Verona by that name is known,
> There shall be no figure at such rate be set
> As that of true and faithful Juliet.

To which Capulet adds, in the spirit of competitive donation: "As rich shall Romeo's by his lady's lie— / Poor sacrifices for our enmity!" The transformation of the dead lovers into statues becomes an emblem of a settling of the feud, with a sense, however, not only of the culpability of the parents but also—despite the best intentions of the builders—of the oblivion to which the families consign their children even in the act of commemorating them.

There is, for all of the genuine grief of the parents, a touch in the statues of what Ulysses in *Troilus and Cressida* calls "monumental mockery" when he is urging Achilles to return to the war:

> Time hath, my lord, a wallet at his back,
> Wherein he puts alms for oblivion,
> A great-sized monster of ingratitudes.
> Those scraps are good deeds past, which are devoured
> As fast as they are made, forgot as soon
> As done. Perseverance, dear my lord,
> Keeps honor bright; to have done is to hang
> Quite out of fashion, like a rusty nail
> In monumental mok'ry.

Of course, it is the fate of the dead that they cannot continually renew their honor through deeds. "The earth hath swallowed all my hopes but she," says Capulet, who is shortly to lose his last hope as well. We know this. But despite an understanding of the finality of death, despite a fear of idolatry, and despite a clear-eyed recognition that monuments cannot defeat oblivion, the fantastic dream of such renewal after death is one of the motives that, even as it used to fuel the cult of the saints, still hovers behind the building of secular monuments. The issue is not simply the honor that accrues to the dead but the benefits that the dead, and more generally the past, can continue to confer upon the living.

I want to go back for a moment before I close to the fear of lifeless matter that I said haunts the building of monuments and makes us generally uneasy with them. I want to add three further brief notes. First, monuments, like graves, are not only expressions of the dream of renewal; they are paradoxically expressions of a dream of containment: through the monument the dead will be given a proper place and kept in this place. We do not want the dead to roam unchallenged in the places of the living; we do not want the grave to open "his ponderous and marble jaws" and to cast up what has been laid to rest. The heavy inertness of matter is present in monuments not only as a melancholy limit but as a friend to the living. The makers of monuments are generally fascinated by the stoniness of the earth, by its hardness, its smoothness, its polish.

Second, again and again in literature dead matter is at once set against the living memory of the name and made to bear the living memory of the name. It is this particular tension between the earth and the name—a tension at least as old as the Hebrew scriptures—that makes monuments in our tradition so fraught. To cut words in matter, to transform matter into a book to be read, is the central memorializing act.

The dream of the monument then is to inscribe the name forever in the earth. One of the reasons that it is not enough to see a photograph of the Vietnam Veterans Memorial has to do with what it means to descend gradually below the level of the ground and to see the book, to see the names cut into the lustrous, polished stone. In that experience, Maya Lin has summoned up the whole impossible history of monuments from the most archaic reaches of the past.

And this leads to my third and final point: the Vietnam Veterans Memorial is a path; it describes, it invites, it requires a movement, a narrative progress from the first few American deaths to the enormous numbers to the closure. I spoke earlier about the benefits that monuments can confer on the living. In a secular world those benefits may be summed up as the making of paths—places to go, places to avoid, routes to safety. My most intense and simple experience of the monument is the cairn—the small heap of stones that marks a path through the wilderness. In California, at least, the critical number of stones is three: two stones may rest on each other at random, but three stones in a heap is rare. In the Sierras once several years ago, I climbed to a very high lake by following cairns across a huge slope of scree: thousands of rocks scraped and dropped along the granite by an ancient glacier. I walked around the high lake, at once extremely pleased with myself at having gotten up there, and also shivering a bit because a Wagnerian storm was rattling around the lake. I then decided to descend. But I had lost my way and could see no cairns at all. Only rocks, endless numbers of rocks, in every conceivable combination except the desired piles of three. I let myself down several boulders, thinking that I would change the angle of my vision and hence see the cairns, but I only found myself in deeper trouble. I realized that I hated and feared the wilderness. I couldn't remember why I had ever gone up there. It was horrible; I was likely to die there. But then I somehow scrambled up the boulders again and somehow fought back my panic and somehow continued around the icy lake—whistling, maybe humming to myself, maybe screaming on and off—until at last I saw what I was looking for: three small rocks piled upon one another. And then another pile in the distance beyond, and another beyond that. I take this to be an experience of what I might call zero-degree monumentality: no names, not even a corpse, except possibly my corpse, associated with the rocks, just the barest trace of an intention, the memory of someone who had been there before and who had left a way out. I was saved. I owe my presence here today to the existence of monuments.

Stanley Saitowitz

I want to tell the story of how I got involved with the New England Holocaust Memorial, which is under construction in Boston and scheduled to open in September 1995.

In October of 1990, I got a poster in the mail announcing an open competition for the New England Holocaust Memorial. It arrived on an ordinary sunny afternoon, and I was really quite taken aback: first with the idea of building a Holocaust memorial that afternoon and also with the question of building a Holocaust memorial in Boston. That night, I began to think about it.

Having grown up in an Orthodox Jewish home, I knew of the Holocaust from my earliest memories. As I thought more about it, I felt a sense of obligation to enter the competition, and the next day I sent in the forty-five dollars for the information package and waited.

I had at the time been teaching at Harvard and flying to Boston weekly. I knew the site across from Boston City Hall. One of the advantages of cross-country commuting is that you build up an enormous amount of frequent-flyer miles. The Premiere Executive Desk of my airline, which probably couldn't believe the number of times I'd flown to Boston, sent me a free ticket, which I had to use by the end of the year for any destination within the contiguous United States. I discovered that Mexico is part of the contiguous United States and booked a flight to Mexico City. The day I was leaving, the competition package arrived. I threw it in my bag on my way to the airport. On the plane I read through it with interest.

On my first day in Mexico City, I went to Teotihuacán. Each time I've been there, I've wondered who the gods were that caused

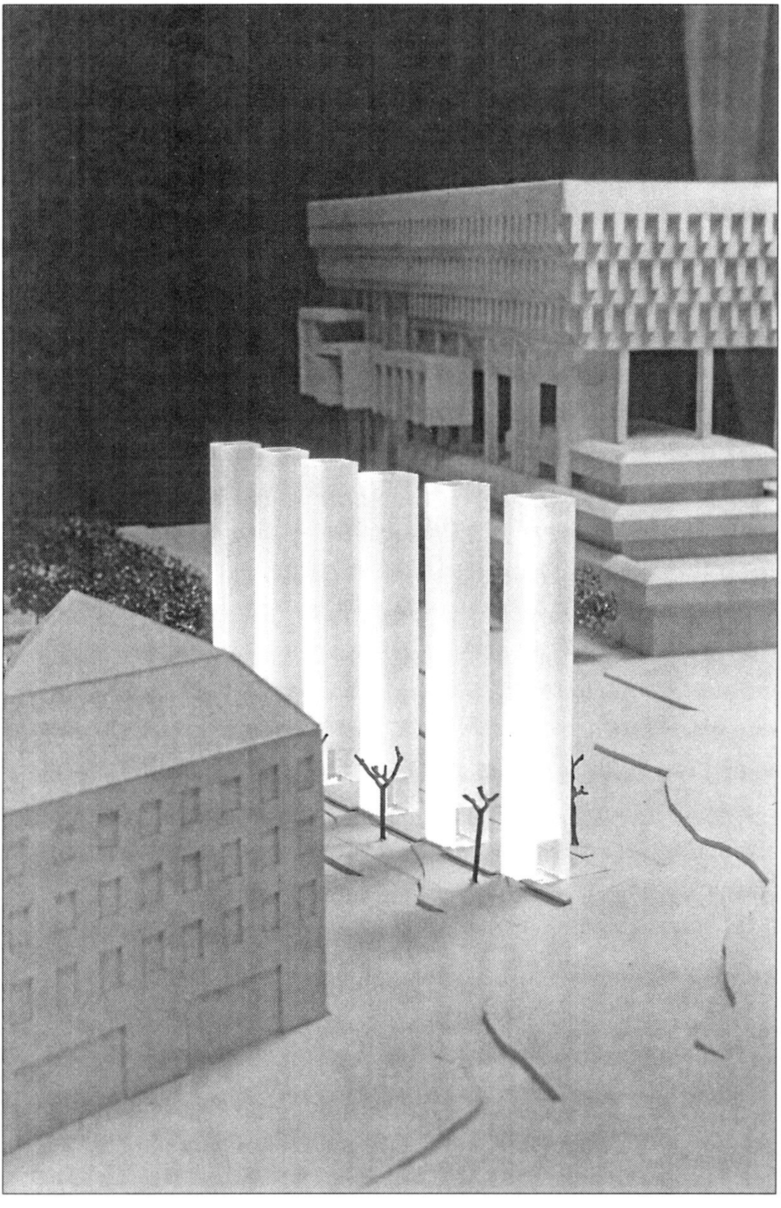

New England Holocaust Memorial, Boston (model)

such magnificent architecture, while I build private houses in the Bay Area.

If you've been in Mexico City in December, you probably know that it is the worst season for pollution. On the bus back that evening, the air was unbelievably thick. It was completely black. Even though I'm not particularly sensitive to pollution—in fact, I love Los Angeles—I began to choke in the bus. I was tremendously inspired by the experience of Teotihuacán, and breathing the polluted air made me slightly delirious. I was thinking about the Holocaust memorial and the six million, and six death camps, and the six-pointed star. In the thick air, suddenly I felt what being gassed must have been like. I went back to the hotel and drew these six towers on the pad next to my bed. The more I thought about them, the more meanings began to attach to the towers. When I got back to my office, I began to tune the towers to the site.

I realized that the towers connected with the columns of Boston City Hall. In getting to know Boston, I was fascinated with this unique American city that is not based on a grid and has a rich variety of urban spaces. I felt that the memorial offered an opportunity to enrich these spaces. The site is part of an undefined plaza facing City Hall. I decided to work only in a narrow segment of the site and to treat the memorial as an urban colonnade which would frame the edge of the plaza.

This is the text I included on the boards. It describes the characteristics and logic of the design.

The construction of the memorial is begun on Remembrance Day.
The horror of the Holocaust is re-enacted in the brutal cutting
of all the trees on half the site. These stumps remain.

Six pits are dug and lined with black granite.
At the bottom of each pit is a glowing fire.
Six glass towers are raised above.

Once completed many meanings attach to the memorial:

Some think of it as six candles,
others call it a menorah.
Some, a colonnade walling the Civic Plaza,
others, six towers of spirit.
Some, six columns for six million Jews,
others, six exhausts of life.
Some call it a city of ice,
others remember a ruin of some civilization.
Some speak of six pillars of breath,
others, six chambers of gas.
Some sit on the benches
and are warmed by the fire.
Some think of it as a fragment of Boston City Hall,
others call the buried chambers Hell.
Some think the pits of fire are six death camps,
others feel the warm air rising up from the ground
like human breath as it passes
through the glass chimneys to heaven.

Etched on the glass towers are
SIX MILLION NUMBERS
which flicker with light.

On the black granite ramp is incised:
DEDICATED TO THE REMEMBRANCE
OF THE *SHOA*,
THE HOLOCAUST.
THE ULTIMATE ACT OF PREJUDICE.
THE NAZI THIRD REICH
SYSTEMATIC MURDER

OF SIX MILLION JEWISH

MEN WOMEN AND CHILDREN.

THE ATTEMPT AT THE

TOTAL AND PERMANENT

DESTRUCTION OF JEWISH LIFE.

THE AIM TO REMOVE JEWS

FROM HISTORY AND MEMORY.

Each of the six burning chambers is named after a death camp:

CHELMINO

TREBLINKA

MAJDENEK

SOBIBOR

AUSCHWITZ-BIRKENAU

BELZEC

The memorial towers rise above a path that is part of the Freedom Trail in Boston. This location gives the Holocaust a place in this mythical path of freedom, and in the history of Boston and the United States. The towers are constructed of a stainless steel skeleton and glass panel skin. Initially I thought about having names etched into the glass, but the impossibility of knowing the six million names led me to choose numbers, which begin with 0000001 and end with 6000000. To accommodate 6,000,000, there are three numbers per square inch covering every face of each tower. I wanted the numbers to be understood with reference to the Vietnam Veterans Memorial in Washington, DC, where there are approximately 59,000 names on a 760-foot wall. Setting the Holocaust memorial in this context gives some idea of the enormity of the destruction of the Holocaust. Below each tower is a six-foot-deep pit named after the six killing machines established in Poland. At the bottom of each pit is a gas fire. These fires produce warm air, which rises up through the grating covering the pits as you walk

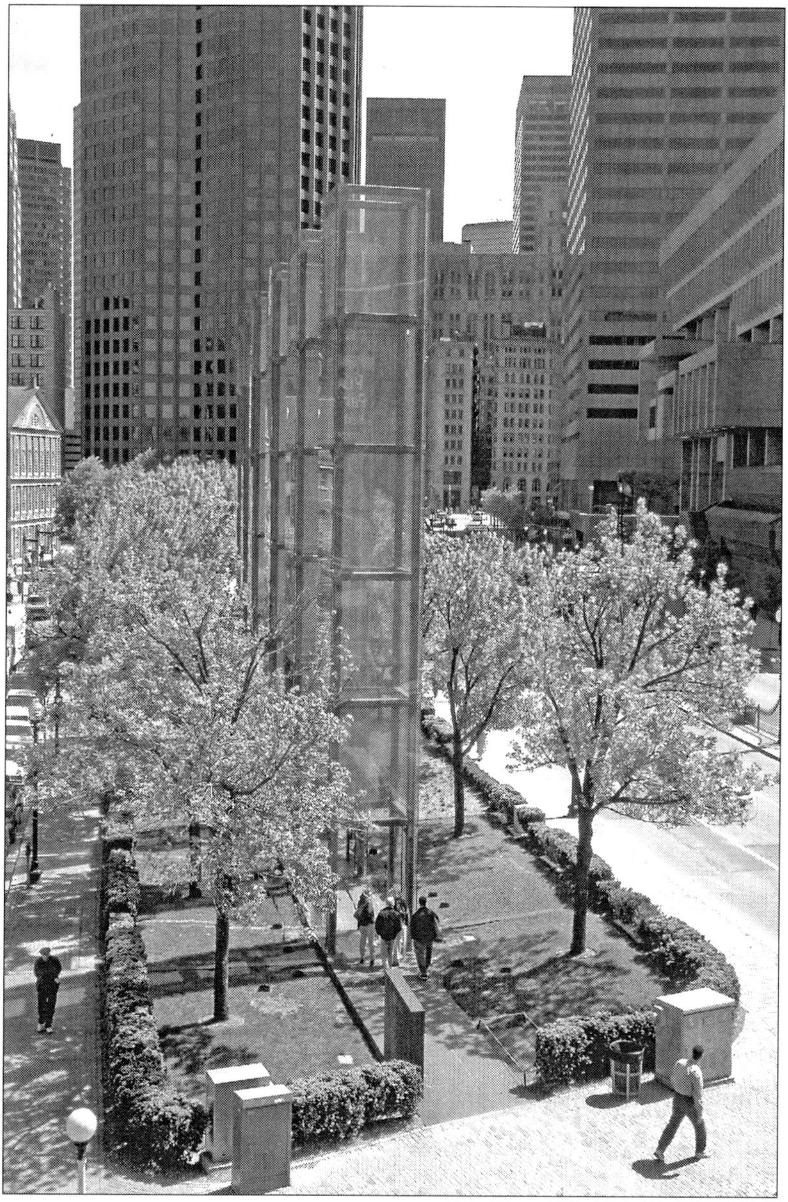

New England Holocaust Memorial, Boston (completed)

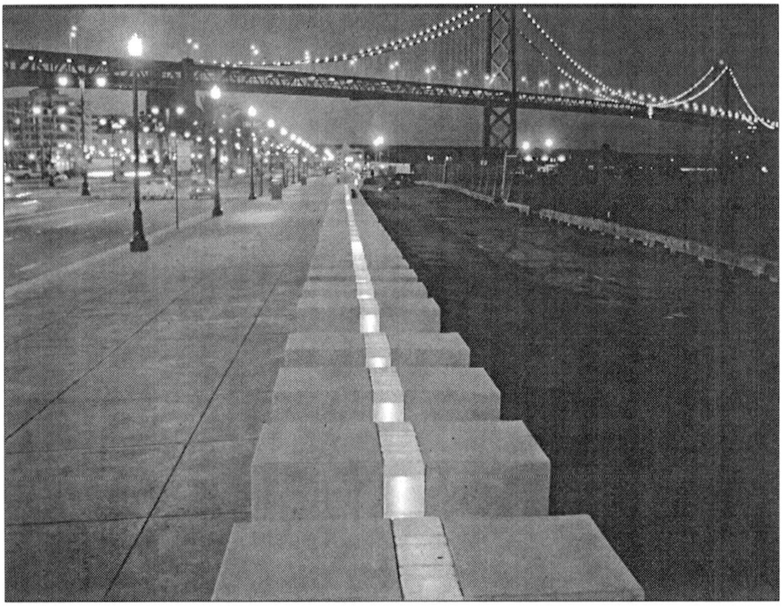

Promenade Ribbon (Ribbon of Light), San Francisco

through the memorial. Light passing through the glass during the day causes the shadows of the numbers to tattoo you, so that you become covered with the traces of these memories. Something of the horror of this experience is captured, through both the names of the camps and the sheer enormity of the list of victims. By day, from the outside, the structure is an innocent player in the making of Boston's urban spaces. At night the monument is lit like the candles of remembrance or the lamps made from the flesh of the death camp victims.

I want to talk about two other urban structures, one in San Francisco, the other in Manhattan. The Promenade Ribbon is a line around San Francisco's waterfront which memorializes the end of the land. It was constructed after the Loma Prieta earthquake, when the freeway was torn down because of structural damage. It marks a line that follows the waterfront for two and a half miles

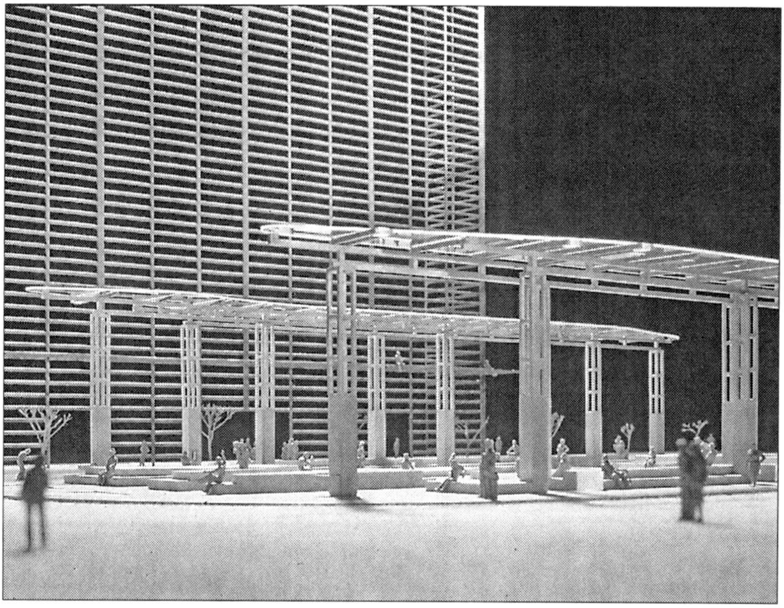

Vesey Square, Battery Park City, New York

at the edge of the city. As it moves through the city, it transforms in relation to the places that it marks with different habitable opportunities—benches or tables or chairs relate to specific conditions like views of the bay or the city. It marks the edge of the land and the water and offers various ways of inhabiting that line. At night, the line is lit with a continuous fiber-optic light.

The last project returns to the idea of place, name, and naming. It is a public place in Manhattan, at Battery Park City. We were given an open square and told to fill it with something. What can you add to Manhattan, which has so much, and so much of so much? I considered making "nothing" and carving out a new kind of urban canyon between these two roofs that establish a street without cars and offers new opportunities for habitation. I wanted to make an urban landscape, a "small" city where buildings are benches, streets patterns, and individuals and the many can find places in it.

In addition, I thought it would enhance the site to memorialize the names associated with the area by marking them on the pavement. The biographies of one hundred citizens, living and dead, who have helped make Manhattan such a mythical place, are etched into the stones. People like Irving Berlin, Leonard Bernstein, and Emma Goldman. Along the crooked street are the names of the "crooked" people of Manhattan: Arnold Rothstein—gambler, bankroller, rumrunner, and labor racketeer; Dutch Schultz—burglar, bootlegger, owner of speakeasies, and police racketeer. The inscriptions provide a picture of the history of this city and inscribe on the pavement the names of people whom, at another time, in a similar public place in Manhattan, you may have shared a bench with.

Maurice Sendak with Herbert Schreier

They Know Everything: Children and Suffering

Herbert Schreier

WE HAVE LEARNED A LOT in the thirty years since we began seriously studying the long-term effects of trauma. Without going into too much detail, there are many kinds of trauma. There are traumas that occur at the hands of human beings and traumas caused by natural disasters. There are kids traumatized individually or in groups, and there are whole populations traumatized. There are also kids who are traumatized repeatedly in family situations. People can be traumatized by situations. Witnesses to trauma, for example, can be traumatized. We also know that kids have an extraordinary memory for trauma and that memory can precede language.

There are two really painful cases in the literature of children who were known to have experienced trauma prior to the development of language. One was an eight-month-old baby who was in a pornography ring. When she was being observed in play therapy, she kept stabbing a baby doll with a pencil in the belly button. Eight months into therapy it just happened that they discovered the cache of photographs, and there was this child with an erect penis in her belly button. If you don't do trauma work, these stories may upset you, but just telling them can give you a sense of what it is to be traumatized. There's a case of a child who watched her mother being blown up by a letter bomb when she was one year old—again, preverbal. At age four, she was not getting on well with her adoptive family. Nobody had talked to her about the event, but she played out in exact detail for her psychiatrist what had happened to her mother on that day. Memory, even eidetic memory, is quite good. Despite the current attacks on repression, dissociation as a defense against facing trauma has been well documented.

What I wanted to present today very, very briefly are the results of the study that we did of the Oakland Hills fire, a fire which in one day destroyed 3,300 homes and 400 apartments, injured 125 people, and killed 25. A frightening thing for the kids was watching the blaze while the television kept reporting that the fire was "out of control." I don't think there are many things more frightening to children than adults being out of control.

After the fire we did several studies, one of them involving an art class. In the school that we consulted there was a wonderful art teacher who had her students do drawings of the fire. (Actually, the assignment before the event of the fire was to imagine that they were Maurice Sendak!) You all know what can happen when you let your imagination wander. We showed these pictures, with drawings from a control group, to art therapists and asked them to analyze them using an adjectival checklist. They overwhelmingly analyzed the emotions in the pictures done by kids who were actually involved in the fire as anger and anxiety. Drawings eight months later showed loneliness. I think this change from anger and anxiety to loneliness reflects our limited attention span for other people's trauma; we expect them to get better right away. The work of Mardi Horowitz is very clear on this matter. It takes a year to two years to get over a trauma and reorganize your sense of who you are in the world, based on having been through that trauma. The nontraumatized, who perhaps could just as easily have been hurt, do not want to think about it.

Another study that we did concerning the fire was to look at kids and their parents. In this case, unlike Anna Freud studying children in the London Blitz, we actually asked the kids how they felt. We found a lot of families in which the kids told us that they were more troubled by the fire than their parents, who were questioned separately, were able to perceive. This is interesting because it raises many possibilities about how we understand other people's suffering. These kids did better at the one-year anniversary when we went back to look at them. But at two years, the anniversary week of the fire, there was a huge fire in Los Angeles, and these kids saw it on television. In the middle of the week, on Wednesday, the kids went out for a fire drill at eight o'clock in the morning, and at ten o'clock in the morning they were called out for another fire drill, which is very unusual for any school. When they looked up in the hills, there was a house on fire. The kids went wild. When we looked at scores for anxiety and posttraumatic stress disorder (PTSD) at that time, the results indicated that when such a discrepancy exists, there is an increased susceptibility to the effects of a reminder of the trauma.

I want to close with a couple of points about trauma, and what happens if you don't treat it. Kids will reenact trauma. They will create games, which often involve the trauma symbolically, and engage other kids in sometimes dangerous and anxiety-provoking play that they don't associate with trauma. (One girl played "bus" on a very dangerous ledge, and got other kids to play with her. The kids didn't make the connection.) Art can be very useful for working out trauma, but if the trauma is not worked through, it becomes posttraumatic play. It just goes nowhere.

An example of our understanding the degree to which kids can be traumatized and of the long-lasting effects of PTSD in kids can be found in juvenile detention homes. Thirty percent of kids in juvenile detention are suffering from PTSD. That study was just done by a researcher at Stanford. If you look at children who murder, 100 percent of them have been traumatized. Despite the finding that 100 percent of them suffered from some sort of psychiatric syndrome besides PTSD, only 15 percent of them had received any form of treatment!

The final point I want to make is also taken from studies by Lenore Terr published in *The Psychoanalytic Study of the Child*. Those who know the paintings of Magritte know that they're weird in a way. There are a lot of faces without features; they are blank. There are pictures where body parts are in the wrong place. Water scenes are very common. The case is interesting because, when he was fourteen, Magritte awoke one night and found his mother missing. She was later found drowned in the Sambre River, her nightgown around her face. Magritte refused to talk of the past and loved Edgar Allan Poe, who as a small child was with his own mother for four days after she died of consumption before her death was discovered. We know Magritte also hated psychiatrists and would not talk to them. He has a famous sculpture of a psychiatrist; it has a birdcage for a chest and no head.

The question of whether the artist was involved in very creative posttraumatic "play" or whether he worked through his trauma is one we might ask Maurice Sendak.

Maurice Sendak

Well, I feel a little bit betwixt and between. I read the article about Magritte that you [Dr. Schreier] gave me, and it was fascinating. I have no doubt, as you have no doubt. Sometimes I'm skeptical that something so abrupt and simple that happens in childhood could have such a long-lasting effect, but I know it's true. A number of things like that have happened to me, and only one of which I'll tell you about because it actually has a lot to do with this issue. I'm one of those people who did not hate psychiatrists. I couldn't afford to. I spent most of my twenties in the psychiatrist's office working out part of this problem. It's something that took me roughly between the ages of three and fifty to solve, and it was solved not through psychiatry so much as through the creative process and working it out through endless books, and then finally clinching it in one book.

I was a very sickly child, which was very typical back in the early thirties, when there weren't drugs or vaccines. You got diphtheria and you got pneumonia and scarlet fever. My parents were immigrants. They were poor. They were tactless. The fact of my mortality was loudly proclaimed all over the house ... in my hearing. My grandmother dressed me in white clothes so that God passing over would assume I was already dead and angelic and go get some other kid. There was no question I could croak at a very early age. At the time I was three, and I was getting over a very bad bout of scarlet fever, which left me impaired in many ways, the Lindbergh case happened.

Some people are nodding, those old enough to remember that case. I will review it briefly for the younger people here who might not know about it. Charles A. Lindbergh was a great national hero, the first man ever to fly nonstop from New York to Paris. He married the daughter of a Mexican ambassador, who was beautiful and poetic and wonderful. She learned how to fly with him, and she flew when she was pregnant upside down doing Morse code. Everyone followed them like you follow now Charles and Di, but they were a lot more interesting than Charles and Di. Well, who isn't? But they were of that princely, royal nature. I knew about them. We all knew about them. But what I knew most about them was that they had a child. That child's face was in the paper, it seemed, almost every day. And that child, of course, was the most beautiful child in the world. He had to be because he belonged to them. He was blond, he was blue-eyed, he was Charlie Junior and we heard about him all the time. And then he was kidnapped.

You must remember, this was a time of no television. I was three years old. There wasn't much conversation between me and my parents. Lots between me and my siblings, but I got all my information from the radio and from glimpsing pictures in the newspapers. I remember vividly Mrs. Lindbergh talking over the radio in a very broken voice about the baby having a cold, and will the person who took the baby rub camphor on his chest and warm his milk for him?

Years later I went to a party in New York and met a news reporter, Gabriel Heatter, the only celebrity I ever wanted to meet in my whole life. I rushed over to him. He must have thought I was totally out of my mind. I said, "You're the guy who introduced Mrs. Lindbergh on the radio." He said, "Yeah." He obviously introduced millions of people, so he couldn't fathom why I was so excited.

We followed the news, of course. Lindbergh flew over the Andes because somebody had seen a blond baby. He flew over the Yangtze because somebody had seen the blond baby, or the Alps or wherever. He was flying and flying and flying looking for a glint of gold somewhere that was his baby's head. Now, I only know this from having understood it later, but you have to accept that this is true—that I equated my mortality, my survival, with Charlie's. You had to see ... I knew I was a poor baby who came from an immigrant Jewish family. He came from a gentile family, and he had a nurse and a policeman and lived in a house with German shepherds guarding it. How did he get out of that house at seven o'clock in the evening? If that could happen to him, what chance did I stand? So my fate hung on Charlie's coming home alive. And, of course, he didn't. He was found dead about three or four miles away, in the woods outside of Hopewell, New Jersey. And that created in me a sense that I had died. There was no question; I could not live if he could not live. That occurred within me without anyone observing. Obviously, I went on eating and drinking and being a pest, but some very fundamental, crucial part of me I declared dead, and it remained so.

Something else happened at that point, too, because when the body was found, I saw a picture, a photograph of the body. I proclaimed this loudly to everybody. My parents were furious at my morbidity, that I went on and on and on about this thing. I did not see the body; I couldn't have seen the body. And they tried in every way to eradicate this bad thing in my head in rather rough ways. So I learned to shut up; I learned to not talk about it. This went on for most of my life. And I never bring it up. At the psychiatrist's office we used it as a symptom, you know, as a fantasy symptom of what had occurred to me. He didn't for a minute accept it as factual.

About fifteen years ago in my little community in Connecticut—and I thought I was hallucinating—it was announced that a man who had just written a book absolving Bruno Hauptmann, who was electrocuted for kidnapping the baby, was going to talk about his book at Ridgefield, Connecticut, at the library. Well, he had a bad agent. Ridgefield, Connecticut ... the Lindbergh kidnapping—nobody's going to be there, except me. And nobody was there, except me. And there's the author up on the stage, looking very distraught because nobody's there except one sort of hysterical looking middle-aged man in the audience. He started to talk about his book, and I was raising my hand. Finally he just quit, and I said, "Let's go out and have a bite, " and went out. He said he would autograph a copy of his book for me, and he was amazed at the details I knew about the kidnapping.

I'd been to Hopewell, New Jersey. I had gone close to the house with a friend who was quite alarmed when we parked the car and I said, "I'll walk to the house." He said, "No, no, no. They won't let you." It was by then a school for bad boys. I wanted to feel what had happened. I didn't time this consciously, but it was seven o'clock in the evening. We parked, and then I walked towards the house. I could hear people talking in the house. I could hear dogs barking. I thought this is how it must have been. It was still light. People are talking in the house, like the colonel and his wife on the first floor. The dog was barking. I went around the corner of the house. I looked up at the nursery window. I had all the time in the world to put a ladder against that window. I went through the whole madness.

Anyway, I told Tony [Anthony Scaduto] over dinner and a lot of wine—I was quite loosened up—about this perverse image I've had in my head, and I said, "I always felt since a child that I'd seen a photograph of the dead baby." He shoved a napkin over and said, "Draw it." Easy. I drew it. Gave it to him back, and he said, "You saw it. You saw it." It was a morning edition of the *Daily News* and it said, "Kidnapped Baby Found Dead," with a hideous photograph of the remains of the child amid a tangle of woods and leaves. You could just see the head and part of the body. It had decayed over two or three months. The newspaper printed a big arrow pointing to the skull, so you could begin to see what it looked like. The colonel threatened to sue the paper if it appeared in the second edition.

This happened to John Lennon, by the way, who was photographed lying on a slab, naked, and Yoko Ono said she'd sue if that appeared in the afternoon edition. Same thing. I'd had the bad luck of seeing it, and children have Polaroid-vision memory. I saw it, I took it, and it stayed there forever. And Tony saved me because he said, "You've seen it. It was there." He told me he had seen it, and then, on another occasion, he gave me a souvenir photograph of that edition, and I could see what I'd seen. It was just what I had drawn.

I can't tell you the relief I felt to know that it was just a simple thing that happened, that I'd just passed a newsstand, probably holding my mother's or my father's hand, and I'd turned and looked as I was taken home. That was the beginning of an endless nightmare for me.

The nightmare ended, more or less, with *Outside Over There*. Every book of mine, every major book of mine has hidden somewhere in it a child being taken away—a dog kidnapping a baby in *Higgledy, Piggledy, Pop*. Over and over again children are being taken away. Or they think they're lost, like Max, who was separated from his mother. Now, I'd always known I would do a trio of books. There would be the little boy, Max, the preschooler. There would be a tiny bit older Mickey, who's now smart enough to investigate a mystery that is erotic and disturbing to him. And then there would be the oldest child, Ida, in *Outside Over There*, who had a whole different problem.

The point of my books always has been to ask how children cope with a monumental problem that happened instantly and changed their lives forever, but they have to go on living. And they cannot discuss this with anyone. No one will take the time. Parents are embarrassed, so they'll shush them up. Of course, this was me that I was talking about all the time, but I had to get older and stronger to do the Lindbergh book, to really get to the matter. And that's what *Outside Over There* is all about.

The heroine is Ida, who is nine or ten years old. That was my sister, who was just ten years older than me when I was born. I gave her the name Ida because we had a neighbor whom I preferred to my mother, which hurt my mother a good deal. I would run across the hall to Ida and sit on her lap and babble and tell her things. She'd be amused, and she would listen, which my mother couldn't do. So I named my heroine Ida. She has a baby sister. I changed the sex of the baby to a sister, thinking, "God, I don't want anybody to track me on this thing." So it's a baby sister. And Ida hates her baby sister and wishes her gone, wishes her dead.

Through art and a magic horn the goblins come, take the real baby away, and leave an ice baby in its stead. Of course, the ice baby was me, a dead baby, and they take the live baby away. Now, I have Ida come to her senses because she's not a psychopathic child—every child will hate her parents or hate her siblings for a moment—and she becomes frightened of what she's done. She isn't yet ready to accept the fact that she has to live with this child. She goes out into the world backwards, and her adventures lead her to an understanding of the situation. She goes into the goblins' den, and finds, to her horror, that goblins are babies. They all look alike. How is she going to tell the difference between goblin babies and her sister baby?

Throughout the journey, the baby always looks like the baby. I'm good at making the likenesses clear. No one ever, in looking at this book, has detected that there's one picture, a center spread of Ida floating through the air, determined that she's going to find her sister, and below, in a small cave, is the baby hidden away from her. It is an exact portrait of Charlie Lindbergh Jr.

I can't tell you how difficult it was to just do it. It was like some kind of obscenity, some kind of strange perversion, but I could not resist copying his features, which I've memorized. It's very easy to do his face.

Before I tell you the denouement of the story, there was another social thing that occurred, which was very important in the thirties. The Dionne quintuplets were born in the mid-thirties, around the time of Bruno Hauptmann's trial and execution. By then, of course, I was talking and completely demented. Those five babies obsessed the world, as did the Lindbergh case. Yvonne, Marie, Cécile, Emilie, Annette. I don't know my birthday, but I cannot forget the names of those girls. That was magic. If anything happened to one, well, the magic was over. If Annette caught a cold, we all held our breath. Of course, this also got us through the Depression. This got us through a lot of rotten stuff that was going on in the world. You could focus on Lindbergh and Dionne. The babies were extraordinarily beautiful. And, of course, historically the first ever recorded from one egg.

They were personally important to me because there were five. There were five Sendaks in my family, so five, as it is with a lot of children, is a very magic number. So nothing could happen to Annette or Emilie, or I was a nervous wreck. Every time one had a cold or diarrhea, I was in a scary depression.

Now, I use five goblin babies, all identical, in the book, an homage to the Dionne quintuplets. I dress Ida in a blue dress, an homage to Judy Garland in *The Wizard of Oz,* who broke my heart. It was the first movie I'd seen—I was about ten—where I wept, and wept not about Oz, but about Judy Garland, because I knew she and I had gone through some kind of serious hell, and that she was using her enormous talent to tell us about that. The blue dress was for her. There's Mozart in the book. I was just designing *The Magic Flute,* and so the two works overlapped, and the solution to the book, of course, was that the only way for Ida to find her baby sister was to play a magic tune. And goblins have to dance. The Grimm brothers tell us that if you're a mother, and you turn your back for a moment, the goblins will come and take your baby. And they'll put a changeling in its place. And if you turn around and look, it looks very much like your baby, slightly cross-eyed and drooling. How do you know your baby from a changeling? You can take a flute and start to play. Changelings have to dance. If it dances, it ain't your kid. Then you pound three times on the table, and the goblins, very grumpy, have to come up and give your kid back and take that thing away. So Ida plays her magic horn, and they all dance themselves into foam; they just disappear into the ether. They just become water, and the only one left is her sister, who welcomes her with open arms. Ida takes her home, and Mozart points the way, because she's now in total harmony with her situation.

She comes home to a depressed mother, who has just gotten a letter from her seafaring father. The first line of the book is "When Papa was away at sea"—like a lot of papas, in one form or another, including mine. The letter says Papa's coming home, and he knows his lovely, wonderful little Ida will take care of the baby. This macho letter drove all of my friends mad, but it's what fathers do. They dump on their elder daughters, and, of course, she adores her father, so she will, indeed, resign herself to her fate and take care of the baby, which is what my poor sister did. With a lot of pinching and poking and black-eyeing she got me through childhood. Telling this story was so hard to do that I experienced my first and only, thank goodness, serious depression and mental collapse during the making of the book.

Somebody asked me last night, "When you take a dive, do you come up all the time?" And I said sometimes you do, sometimes you don't. Sometimes you come back a little bit less than when you went in, and it's risky. It's very risky. This was the riskiest book I ever did because I couldn't get out of it. And I couldn't finish the book without the help of friends, psychiatrists, pills. I took six months or eight months off from the book. Then I went back and I did the deed. And, in fact, I finished it. I mean I can talk about it now as if it were a very severe fever that I had for most of my life.

I met the daughter of Lindbergh, Reeve Lindbergh, a marvelous young woman who happens to be a children's book writer. I was shaking because I was sitting next to a Lindbergh, and I leaned over to her and I said, "I did a book, " and before I could finish it, she looked back and she said, "And it's called *Outside Over There*, and it's about my brother, isn't it?" And she quite frightened me. She quite frightened me. I also frightened her because it was a Lindbergh thing. Charles Lindbergh was a very, very dictatorial man and, as we learned later, not a very good man in my terms. Nothing was to be said about this child, ever. Mrs. Lindbergh was pregnant when it all began, and he was afraid she'd miscarry. She had her second son some months after the trial. And then five other children, Reeve being the last. Reeve said, "I know nothing, nothing about the case. My parents didn't want us to know anything about it, and so I have been loyal to my parents, and I've never read anything about it. I've never looked at pictures. I've never..." And I said to her, "Do you want to? Or do you not want to?" And she said, "I want to." She was forty at this point. So I told her about her little brother, and you can only imagine what this did to me, to be talking to this person, who looked so much like her father. But then it was over.

So I am the case Herb's talking about, and I am the book you're talking about, and how it is, indeed, worked out, or at least attempted. And it isn't because you pedantically think you must. You have no control. It's a repetition business. You've got to tell the story, like the Ancient Mariner. You've got to tell the story until the story's finished.

It's hard for me to even tell you now. I didn't think it would be this difficult, and I thought I was quite clear of it, but it's still there. I saved all my Lindbergh souvenirs that Tony gave me, that I collected over the years. The mother, Mrs. Lindbergh, lives two towns away from me, and I've had many fantasies of going to her house, thinking, "What would I say to her?" And then the absurd thought came into my mind: I'd rush over and say, "I'm Charlie! I've come back!" *That* would kill her.

Seamus Heaney with Robert Hass

Sounding Lines: The Art of Translating Poetry

ROBERT HASS: So, Mr. Heaney, do you have a theory of translation?

SEAMUS HEANEY: I don't have a theory of it, no. I have done it different ways, and I know that there are different motives. One motive is the writerly motive, slightly predatorish. The writer hears something in the other language and says, "I would like that, that sounds right, I need that."

I have not a theory but a metaphor for it. It's based upon the Viking relationship with the island of Ireland and the island of Britain. There was a historical period known as the raids, and then there was a period known as the settlements. Now, a very good motive for translation is the raid. You go in—it is the Lowell method—and you raid Italian, you raid German, you raid Greek, and you end up with booty that you call *Imitations.*

Then there is the settlement approach: you enter an oeuvre, colonize it, take it over—but you stay with it, and you change it, and it changes you a little bit. Robert Fitzgerald stayed with Homer, Lattimore stayed with him, Bob Hass has stayed with Czesław Miłosz. I stayed with *Beowulf.* But I also raided Dante in the late '70s, when there were people on what they called the "dirty" protest in the H-Blocks in Long Kesh. There was an intense and violent intimate atmosphere not only in the prison but in Northern Ireland in general. At the time, I was reading *The Inferno* in translation, not a very good translation maybe, but one that I liked. Anyway, I came upon the Ugolino section, and I thought, "This is cannibalism." There's an almost sexual intimacy between the two people, between Ugolino and Archbishop Roger, which seemed cognate with the violence and intimacy of Ulster. So I raided that section. I was thinking of dedicating it to the people in the prison until I met a Sinn Fein fellow who said, "You never write anything for us," and I said, "That's right." What I meant as a gift was suddenly being levied, so I didn't do the dedication.

Anyway, I interfered with it a bit; I did a Lowell-esque translation. I put in a couple of images, and thickened the texture of the Italian up, and then somebody said to me, "You should try the whole thing." But when I thought of trying the whole thing, I realized I didn't know Italian well enough, although I did do a version of the first three cantos. I raided for Ugolino, but could not manage to establish a settlement. But I settled with *Beowulf* and stayed with it, formed a kind of conjugal relation for years.

ROBERT HASS: You don't have the Ugolino here?

SEAMUS HEANEY: I don't know. It's a bit long. It's in a book called *Field Work*. I'm sorry, I forgot it. Oh, someone in the audience has it! Are you sure you want to do this so early?

ROBERT HASS: Do some of it, yes.

SEAMUS HEANEY: Well, you know the situation: Dante is walking, down on the ice of the ninth circle of hell, and comes upon these two characters in the ice. Incidentally, the beginning of this echoes the beginning of the Old English poem *The Battle of Maldon*. The early part of the English poem is lost, so it starts with a strange, floating half-line, one of my favorite openings. It says: "It was broken." Then the poem proceeds. So "Ugolino" begins as Dante breaks off a previous encounter:

We had already left him. I walked the ice
And saw two soldered in a frozen hole
On top of other, one's skull capping the other's,
Gnawing at him where the neck and head
Are grafted to the sweet fruit of the brain
Like a famine victim at a loaf of bread.
So the berserk Tydeus gnashed and fed
Upon the severed head of Menalippus
As if it were some spattered carnal melon.
"You," I shouted, "you on top, what hate
Makes you so ravenous and insatiable?
What keeps you so monstrously at rut?
Is there any story I can tell
For you, in the world above, against him?
If my tongue by then's not withered in my throat
I will report the truth and clear your name."

That sinner eased his mouth up off his meal
To answer me, and wiped it with the hair
Left growing on his victim's ravaged skull,
Then said, "Even before I speak
The thought of having to relive all that
Desperate time makes my heart sick;
Yet while I weep to say them, I would sow
My words like curses—that they might increase
And multiply upon this head I gnaw.
I know you come from Florence by your accent
But I have no idea who you are
Nor how you ever managed your descent.

> Still, you should know my name, for I was Count
> Ugolino, this was Archbishop Roger,
> And why I act the jockey to his mount
> Is surely common knowledge; how my good faith
> Was easy prey to his malignancy,
> How I was taken, held and put to death.... "

Some things I added: the melon image. And the phrase, "Why I act the jockey to his mount," I don't think is in the original. Also, the whole movement of the lines is different. The Italian swims. But my translation is sluggish. I liked it like that. I've often said that Dante's movement is Chianti-pour, but that mine is poured concrete. I thickened it up. But I think there is a different covenant with a work if you do the whole thing.

The translation I like of Dante is Dorothy Sayers's, which is in terza rima. It has no pretentions to decorum. There is a touch of Gilbert and Sullivan in the rhyming—she's just sketching it out. The feeling is that she is saying to you: "It goes more or less like this, and it rhymes more or less like this." Its swiftness makes it very readable.

ROBERT HASS: So how did you come to the *Beowulf*?

SEAMUS HEANEY: Well one simple answer is that an editor wrote to me and said, "We would like you to translate *Beowulf*." I had done Anglo-Saxon at University. I dwelled with it for three years on and off, from about 1958 to '61; it was part of the course. I gradually realized that I really got something from it. I liked, as I mentioned, *The Battle of Maldon*, I liked *The Seafarer, The Wanderer*. The grayness attracted me, I think. The sleet and the rock in it. At the same time, there is something tender at the center of it. And then, when I began to write as an undergraduate, I was animated originally by Gerard Manley Hopkins, who is basically an Anglo-Saxon poet writing naturally in the stressed English of the native pre-Conquest tradition. Anyway, when this offer came I thought it would be good for me to translate *Beowulf*, to steady myself, to go back to that language, to my original stressed speech. When I began to write I had wanted the verse to thump and the language to be thick and so on.

In the 1970s I did an essay and I quoted a Northern Irish poet called W. R. Rodgers, Bertie Rodgers. What interested me was Bertie's description of the Northern Irish speech—a speech which really equips Northern Irish people to translate *Beowulf*. He says:

> my people an abrupt people
> Who like the spiky consonants of speech
> And think the softy one cissy; who dig
> The *k* and *t* in orchestra, detect sin
> In synfonia, get a kick out of
> Tin cans, fricatives, fornication, staccato talk,
> Anything that gives or takes attack,
> Like Micks, Tagues, tinkers' gets, Vatican.

And I've often said that if you gave Anglo-Saxon poetry to the Reverend Ian Paisley, he could speak it perfectly. It's really big-voiced.... *Hwæt, wē Gār-dena in geārdagum, þēod-cyninga þrym gefrūnon*. Seriously, I think this has to do with the nature of the stress in the Northern Irish accent. Anyhow, I did about 150 lines of *Beowulf* in 1984–85 and then said, "I can't do anymore, it's too difficult." The words of the original are so big and the alliterative principle so strong. In Anglo-Saxon you have these huge monkey wrenches which are sort of welded together. All you have in modern English are little words like spanners to hang on the line. So I said I wouldn't proceed with the commission.

And then eventually—this has less to do with translation than with the psychology of poets—about ten years later, the editor wrote and said, "I know you don't want to do it, but could you give me the names of two other people you think *could* do it." And at that point I knew exactly who should do it.

But basically, I took it on because of the language. I felt it was in me, I felt there was some trace element of it in my own first speech, the dialect of Northern Ireland. And there was an Anglo-Saxon growth-ring in my ear from having studied it at university.

ROBERT HASS: You had 150 lines that you were more or less satisfied with, and then when you sat down to the task, did you know what you wanted to do, or did you have to invent it all over again?

SEAMUS HEANEY: From the start, I realized I couldn't do anything unless I found a way of getting started. OK, that's a truism, but how do you enter Anglo-Saxon, how is your own English going to move and sound? You know there are four stresses to the line, you know it can be linked together with alliteration, but how will it be paced? And then I thought of a voice—a voice that belonged to a cousin of my father's. One of three old country men who lived together in a house in a very quiet lakeshore district. When I was a youngster we used to go down there; I would be with my father—five males on a summer evening, no lights on in the house, twilight darkening slowly. Not much spoken, but occasionally one of them would break the silence and say something, like "We were at the corn today," or "We'll be at the corn tomorrow."

Still, there was a terrific verity about everything they said, and that chimed perfectly with that aspect of Anglo-Saxon poetry which is gnomic, that can say, "Water is wet," and get away with it. You need some way of echoing this. And so when I thought of this voice, Peter Scullion's voice, I thought, "That is the way." In *Beowulf*, there is a kind of proverbial wisdom-speaking which is matched by that country-speak they had. In the opening lines of the poem, for example, the young son is commended for helping and fighting for other people because then, in the end, when he becomes king, those people will stand by him. And then comes a gnomic observation—it's an Anglo-Saxon line, but in my version it belongs entirely to Ulster country-speak, in cadence and attitude—"Behavior that is admired / is the path to power among people everywhere." That could be said by an old farmer at the gable, you know, nodding and repeating it.

ROBERT HASS: Did you have a sharp sense after a while of what you weren't getting, of what you had to let go, to do what you could do?

SEAMUS HEANEY: Yes. I didn't get enough of the Anglo-Saxon weather, I mean the weather of feeling, of diction, the weather of the language. Pound manages it in his *Seafarer.* Pound writes wonderful Anglo-Saxon, modern Anglo-Saxon poetry. I may as well come out and say that the people who were asking me to do the translation were the Norton Anthology, and since I had been teaching for years myself, that kind of affected my covenant, not only with the text but with the commission. I felt it should be line-for-line, what the original said. No "spattered carnal melons" allowed. [Laughter] Yes. No Lowell-izing of the text, you know? Which is a great pity.

The example I have used to show how correctness won out over pleasure is a line very early on, when the big funeral is taking place and the poet tells us how the ship is ready to go out with the body of Scyld Scefing on it. The funeral ship is in the harbor, and it is *ut-fus,* a wonderful Anglo-Saxon word, out and fusing to go, eager to go, *ut-fus, æþelingas þæs,* fit for a prince, *isig,* icy.

In my original version, I had a line which I was delighted with, which I would have wished to keep. The boat, it said, stood in the harbor, "clad with ice, its cables tightening." There are no cables in the Anglo-Saxon of course, but I felt that this is *ut-fus,* you know, ready to move. Then my censor came at me and said, "Come on, take that out, kill your darling. Take out the cables. Lose your lovely tight alliteration." So I did. I mean it was a sin against the gift, against the grace of the line, but in order to be faithful to the literal sense, I ended up with "Ice-clad, outbound, a craft for a prince"—fine, it's what's in the line, but it's not as alive, as eager, as *ut-fus*.

ROBERT HASS: It's worse when your censor is alive. [Laughter] Robert Pinsky and I were collaborating on a translation of a very great poem written by Czesław Miłosz in the middle of the Nazi occupation of Warsaw, called "The World." Everyone was writing protest poems and Miłosz wrote a poem in a series of short song-like quatrains, almost like children's verse, about a family in a Lithuanian village. And in one section of the poem, the mother tells the children a parable, and the parable is called "Parable of the Poppyseed." The poem had never been translated because Miłosz was convinced that it had to rhyme and sound like children's verse if it was going to be translated. And so we said, "Let us give it a try." I think a literal translation of the Polish would go something like this:

> On a poppy seed there was a tiny house.
> Inside the house were people and a cat.
> Outside poppy-seed dogs bark at the moon,
> Never imagining that somewhere is a world much larger.

In my first effort to try to write a naive-sounding poem and make it rhyme I gave myself some latitude. I think it went like this:

> On a seed of poppy is a tiny house.
> Inside are people, a cat and a mouse.
> Outside in the yard, a dog barks at the moon.
> Then, in his world, he sleeps until noon.

I thought, "not bad, I'm on my way." I showed it to Czesław Miłosz, who would sometimes come around late in the afternoon to see what we were doing. He read it and he said, "Mouse?" [Laughter] Back to the drawing board.

ROBERT HASS: I thought that it might be interesting for you to hear a little bit of the beginning of *Beowulf* in a couple of the available translations. This one was done in 1957 by David Wright, who says, "My aim in translating [this poem] has been to produce, if I could, a readable version in contemporary English prose. It begins:

> Hear! We know of the bygone glory of the Danish kings, and the heroic exploits of those princes. Scyld Scefing, in the face of hostile armies, used often to bring nations into subjection, and strike terror in the hearts of their leaders. In the beginning he had been picked up as a castaway; but he afterwards found consolation for this misfortune. For his power and fame increased until each of his overseas neighbours was forced to submit and pay him tribute. He was an excellent king.

This translation by Constance Hieatt says that in this version of *Beowulf* readability was a primary objective; literal translation was out of the question. "I wanted to bring out the intense qualities of ornamentation" in Anglo-Saxon verse, she says. And this begins:

> Indeed, we have heard of the great Danish kings in days of old and the noble deeds of the princes. Scyld Scefing often drove troops of enemies from their mead-hall seats; he terrified the lords of many tribes, although he had once been a destitute foundling. He found consolation for that: he prospered under the heavens, and grew in glory, until every one of his neighbors over the sea had to obey him and pay tribute. That was a good king.

[Professor John Niles reads:]

> Hwæt, wē Gār-Dena   in geār-dagum,
> þeod-cyninga   þrym gefrūnon,
> hū ðā æþelingas   ellen fremedon.

Oft Scyld Scēfing sceaþena þrēatum,
monegum mǣgþum meodo-setla oftēah;
egsode Eorle, syððan ǣrest wearð
fēasceaft funden; hē þæs frōfre gebād:
wēox under wolcnum, weorð-myndum þāh,
oðþæt him ǣghwylc þāra ymb-sittendra
ofer hron-rāde hȳran scolde,
gomban gyldan: þæt wæs gōd cyning!

ROBERT HASS: Do you want to follow that? Did you look at other translations?

SEAMUS HEANEY: I looked early on at some verse translations, but I worked with scholarly prose. What I used as a crib was the Donaldson translation, the one in the Norton Anthology, and it could be said of it (in a negative way) that it is "no language." Ben Jonson said that of somebody: "He writ no language." At the same time you could also say that Donaldson's work has the complete otherness of the Anglo-Saxon. It is faithful to the kennings; it keeps the appositional style; you are in the midst of a different way of making sense. And it certainly has no cajolement for a contemporary reader; it doesn't set out to write contemporary English prose, and it doesn't set out to attract the undergraduate. So you begin and you think, ah well, at least I'll be writing in clearer English. Then you finish your work and you think, there's a lot to be said for Donaldson, you know, that strangeness.

So I used the Donaldson and I used the Tolkien and the Barber, the Oxford school's version. Then I came across a translation that Bill Alfred had done for the Modern Library in prose, and I had to beware of it because the word choice was very good, the diction was excellent, and I found myself attracted to Bill's solutions, so I schooled myself to keep away from it. But I read it afterwards for a reward.

Still, I couldn't start until I had translated the first word, *hwæt.* So I translated it into Irish English, with the word "so," a particle which obliterates all previous narrative and announces your intention to proceed with your own.

The first time around I imitated more or less what Peter Scullion would say. And I liked another phrase which was still used in the country, about people who were famous or in control. It was said that "they held sway." I thought that was good for a warrior culture, so I began the poem,

> So, the Spear-Danes held sway once.
> The kings of that clan are heroes to us
> because of their bravery. Those were princes who dared.

And then I began to get a conscience: *Hwæt, wē Gār-Dena in geārdagum*—there is a nice alliteration in that but also a kind of cajolement between the vowels, and eventually I got, "So the Spear-Danes in days gone by..." There you get the alliteration and the "a"s and the same word order. I wish I could find similar equivalents for the other 3,181 lines. Anyway my version went:

> So the Spear-Danes in days gone by
> and the kings who ruled them had courage and greatness.
> We have heard of those princes' heroic campaigns.
>
> There was Scyld Scefing, scourge of many tribes,
> a wrecker of mead benches, rampaging among foes.
> This terror of the hall troops had come far.
> A foundling to start with, he flourished later on
> as his powers waxed and his worth was proved.
> In the end, each sept on the outlying coasts
> beyond the whale road gave in and obeyed him
> and began to pay tribute. That was one good king.

And then there is scansion. One of my favorite lines occurs in the description of Beowulf's boat journey across into Denmark from Geatland. It says, "the boat was on water / in close, under the cliffs." A couple of people who have read it have questioned "in close, under the cliffs" as a line—they don't get the Ulster stress; that to me is a spondee, *in* close. And I want to stick to my own cadence even if standard English dictates otherwise.

What about your difficulty with cadences? I know you are translating another strictly metrical Polish work.

ROBERT HASS: Well, yeah. It is a different set of problems, compounded, for me, by the fact that over the years of doing this I've never really learned Polish. I work directly with Miłosz. I can now pick my way through a newspaper but I've never lived in Poland, I've heard Polish speech only rarely. So my sense of it is a book-sense. Miłosz wrote a poem—almost the only major work of his now that hasn't been translated into English—that is in a rather strict meter that is maybe the Polish equivalent of blank verse. It is an eleven-syllable line for the most part—it depends a lot on the way the pause moves around; sometimes it is five syllables and then six, sometimes it is six syllables and then five. The Polish scansion system—which they call syllabotonic—they say, is not really quite so metrically regular as English. There is a little more freedom with nonaccented vowel sounds. So this is again a poem that probably should be translated—it is very long—into something like blank verse. I don't know if that slight tightening up would represent the sound of the poem accurately. I have only just begun working on it; we did a section of it.

We start with making a literal translation and what happens, really, is that Czesław frames the terms of the rhythmic conversion into English and the grammar may be quite rough. Sometimes the lines are just wonderful; they don't have to be touched, but the whole thing has to be articulated. Before I was working with him directly, when I started on this project, my friend Renata

Gorczynski would tape the poems so I could hear them. And then I would try to find an English equivalent. Sometimes you hear one and sometimes you don't.

The difference with this project is that in one way my job is to get this work that people are interested in into English, period. Later on, people are going to sort through this body of work and someone who knows Polish very well is going to decide, as someone might with a Baudelaire poem, "I want to make it better." Some of these works will be retranslated and retranslated. So my work is to get the word out, in a way. I was saying to Seamus the other night that for Miłosz the poem is in Polish, so one of the things that happens when we work is that "good enough" is good enough for him, whereas I want to say, "Let me work on this line for a couple of weeks." He says, "No, let's get this done." Because it is after all a poem in Polish, not a poem in English. "This is pretty good, it sounds all right." So this quite pragmatic attitude qualifies my task.

ROBERT HASS: Do you have a sense of people looking over your shoulder when you're dealing with Irish material?

SEAMUS HEANEY: Absolutely. First of all, the dead generations of previous translators. Many of the poems have been translated before, famously, and some versions are canonical. It's like translating Dante except it's not as big a deal and usually they are shorter poems. But you are aware of how the lines have been translated by earlier poets.

ROBERT HASS: What about your translation of Raftery? Did he compose orally?

SEAMUS HEANEY: Yes, I think so. There is a famous one, an unusually perfected little thing, an unexpected, apparently extempore lyric.

ROBERT HASS: Are you going to read it?

SEAMUS HEANEY:

> I am Raftery the poet,
> full of hope and love,
> my eyes without eyesight,
> my spirit untroubled.
> Tramping west
> by the light of my heart,
> worn down, worn out,
> to the end of the road.
>
> Take a look at me now,
> my back to a wall,
> playing the music
> to empty pockets.

The question arises with lots of work, especially traditional work: what do you do about the meter? Do you translate metrical verse metrically? There is no one answer, there are only the choices people make. Does it rhyme, and if so do you translate it into rhyme? A sonnet, for example; a sonnet is partly its movement. It is whatever tension and checks and balances are in the movement of it. And after all there is a turn in a sonnet, in an eight-and-six sonnet, it should shift itself, move within itself, and the rhyme is part of the gear system, as it were, even though it may not be noticed that much. I found myself thinking more about these things when people were translating my own poems into other languages, like into French. Some sonnets of mine were being translated into French with no rhymes in them and no meter, just a free verse crib, and I thought, "Well, why bother?" It doesn't move. And then I thought, "What happens when these poems go into Japanese?"

In Russian, it would probably be OK. Seeing Bob Tracy here reminds me of his work on Mandelstam. I had read with delight W. S. Merwin's and Clarence Brown's translations. Then in between I met Joseph Brodsky, who said what he usually said about anything: "No, no, no! When you are listening to Mandelstam in Russian you have to think something like late Yeats. This is sturdy quatrain metrical stuff." And indeed when Bob Tracy's versions came out, you felt the four-squareness, the architectural stone principle working in them. The meter and the rhyme gave the poem a different kind of verity. The virtue of Merwin's work was in making the poems available—getting Mandelstam into the ear, saying, "Listen to this." He said it in Merwin-speak, naturally. The original became slightly more beguiling and more sinuous. The Tracy versions were more plonked down à la Mandelstam. I suppose it is inevitable that people speak in their own voice in translation. But the older I get the more obedient I tend to become.

ROBERT HASS: I set my students the task of translating a poem from the Oglala Sioux of Sitting Bull as recorded by Francis Densmore, who heard it sung in about 1899 by someone who had known Sitting Bull, and it goes something like—a literal translation would be (this was after Little Big Horn, after he had taken his people into Canada, they had starved through two winters, and he then brought them back to the United States and saw them herded into reservations):

> A warrior I have known how to be, hey. Now that is all over,
> hey. Now I know how to crash against hard things.

That is the whole poem, sung. There are two puns in the Sioux on the word for "bear," because "to know" has the same root as "bear." So, in the song, a warrior is a bearish person and also a knower. To get that, you would have to put in a couple of puns on bearishness that carried some of its meaning for the Oglalas. To make matters worse, Francis Densmore (who was basically an ethnomusicologist) records that, as sung, in a series of descending sevenths, it basically imitated the song of the midwestern plains meadowlark, which was the bird that Sitting Bull had encountered as a young man on his first vision quest. So in order to demonstrate how easy translation was, I gave my students a word-for-word version of this poem and told them, if they could, to include two puns on "bear" and make it sound like the song of a plains meadowlark.

There is a good part of translation that in that way is just impossible. Another Miłosz story: I was working with my friend Renata Gorczynski and there was a line in a poem that Miłosz wrote in Berkeley in the mid-'70s—he had been here twenty years—when he felt that, except for the friendship of Peter Scott and their translations together, he was writing poems about the sun going down over San Francisco Bay for about six people. His poems could not be published in Poland and were published by a small emigré press in Paris. Very few American poets knew who he was, though a number of them would show up to audit his classes. And he began a long poem called *The Separate Notebooks*, one section of which begins, "Now you have nothing to lose. My cunning, my cautious, my hyper-selfish cat. Now you can make a confession into the void because nobody cares. You are an echo," and, as Renata translated it for me, "You are an echo that runs tippy-toe through an amfilade of rooms." And I thought, "Well, we're going to have to work on that line." [Laughter]

Amfilade it turns out, is a French architectural term meaning a series of rooms of French doors opening one to another, and we were able to work this one out by looking up *amfilade*, the Polish word, in the French dictionary and then going to the English dictionary and finding that the English word was amfilade. And you don't want it to sound like a translation, but it is not such an unusual term in Polish as it is in English. So what do you do?

The next word, the word that she had rendered "tippy-toe," was *tupotem*, an adverb. I said, "What does *tupotem* mean?" and she said, "Well, it's an onomotopoetic word and the best way to tell you what it means is the typical name in eastern Poland for a pet hedgehog is *tupotcya*." So *tupotem* is like the sound of a hedgehog running across a hardwood floor. That's like the meadowlark. There are things that you just give up on.

SEAMUS HEANEY: What did you do?

ROBERT HASS: "Skittering."

SEAMUS HEANEY: Ah!

ROBERT HASS: And I changed *amfilade* to "train" and then decided to stay with *amfilade*. Sometimes it is better to have the recalcitrant strangeness and accuracy.

ROBERT HASS: I want to ask you about Virgil and "Seeing Things—another raid?

SEAMUS HEANEY: Yes. When I was at boarding school, the Virgil that was set when I was doing my exam was *The Aeneid*, book 9, Nisus and Euryalus and all that. But the teacher was a wonderful teacher. He taught obliquely, because he kept saying, "Oh boys, I wish it were book 6." [Laughter] All through my life, then, I thought, "book 6." And of course it's irresistible, once you read it. The journey into the underworld, the golden bough, and so on.

When I met Robert Fitzgerald, who was at Harvard and had translated *The Odyssey* and *The Iliad*, he was translating *The Aeneid*. We spent an afternoon playing with "How could you translate the first three or four words?": *Arma virumque cano*. Robert was faced with that. Do you just say: "I sing of arms and a man"? Do people still sing? He said he might just begin with *Arma virumque cano* and then proceed with the English, but in the end, without triumph or pleasure, he settled for "I sing of warfare and a man at war."

Then when Robert died, there was a memorial reading held for him. And I thought, "book 6." I thought of the bit where Aeneas meets his father in the underworld, because Robert had been a father figure in my life at Harvard, so I read this and then thought more about the underground journey, going down, getting back. I'd been translating the opening sections of *The Inferno* and was interested in the whole theme of descent. And I had been thinking of the finding of the golden bough and of being given the branch as symbolic of being given the right to speak. Then my father died, and I had a number of poems about him, and next thing someone asked me to contribute a piece to an Irish issue of *Translation* magazine, and I thought, "I'll go and get permission to go down to the underground to see him." So I began to translate the bit where Aeneas goes to see the Sybil and she tells him that in order to go down to see Anchises he has to find the golden bough. It is a perfect little narrative in itself, and it ends with that moment of discovery and triumph when Aeneas finds the bough and the bough comes away in his hand and he has been given the right of way. It's like finding a voice, the beginning and end at once. So that was a raid, and it led into a book where I met my father in a poem called "Seeing Things."

As ever in the raid system, there was something out there in the other language that I needed. For vague reasons. My favorite raid is the sonnet by Wyatt: "Whoso list to hunt, I know where is an hind," a translation of Petrarch. I think it may be one of the very first sonnets in English. I actually prefer it to any other Renaissance sonnet.

ROBERT HASS: Can you say it?

SEAMUS HEANEY: Yeah ... But this is not an exact translation. In the original the speaker meets a bejeweled type of deer, and Petrarch clearly has some class of allegorical deer in mind. But next thing Wyatt comes along and the deer comes physically to life. This is a hunter who has been after actual deer. The tradition, as you may know, says that this poem is about Ann Boleyn, after she had been married to Henry VIII. Because after the marriage history records that Sir Thomas Wyatt was locked up in the Tower of London for a little while. Just to keep him, probably, out of the chamber.

ROBERT HASS: I remember one of my teachers remarking that falling in love with Ann Boleyn in early Tudor England was a little bit like taking a shine to Stalin's girlfriend. Not a safe thing to do.

SEAMUS HEANEY: That's right. But in the poem the woman certainly is untouched. *Noli me tangere* is in the Petrarch original, and so is the general shape of the thing. But the wild energy isn't there.

> Whoso list to hunt, I know where is an hind,
> But as for me, alas, I may no more.
> The vain travail hath wearied me so sore,
> I am of them that furthest come behind.
> Yet may I by no means my wearied mind
> Draw from the deer, but as she fleeth afore,
> Fainting I follow. I leave off therefore
> Since in a net I seek to hold the wind.
> Who list her hunt, I put him out of doubt,
> As well as I may spend his time in vain.
> And graven in diamonds, in letters plain,
> There is written her fair neck round about:
> *Noli me tangere* for Caesar's I am,
> And wild for to hold, though I seem tame.

It is quite wonderful, the full rhyme of "wind" with "behind"—the movement.

Sebastião Salgado with Orville Schell

Migrations

Sebastião Salgado

I'M VERY HAPPY to have this show at the Berkeley Art Museum, this museum linked with the university. The pictures that we will show in this exhibition are a bit of a cross section of our life, the life of all of us as human beings. I was recently at a small reception in the museum, and I was looking at a few migrant workers there, you know, in the museum, serving, working. They reminded me of the many people I've met, crossing the borders, the border between Guatemala and Mexico, coming from South America, from Central America, and jumping the trains, traveling three thousand miles to arrive here in the US. They take many risks. For what? They come here just to work.

Once when I was with a group of these migrants, we stopped in a town in Oaxaca, in Mexico, and waited for another train to jump. These were fourteen-year-old boys, kids, sixteen-years-, nineteen-years-old; the older ones were twenty-two-, twenty-three-years old. I asked them, "Why you are going to the United States? What are you expecting to find there?" And they said, "Well, we can have work. We can probably work seven days a week. And who knows, once a month we can have some rest. And one day, maybe our girlfriends will come, and we'll buy a used car and get a small house." To my mind, that's the minimum that every human being must have. That's the minimum. These guys were looking just for their dignity; they just wanted to get enough money or security to live their life. I respect them a lot because it was so hard for them to reach this land.

I also met many people crossing the border between Africa and Europe in Gibraltar, you know, in boats, taking huge risks with their lives to be in Europe, just to get a job. And why do we imagine that this is happening, on the scale that it is, on the planet today? Of course, migration always exists, but it has not always existed at the level at which it's happening now.

My country, Brazil, in thirty years' time moved from having 8 percent of the population being urban to today's statistics, where about 80 percent of the population is urban. The United States, by comparison, took about two hundred, three hundred years to become urban. Brazil did that in thirty years. Mexico, in the same number of years, about thirty years, changed in such a way that what was once a country with a 92 percent rural population, today is close to a 75 percent urban population. It is important, then, to remember that when we speak of migration, most of the migration occurs within countries, from rural areas into the towns, in third-world countries. And why has that happened? That's the question that thus far has not been raised. It didn't just "happen" like this. Something must have provoked all this displacement.

That's the point of my work. Prior to my current work I did a show called *Workers*. That story was a kind of homage to the working class around the world. We also produced a book, named *Workers: An Archaeology of the Industrial Age* (Aperture, 1993). Earlier in my life I was an economist. I made my living in that way.

As I was skilled in photography, one day I made the decision to pay homage to this working class that was the center of my studies when I was an economist. I traveled around this planet photographing workers because I feel that we are at the end of the first big industrial revolution. The arrival of new technologies and production methods geared toward the new needs of consumers has changed something about industry. Touring around the planet, I started to see that this change was a much bigger revolution. All of society on this planet was headed for a big change, because what we now call globalization was happening and had been happening for a very long time. Now we have realized this, of course, and it has been named "globalization." We have changed the scale of value of the goods produced here in the northern part of the planet: the computers, the high-technology products. They have a price, a very inflated price. And the prices of the goods produced in the southern part of the planet, they have another price, and that price keeps decreasing.

In the end, globalization—I came to understand during those years—is an incredible system that we have created in order to transfer wealth from one part of the planet to the other. It is not that you in the United States work more than the others, not that the French work more than the Africans; that's not true. I went to Rwanda, for example. In Africa, I saw these guys working hard, working twelve hours a day to produce. They produced a lot, they worked a lot, and what can they buy with their products or earnings? They can buy some clothes, bad clothes; they cannot even buy shoes. They cannot buy health services; they cannot buy a house; they cannot buy education. But they work as much as we do. And when they export their products, they export a negative price. They pay us to consume their products. When you go to Sierra Leone or to the Ivory Coast to see these guys produce the cocoa that we consume here—chocolate—or the guys producing coffee, it's exactly the same. The people who fix the prices of these goods don't produce one gram, one pound, of coffee, of cocoa, of tea. The price is fixed in London; it's fixed in New York; it's fixed in Chicago, and the prices keep going down, and the prices here keep going up.

These people, whom I met on the road, whom I photographed on the road, who are pictured in my work, they worked as hard and long as any of us. And they don't understand why they've lost their houses, their jobs. They don't understand why there are so many wars going on. They were just on the road, headed elsewhere, looking for another point of equilibrium for their lives. In the past, they had worked hard and they had been living in equilibrium. They had a house; they had a job; they had their dignity. They had their children. They were poor, but they had these things. And now they have nothing. These young kids that I met on the train coming here, they were just looking for a way to defend their dignity, a way to live. They had come just to be able to work. Ninety-nine percent of the people who arrive in this country come to work, to produce. It is the same with the migrants who arrive in France via Gibraltar. It is the same thing.

That, my friends, is globalization. The word "globalization" is big on this side of the planet. We speak of the globalization of finance, the globalization of the economy, the globalization of information, the globalization of any kind of thing that we want. But we never speak about globalized people. Globalized people don't interest us. But we must pay heed to the others.

In my country, Brazil, we have no tradition of producing oranges. Brazilians don't consume oranges and never have. Orange juice for us means nothing. Yet in the last few years, Brazil has become the first producer of oranges on the planet. For what? For this country here. When you had oranges produced mostly in Florida, and unexpected cold weather killed Florida's orange trees, it was necessary somehow to guarantee some orange trees for this market. Where did that market look to? It looked to São Paulo, Brazil. The Brazilians took the land where they were producing rice, beans, potatoes—all that was necessary for the Brazilian people to eat—and sold it. This was a region of big colonization, of Italian and Japanese people. Big companies came and bought the land; they paid the market price. But Brazil's currency was hugely inflated. Those who sold their farms put the money aside. Six months later they couldn't buy a bicycle with that money.

While I was shooting *Workers*, I went to these orange-producing farms. I also visited farms where they produce sugar cane. Brazil has become the biggest exporter of sugar, too, and soybeans. Brazil is the second biggest producer of soybeans on this planet. Brazilians don't consume soybeans. These products are produced for a global lifestyle, an international lifestyle, but not a Brazilian one. Millions of small farmers were pushed out of their lands. They moved to towns not far away. These small towns, in a few years, became huge towns. Whenever the now-large farms need workers, they send a truck to town. They employ people on a day-by-day basis. When they have no more jobs, they don't send trucks. And sociologists study the patterns. Sociologists and anthropologists conduct their studies as if this has always existed in Brazil. But thirty years ago, there was nothing like this. It is a product of globalization.

While doing these shoots, I met a lot of guys who work on what was once their own land—the land they lost to these big farms. And the orange juice keeps coming. When you drink juice, you don't raise these kinds of questions, but you should. Because in the end, all the health that you have accumulated in this country is the health of the rest of the world. And if you want, in a sense, to live together, if you want to live in a society that's a society for all, we must find a way to remedy this. The immigrants who risk everything to come here would not even be coming if they could find a job at home, if they could keep a house and a way of life.

We are working on a project in Brazil. When I was a kid, more than half of the land that is now farming land was rainforest, with crocodiles in the rivers, with monkeys. There were small farms, with thirty-five families working the land, producing any kind of produce; they created a society at equilibrium—a poor society, but they could sustain themselves. They were not unhappy. But slowly we cut down the forest for logging, for coal, and most often to plant grass for grazing land, for meat. The United States has 93 million head of cattle; Brazil has 170 million head of cattle. We have more cattle than we have people in Brazil. Brazil cannot consume all this meat. The meat is for export, for foreign markets.

And that is the point. It's not that I'm saying we can come back from globalization. But we probably can find a much more human, or humane, way to globalize the world. We can mine in a different way. And imagine how we waste resources in rich countries like this. I'm not saying it's only the United States, but rich countries in general. You see the new bombers that you have here, the B-1s and the B-2s, each plane worth $200 million. One tractor for agriculture costs about twenty thousand dollars. With the money it takes to build one of those bombers, we can build ten thousand tractors. My friends, with ten thousand tractors, we can begin a huge agricultural revolution in many countries around this planet, just by forgoing one bomber.

The forests we're trying to plant in Brazil, with the organization I work with, are very important; we need to get resources back into these forests. We are planting about 1.5 million trees, and we are creating an environmental school. At present we do not have enough resources to get all the trees we need. The organization runs on small amounts of money and donations that we get here and there. We have finally gotten some help from the surrounding community. They are putting 10 percent of their budget into rebuilding the forest, because the region has no more water. There are so many rivers that twenty or thirty years ago had crocodiles living in them and today have no more water. Because we cut down the forest, the rivers cannot retain the water during the rainy season, and big erosion kills the small rivers.

We are fighting with a lot of different institutions to get funds, in order to multiply the amount of money we are spending on this project. That means about $50 to $60 million. In thirty years, if we keep at it, we will have planted 60 to 70 million trees. It would be a green revolution. And I assure you that in order to accomplish a green revolution, we would have to change completely the face of the planet down there. The cost of this is equal to one-quarter of one bomber plane, of which you are producing hundreds in this country. Congress just voted now at the end of October [2001] to approve a contract for $400 billion for producing new bombers—$200 billion will be for this country, and $200 billion will be for England, Denmark, Spain, Turkey. And that's just one kind of plane. Then there are the tanks, the weapons, the Star Wars program. How many billions of dollars are going to be spent? And for what? In thirty years, this all will be obsolete and will have to be rebuilt.

And, sure, we can point our fingers like this at the American government. But the American government is all of you inside of this room; it's all of you who are in the streets. That's the point. How we can build the kind of society that will be a society for all? How can we become a planet that regrows its lost forests? How can we live on a planet such that every human community can live with dignity, including the communities of the future? It seems that we have forgotten that there is a future for Africa, though we speak all about starvation now. You remember, people of my age—I just turned fifty-eight a few days ago—we remember when we were kids the myth that surrounded Africa, with the jungle, the animals, the mysterious culture. Now we speak only about starvation in Africa. We speak only about the wars in Africa. But what planet are we building? Is this what we are working for? Is this what we will leave to our kids?

That is why I always hope that my pictures will provoke a debate. I know that these pictures alone are nothing. But these pictures, together with humanitarian organizations, with the newspapers, and with the children, all together, can probably build a new society. And the question is how to do so. I believe we can do this by opening up a dialogue. We must open our minds to a discussion. We must start the discussion with our neighbors, in our streets, with our community. Maybe this would cause us to elect responsible people who compete to bring forth new, good ideas. The people want new ideas.

My first book is about workers, and the second is about migration. When I finished photographing the book on workers, I was very proud of humanity because I had shot photographs in shipbuilding factories, automaking factories, big mines, and I was so moved by how humans are capable of transforming the world around them. We are an animal made to transform goods. It's incredible to see how we can produce a ship. We get flat steel—a square that's produced in a steel plant from material that comes from a mine. Then these small men inside the shipyard produce something the size of a great ship. They are capable of putting all this together. They tie this flattened steel, slice by slice, into an incredible ship that then tours around on this planet. The ship gets shirts from Bangladesh and brings them to people here in San Francisco to consume. These shirts are made with a textile that came from India. It's incredible how sophisticated we are at producing things. So when I finished photographing the workers, I was 100 percent sure that humanity was in evolution. And for me this evolution was a positive one.

But now that I've finished photographing the work on migration, I've come to see that evolution can be a downward curve as well. We are going to the death. What's incredible in what I saw when shooting this is the capacity of adaptation that we have as humans. We have adapted to so many kinds of situations. When I came to photograph the refugee camps of people who had come out of Rwanda, it was incredible. I saw on one day thousands of dead people, a mountain of dead people, probably ten thousand or fifteen thousand dead people. There were so many it was not possible to bury them one by one. It was necessary to dig a huge hole and use a bulldozer to move a hundred bodies at a time into the ground. Total degradation.

A man walked up with a child in his arms, and discussed something with someone nearby. Then he walked up to the pile of bodies and threw the child on top. I ran up to him and said, "Old man, who was this child?" And the man told me it was his child who had died the night before. He just threw him on the pile and left. He had completely adapted himself to this world of death.

This violence that we live with on this planet today, and the violence in my country—thirty years ago it didn't exist. Now Brazil is one of the most violent countries on this planet. This is what we have become. I'm not certain that we can survive this.

We need to understand two things: solidarity and community. If we have a real idea of solidarity and a real idea of community, we might survive. Brazil will probably disappear. The dinosaurs were stronger than us; they lived about 150 million years ago, they lived for a while and they're gone. And probably if we don't pay attention, we will end that way too.

When I was on the road photographing people, they all had this in common: the hope of survival, the instinct of survival. If there is a god for us humans, it is our instinct of survival. I believe that it is in this sense that we must act; we must work together to protect ourselves. Our instinct of self-preservation should be one of protection common to us all. We cannot protect only the Americans or only the French; we must protect all of us together. We cannot survive alone; we must live together.

Conversation: Sebastião Salgado and Orville Schell

ORVILLE SCHELL: That's a pretty bleak view of things. And I'm kind of curious to know, what keeps you going?

SEBASTIÃO SALGADO: That has been my life, where I come from. I was born on a farm, and moved to a small town when I was four or five years old with my family. I have seven sisters. When I grew up I moved to a bigger town—Vitória, the capital of the province—and started to work. There I met Lélia, whom I married. I went to college in economics and graduated from the university in São Paulo. My wife and I were active in movements against the dictatorship in Brazil and were pushed out of the country.

Today, thirty years later, we live in France part of the time and in Brazil part of the time. We are in France most of the time; we too are migrants, or refugees, who have had to live in a foreign country. So I understand this way of life.

But I don't work alone. When we see pictures, we tend to make the photographer into the sole creator, some heroic person, because it's only his name on the photo. But no one works alone. We have a team. I work with Lélia and with a group of people in the laboratory who edit the shots. We also work with a number of humanitarian organizations that use these pictures. I had a meeting recently in Oakland with the Tides Foundation, who had arranged to show my photographs, and that means we do not work alone. I work with friends and with strangers all over the world.

We are all working at pushing this debate, provoking discussion. With the environmental project in Brazil, we are probably the biggest employers in our region. We employ ninety-two people. Lélia and myself represent the group and go around the world speaking and begging for money to support this project, telling the world that we must plant these trees. That's what Lélia and I do for the organization. But we also have the guys there planting; we have the biologists taking care of the ecosystem, monitoring it. That means we are not alone. That's the point. Not being alone gives us power to keep going; even when the situation is not easy, we retain hope.

ORVILLE SCHELL: Do you think in the last ten years, fifteen years, you've become less hopeful or more hopeful?

SEBASTIÃO SALGADO: To be honest, I have become less hopeful. I have become less hopeful, in the sense that I have traveled a lot. I've probably been to more than a hundred different countries on this planet, and revisited many countries multiple times. It is rarely the case that the countries in the third world are in a better situation on the second visit or the third. As time passes, the situation only gets worse. Each time I see more degradation, more difficult situations.

ORVILLE SCHELL: Did you ever think of just giving up?

SEBASTIÃO SALGADO: No. I'm not giving up. I worked for seven years shooting the pictures for *Migrations*. The people that I met all over the world, they were distressed, but they were not depressed. They were hopeful, full of energy to get to a new point of equilibrium. Seeing that gives you a lot of hope.

But it's very complicated. We've just come back from Mexico City. In the 1990s, I went to do a story in Mexico. I went to Oaxaca to shoot a group called the Mixes. These are incredible people. These Mixes, they were musicians. For the people in this society who were supposed to play an instrument or to sing, it was not necessary to work in a hard job. Music is their work. And they had incredible songs, incredible music. In 1998, I went back to Mexico to work with the Zapatista's movement and to work with migrants crossing into this country. I based the story out of Mexico City. While I was there I went to the Mixes' country, but they weren't there anymore. They had abandoned their land.

We did a book about the landless movement in Brazil, a book named *Terra: Struggle of the Landless* that can be found in this country because it was published in England by Phaidon (1997). We had a lot of shows, and Lélia designed a series of posters for the exhibition. The landless movement is about peasants who do not have land or citizenship. Despite their hardships they create cooperatives and fight for citizenship and land. When I met with the leaders of the landless movement, they told me that we are probably losing the fight because they are able to help about fifty thousand families a year, seventy thousand families maximum. But there are more than two hundred thousand families per year that abandon the land and go to the towns. This is a system that must be changed.

ORVILLE SCHELL: Do you think it's really a system, or is it just sort of happening out of control? I mean, at the heart of this whole proposition is the question of globalization. Have you analyzed that? Is it hopeless? What's the alternative?

SEBASTIÃO SALGADO: I don't believe that these things happen just because they happen. We live in a world where we provoke changes, and those changes create big waves of reaction on the other side. Here is an example dealing with Europe: about a year and a half ago, European chocolate manufacturers changed the composition of the chocolate in order to consume more fatty material from European agriculture. They've added 5 percent more fat material to the production of chocolate. That's great for the people at Nestle, who get to produce chocolate at a lower price for a larger profit. Their stocks go very high in the Dow Jones numbers because they profit. But in the Ivory Coast and in Sierra Leone, that produces millions of unemployed workers, since the demand for cocoa decreases. These things are without a doubt related. Of course it is a complex problem that also has to do with local officials and government in Africa. But these things are related. We must look for a solution.

We are acting in a global order that is not profiting the majority of the people. And I believe that we must look at the full model, not just the profit margin. When I was photographing *Workers*, I went into a small factory in Bangladesh. This factory is not producing goods for Bangladesh. It's importing globally. We are living in that kind of a system, completely integrated.

In my country we have the Workers' Party, which possibly will gain power in next year's elections. But even so, even if we elect a Workers' Party president, he will probably find it impossible to take Brazil out of that globalized system. If you take Brazil outside of that system, Brazil won't exist anymore. What can we do?

ORVILLE SCHELL: Well, that's the question I want to ask you.

SEBASTIÃO SALGADO: I can't have all the answers or the only answer. I'm just one factor in the equation. I take pictures and bring them here and try to provoke a discussion. The question you ask me is better put to the sociologists and the anthropologists here. This is a fabulous college, probably one of the best universities on this planet. You probably know where we are going. No?

ORVILLE SCHELL: I'm not sure.

SEBASTIÃO SALGADO: So that's the reality. And I try to link things together, to show people what I've seen, to get a discussion going. This work I do is the most important thing to me. But I have no solution. I don't know what the solution would be. I believe that we must work together to find the solution. Me, with you, and with all the people in the streets, all around, together. We must have debate; we must have discussion. I'm willing to bet that the solution will not be found only in Brazil, or only in Africa, but probably the solution is here, in the way that we live here. We can live differently. We can be less egoistic. That is probably the only solution.

We live in a cynical society, and that is a problem. The press is especially cynical, and they create the news, no? Start with the journalists. I had a show in New York from June to September [2001]. A critic in the *New York Times*, the art critic who criticized my work, in the end, criticized himself. He told me that I was not cynical enough. That judgment is a big problem, you know.

ORVILLE SCHELL: And he also said your photographs were almost too beautiful.

SEBASTIÃO SALGADO: They were almost too beautiful. Compare me to the American photographer Walker Evans. In the end, Walker Evans has a kind of cynicism. So they think that it must also be necessary for me to have a little bit of cynicism inside my pictures, no? And this is a big problem in the society that we live in. I work with many journalists, and they are basically cynics. It's terrible, this society that we are living in today. If we eliminate a little bit of the huge pretensions that we have, probably we can live in a better world.

ORVILLE SCHELL: You're a real idealist, aren't you?

SEBASTIÃO SALGADO: Yes, I'm an idealist.

ORVILLE SCHELL: It is interesting to hear you, who are one of the best-known photographers in the world, and yet hearing you speak, you would hardly know you're a photographer at all. I mean, you're almost an evangelist for this global dilemma that you find yourself in. It's a rather striking comment.

SEBASTIÃO SALGADO: Well, we can speak about my photography. I don't mind that. But consider this: I'm sure that inside this room there are many people of my generation who did what I did at a younger age and tried to learn Esperanto, no? In order to learn a language in which it would be possible to communicate with the entire world. We had this big illusion that that was possible. And we tried. And now that has disappeared as if it were not the truth. Then we began to think that English was the universal language. But in the end, finally, the photograph is, for me, the universal language. The image. Not only the photograph but the moving image. Photography is a universal language, a very powerful language. What you write in this language in Africa, we can read here with no translation. What you write in India, we can read in China. That's a very powerful language.

In that sense, I use this language. I am a writer in this language of photography. I have the passion of a photographer, which was, of course, the first motivation that made me begin taking photo-

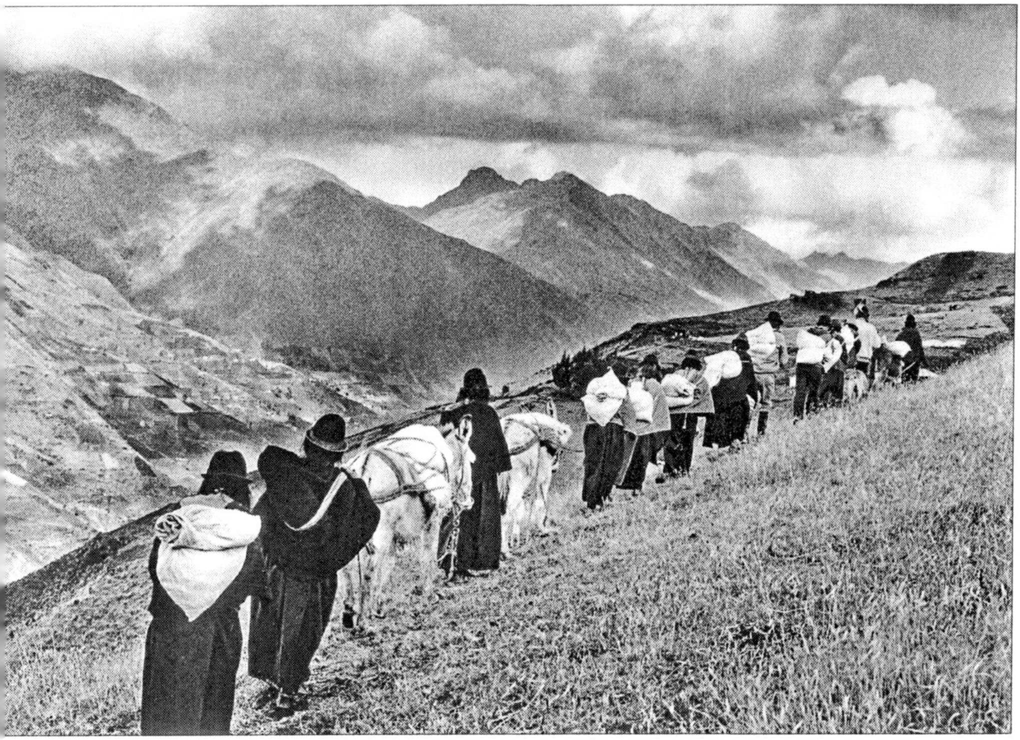

Sebastião Salgado, *Equador, 1998*

graphs. I love photography. It's a pleasure to be close to people, to approach them with a camera. And the people love you to observe their life. They tell you their stories, and they accept you. And it's fabulous because I never pose people. I don't organize people into a frame for a picture. But when you approach with a camera, people act for you. People accept you. When I'm shooting I work mostly alone, and when you come alone, you are accepted. Humans are animals made to live in a community, made to live in a group. But they welcome others in, too.

This is photography. I write with this aesthetic language. It's a formal language. That means it must be aesthetic, of necessity. But it's very powerful. The photographer has this possibility to approach people, to live with people, to freeze a moment, a fraction of a second. Each of the photographs in this show, if added up according to the time of their exposure, might add up to a second or two. It's a fraction of time. But it's powerful. You begin to understand the story of the people you see. You understand the distresses of this society we all live in. We understand a bit of the aesthetics. We understand something about photography.

It's a pleasure to be photographer. I can shoot from the morning to the evening. But, you know, these are not objects in the sense that I made them for this show. I speak about my photography, how I made a composition, how this aperture was set, how the light is there. These pictures, they are not objects. They are a history, and the subjects speak in these pictures about our history. For me, it would be difficult to come here and speak only about photography. It is more important to draw attention to the society that we are living in, the society that created these pictures. This is how I make my way of life.

ORVILLE SCHELL: How do you view America? In this global society that we are evolving into, the United States figures very prominently. When you look at America, what do you see? And what would you say to our president if you were asked to say a few words?

SEBASTIÃO SALGADO: Well, you know, for me it is simply unimaginable that I might say something to the president of the United States. Not that I'd never have access to him, but, really, how could I speak to a person that represents an incredible machine, an incredible system? I'm not sure if I were to say something to the president of the United States, that the president would be capable of changing anything. There are so many powers—military power, industrial power, economic interests—that probably a president is just one point in a system. Maybe I could go to tell something to the House of Representatives; that would be incredible. Because in the end these are the guys that represent the people who are here, no?

At this point in time, there are so many things to say, so many things to discuss, you know, so many evident things. But the machine that we build—what are we to think when we see what happened in this country on September 11? It was terrible, terrible to see, to watch television and to see these planes crashing into buildings. To see the fire burning the buildings and the humans hanging out of tiny windows, and there being no way to save them. This is such a powerful country, so rich in technology, and still there was no way to save these people. And so they jumped into empty space. I thought to myself, now it is truly time for a dialogue on this planet. Because now we must understand that this country is rich, very rich, that these two buildings in a way represent all of the wealth of the planet, because this is the financial system that dominates the world economy. But we need to open a dialogue about *peace*.

But what happens when the president of this country can speak only of the vengeance of war? He went for bombing and very quickly we destroyed Afghanistan's already ailing infrastructure. What can happen now? I have no idea. It seems that the "terrorists" had more reasons to use force than they did to enter a debate or dialogue. And now the US is thinking of bombing Iraq? We are not entering a dialogue: we are pushing a military situation. We are provoking more war. This is not a solution.

This country has so many economists, so many sociologists, so many anthropologists who must know the truth of this. But instead we increase military spending. When you see the kinds of budgets that were passed by Congress after September 11, the warlike intentions become apparent. When the planes smashed into the World Trade Center, the Dow Jones average was not too high, and the NASDAQ was at its lowest level. The American economy was heading toward a depression, and now, after September 11, we've seen a lot of investment in the country. There are those new planes I spoke of a few minutes ago—the first agreement is $400 billion. Then there's the Star Wars system. The military systems are getting more and more power. That means you can't begin to come out of the recession. And these men who control the military industry do not think about ecology. They are not concerned with the health of the planet.

ORVILLE SCHELL: But do you think photos might have the power to make people ... Do you think your photographs ... ?

SEBASTIÃO SALGADO: No, I'm not speaking about my photographs.

ORVILLE SCHELL: Well, let's just say photographs in general.

SEBASTIÃO SALGADO: I don't believe that they are powerful.... You know, the photographs alone are nothing. They are nothing, the photographs.

ORVILLE SCHELL: I'm grappling here to know how ... What's the answer?

SEBASTIÃO SALGADO: Your question is the answer. The question: what's the answer? I don't have the answer. Because, you know, the photographs, as I said a few minutes ago, must be just one part of the whole. They are just one element of the full debate. And they are more a question than a reply.

Contributors

KWAME ANTHONY APPIAH, philosopher, cultural theorist, and novelist, is Laurance S. Rockefeller University Professor in the Department of Philosophy and the University Center for Human Values at Princeton University. His most recent book is *The Honor Code: How Moral Revolutions Happen* (2010).

IVAN KLÍMA is a novelist, essayist, and critic whose novels, written in Czech and widely translated, include *My First Loves*; *Waiting for the Dark, Waiting for the Light*; and *Love and Garbage*. His autobiography, *Moje šílené století* (My mad century) was published in two parts in 2009 and 2010.

PETER SELLARS is a director of opera and theater noted for his unique contemporary stagings of classical and contemporary works. His production of John Adams's opera *Nixon in China* was staged in 2011 for New York's Metropolitan Opera. He is Professor of World Arts and Cultures at the University of California, Los Angeles.

MIKE DAVIS, best known for his book *City of Quartz: Excavating the History of Los Angeles*, is an urban theorist, historian, and political activist. He is a Distinguished Professor in the Department of Creative Writing at the University of California, Riverside, and an editor of the *New Left Review*.

ARTHUR DANTO is an art critic and Johnsonian Professor Emeritus of Philosophy at Columbia University. A selection of his published books includes *The Philosophical Disenfranchisement of Art, After the End of Art,* and *The Abuse of Beauty.*

MICHAEL IGNATIEFF, author of *Isaiah Berlin: A Life,* is a historian, journalist, and former member of the Canadian Parliament. He has held senior academic posts at Cambridge, Oxford, and Harvard and is currently a Senior Resident at Massey College of the University of Toronto.

J. M. COETZEE, a novelist and 2003 Nobel laureate in literature, is an Honorary Visiting Research Fellow at the University of Adelaide, Australia. His many novels include *The Lives of Animals, Elizabeth Costello,* and *Diary of a Bad Year.*

KENZABURŌ ŌE received the Nobel Prize for literature in 1994. He is best known outside Japan for the novels *Teach Us to Outgrow Our Madness, Somersault, Death by Water,* and, most recently, *The Changeling* (2010).

ANTHONY GRAFTON is the Henry Putnam Professor of History at Princeton University. Grafton is the author of *What Was History? The Art of History in Early Modern Europe, Codex in Crisis,* and many other books. He received the Mellon Foundation's Distinguished Achievement Award in 2003.

MICHAEL POLLAN is the author of *In Defense of Food: An Eater's Manifesto, The Omnivore's Dilemma, The Botany of Desire,* and other books. He is currently Knight Professor of Science and Environmental Journalism at the University of California, Berkeley.

THOMAS LAQUEUR is Helen Fawcett Professor of History at the University of California, Berkeley. He is best known for his book *Making Sex: Body and Gender from the Greeks to Freud* and is the recipient of a 2008 Mellon Foundation Distinguished Achievement Award.

MAYA LIN is an artist and architect acclaimed for her design for the Vietnam Veterans Memorial in Washington, DC. She is currently working on the Confluence Project, a multisited installation spanning the Columbia River system in the Pacific Northwest that intertwines the history of Lewis and Clark with the history of the Native American tribes who inhabit those regions.

ANDREW BARSHAY is Professor of History at the University of California, Berkeley. His books include *The Social Sciences in Modern Japan: The Marxian and Modernist Traditions* and *State and Intellectual in Imperial Japan: The Public Man in Crisis.*

STEPHEN GREENBLATT is John Cogan University Professor of the Humanities at Harvard University. He is the general editor of *The Norton Shakespeare* and the author of numerous books including *Will in the World: How Shakespeare Became Shakespeare* and, most recently, *The Swerve: How the World Became Modern* (2011).

STANLEY SAITOWITZ is Professor Emeritus of Architecture at the University of California, Berkeley, and Design Principal of Stanley Saitowitz-Natoma Projects Inc. in San Francisco. His design for the New England Holocaust Memorial in Boston, Massachusetts, was awarded the Henry Bacon Medal for Memorial Architecture by the American Institute of Architects.

MAURICE SENDAK is the author and illustrator of many noteworthy children's books, including *In the Night Kitchen*, *Where the Wild Things Are*, and *Outside Over There*. He has also designed and produced ballets and operas, most notably Mozart's *The Magic Flute*, Prokofiev's *Love for Three Oranges*, and his own operatic version of *Where the Wild Things Are*.

DR. HERBERT SCHREIER has practiced psychiatry at Children's Hospital in Oakland since 1977, specializing in treatment of emotional and behavioral disorders. He is also the co-author, with Judith A. Libow, of *Hurting for Love*, a detailed examination of Munchausen by Proxy Syndrome.

SEAMUS HEANEY, winner of the Nobel Prize for Literature in 1995, is the author of *Field Work*, *Station Island*, and *The Haw Lantern*, among many other works of poetry and prose. His translation of the Old English epic poem *Beowulf* was the winner of Britain's Whitbread Award. His most recent volume of poetry, *Human Chain*, appeared in 2010.

ROBERT HASS, Professor of English at the University of California, Berkeley, was Poet Laureate of the United States and Poetry Consultant to the United States Library of Congress in 1995–96. His published work includes *Field Guide*, *Praise*, *Sun Under Wood*, *Time and Materials*, and *The Apple Trees at Olema*. He has received numerous awards, including the National Book Award and the Pulitzer Prize.

SEBASTIÃO SALGADO, a Brazilian photographer, has dedicated himself to chronicling the lives of the world's dispossessed, work that has filled ten books and many exhibitions and for which he has won numerous awards. He is a UNICEF Goodwill Ambassador and an honorary member of the Academy of Arts and Sciences in the United States.

ORVILLE SCHELL, former Dean of the Graduate School of Journalism at the University of California, Berkeley, has devoted most of his professional life to writing and reporting on Asia. The author of fourteen books, he has also written widely for national magazines such as *Wired*, the *New York Review of Books*, the *New Yorker*, and *Harper's*.

Photo Credits

Menin Gate, Ypres, Chrislofoto / shutterstock.com

Interior, Menin Gate, Mark van Vuren / shutterstock.com

Thiepval Memorial, France, Dr. J. Bowman / fotolia.com

Thiepval Memorial, Andrew Emptage / dreamstime.com

Lawn and cemetery at Thiepval Memorial, René Lubberdink / iStockphoto.com

Vietnam Veterans Memorial, Washington, DC, Caitlin Mirra / shutterstock.com

Lettering detail, Vietnam Veterans Memorial, Vacclav / shutterstock.com

Yasukuni Shrine, Tokyo, IZO / shutterstock.com

New England Holocaust Memorial (model), courtesy Stanley Saitowitz

New England Holocaust Memorial (completed), courtesy Stanley Saitowitz

Ribbon of Light, San Francisco, courtesy Stanley Saitowitz

Vesey Square, Battery Park City, New York, NY, courtesy Stanley Saitowitz

Equador, 1998, courtesy of Sebastião Salgado

CPSIA information can be obtained at www.ICGtesting.com
Printed in the USA
BVOW010347081211

277765BV00002B/44/P

9 780982 329436